Behind Prison Walls

A Jewish Woman Freedom Fighter for Israel's Independence

Behind Prison Walls

A Jewish Woman Freedom Fighter for Israel's Independence

By

Tzila Amidror Heller

Foreword by

Menachem Begin

Translated by

Elizabeth Maor

KTAV Publishing House, Inc.

Copyright © 1999
Tzila Amidror Heller

Translated from the Hebrew
Copyright © 1961
Jabotinsky Press

Library of Congress Cataloging-in-Publication Data

Heller, Tzila Amidror
   [Ba-ma' atsar be–Vet–Lehem. English]
   Behind prison walls : a Jewish woman freedom fighter for Israel's
independence / by Tzila Amidror Heller ; foreword by Menachem Begin :
translated by Elizabeth Maor.
       p. cm.
   ISBN 0-88125--631–5
   1. Heller, Tzila Amidror. 2.. Revisionist Zionists—Biography.
3. Women political prisoners—West Bank—Bethelehem—Biography.
4. Irgun tseva 'i le 'umi. 5. Lohame herut Yisra 'el. 6. Palestine–Biography.
   I. Title.
DS151.H364A3   1998
956.9405'092—dc21
[B]   98-28595
                                                              CIP

Manufactured in the United States of America
KTAV Publishing House, Inc.
900 Jefferson St.
Hoboken, NJ 07030

✳ ✳ ✳ ✳ ✳ ✳

Table of Contents

✳ ✳ ✳ ✳ ✳ ✳

Foreword

The Fighting Jewish Woman

The fighting Jew has arisen from the dust, from the ashes and earth in which he was buried. The dust was his humiliation, such as had never been experienced in the annals of the human race. The ashes were the murder, the destruction, the extinction, the crushed skulls and the gassed children——all endured with only the slightest resistance, too little too late, and not in the name of life and liberty, but in the name of an honorable death. The earth is simply the earth, the earth of our homeland, and as we were exiled from it, our nation was diminished in valor. It was that valor which united Israel in the days of old, and which, now that we have returned to the homeland, has given the survivors of the ghettos the spirit to conquer, and has turned unarmed slaves into fearless rebels.

The rise of the Jewish warrior is the most wonderful of the miracles performed by the Almighty since our people's exile from its land, and was a precondition for the rebirth of our nation. For nineteen centuries the gentile knew and hated the Jew wherever and in whatever condition he found him: smart, sober, merchant, wanderer, rich, poor, despised, despising, trodden underfoot, silent, beaten, weeping. A fighting Jew? A contradiction in terms, *contradictio in adjecto.* Yet he rose up, the fighting Jew, before their astonished eyes.

By the side of the fighting Jewish man rose the fighting Jewish woman, and with her appearance came the glory of

vii

national renaissance. The Roman historian Tacitus, in his book
on the resistance of Judea Minor, "which caused great anger"
because it was the only revolt which continued after all the
other nations had surrendered to the conqueror, mentions that
the women of Judea also fought in the rebellion. But seventy
generations passed, and while the spirit of love accompanied
the Hebrew wife, mother, and sister, the spirit of war was dor-
mant. In our day that spirit has reawakened.

Our sister-in-arms is like Hannah, she who preferred, in her
supreme bravery, to see her sons die rather than abandon their
God. Hers is the valor of our matrons in the days of revolt and
resistance. Those matrons knew well that the deeds of their
sons entailed danger and sacrifice, but they neither objected
nor complained nor tried to prevent them from their actions;
rather, they provided them with aid, comfort, and encouragement, as did Hannah.

The Jewish fighting woman of our day did more: her contribution to the war of liberation was not only that she sent her
sons, but that she herself participated. She proved that the
Jewish resistance movement hastened victory and could not be
broken. She suffered in silence, fought actively in military operations, and served long prison sentences.

Tzila Amidror, a student of Jabotinsky, a fighter in the
National Military Organization (the Irgun), wrote one of the
most wonderful chapters in the story of the national war of liberation. It is the story of the stand taken by the Jewish women
who rotted for years behind the walls of the Bethlehem prison.
I am certain that those who read this book will find their hearts
filled not only with compassion but with pride. The figure of
the fighting Jewish woman presented in this book is the result
of personal experience seen through the eyes of love. It is both
a historical and an educational document. Our sons and
daughters should read it, that they might know and understand.

Menachem Begin
1961

※ ※ ※ ※ ※ ※

Preface to the First Edition

Nineteen years after my first arrest and imprisonment, four-teen years after my final release (during those five years I was arrested and released several times), and twelve years after the establishment of the State of Israel, I sat down to write this book in an attempt to tell the story of the war of the women of the fighting underground, the soldiers of the National Military Organization (the Irgun) and of the Fighters for the Liberation of Israel (the Lehi).

When I decided to write this book there was no printed material I could turn to, no records, no sources to research. The only thing I could rely on was my memory. As a result, many important things may have been left out, especially things to which I was not an eyewitness. I wrote according to subjects and not in chronological order.

When a prisoner or detainee is mentioned by name, it does not mean I intended to give her preferential treatment. It is only natural that I would give the names of the women who were my cellmates or with whom I was especially friendly, whose lives and experiences I shared, but this is not meant to belittle the contribution of those whose names are not men-tioned.

My readers will understand how difficult it was for me to undertake the writing of this book. I knew what a great respon-sibility I was taking on myself, and I knew how hard it would be for me to write, being neither a writer nor the daughter of a writer. The irony is that I have to thank the Minister of Foreign

Affairs, Mrs. Golda Meir, whose statement I have included here, for my final decision to take pen in hand. When there are those who shamefully distort history, someone must stand up and call them liars!

Here is what Mrs. Meir said, as quoted in the Hebrew newspaper *Yediot Ha'achronot*, November 11, 1959:

WHY DIDN'T THEY ARREST GOLDA?

> Some young people came to tell Golda Meir that she had been elected to the Knesset, and a few of them asked her for an autograph. Incidentally she mentioned the fact that she had not been arrested on "Black Saturday," along with all the other members of the Jewish Agency Executive. There was, she said, a simple reason: *During the time of the British Mandate there was no detention camp for women.*

There are many people in Israel, among both the younger generation and the new immigrants, who drink the poisoned water of the wells of historical distortion, and it is for them that I have tried to provide "water out of the well of Bethlehem, that was by the gate" (2 Samuel 23:15).

My intention was not to write an account of my own imprisonment, or that of other underground resistance fighters, nor a history of the prison at Bethlehem, but rather to provide a selection of our experiences behind bars. The prisoners' rabbi, Ari Levin, *shlita*,[1] used to call us "the women of Israel in captivity," who openly and secretly made our contribution to Israel's war of independence, and who belonged to the school of Jabotinsky, persecuted on all sides, fighting the war for their people until victory was achieved.

If this book makes the smallest contribution to the knowledge of how we got to where we are today, and who brought us there, that will be my reward.

My thanks to everyone who helped to make this book possible, with special thanks to the staff of the Jabotinsky Institute.

December 1961

---

[1] Hebrew abbreviation sometimes appended to the name of a rabbi, meaning, "May he live long and happily, amen."

※ ※ ※ ※ ※ ※

Preface to the English Translation

This book first appeared in 1961, published by the Israeli Ministry of Defense, and went through seven reprintings, the last appearing in 1981. It was written to explain to the reading public about the war the Irgun fought and to document the conditions under which the underground resistance fighters were arrested and detained in Bethlehem.

This book describes events that occurred when Israel was called Palestine and the country was ruled by the British, who had been given a Mandate by the League of Nations to help the Jewish people establish a national home there. Jabotinsky and the members of his movement realized early on that the British had no intention or desire to fulfill the duty given them by the Mandate, but quite the opposite: they sided with the Arabs against the Jews. They passed laws decreeing that Jews coul not buy land and could only come to the country if they had certificates that were parceled out in the smallest number possible, while they permitted Arabs to immigrate into the country freely with no bureaucratic restrictions whatsoever.

The leaders of the Yishuv favored restraint. The Arabs viewed this policy as weakness and were encouraged by it to slaughter Jews at will, the main riots occurring in 1921, 1929, 1936, and 1939. David Raziel, commander of the Irgun, knew that the only law the Arabs respected was "an eye for an eye"; he decided to fight back, and the Arabs were quelled toward the end of 1936.

This was not the Irgun's sole aim; it was first and foremost interested in the establishment of a Jewish state, which could not be accomplished as long as the British were still in the country. The movement had no intention of going to war with the entire British Empire, it was only interested in having them leave Palestine, since only then could a real country be established. The Irgun's aim was to hit the soft underbelly of the British: their honor and self-respect, and to avoid actual bloodshed insofar as was possible. Jabotinsky wanted the Jews to be gadflies for the English, thorns in their side, to bring them to the point where they would be only too happy to see the last of us.

In the meantime the Second World War broke out, and the Irgun decided to put the war against the British on the back burner and to concentrate on fighting the Nazis. When the war in Europe ended, Begin, then the commander of the Irgun, officially announced that our aim was to get the British out. The Irgun only had a few thousand fighters, whereas there were more than one hundred thousand British soldiers in Palestine, so every operation had to make waves. We "confiscated" their weapons, bombed the King David Hotel (an operation which backfired, the true story of which is known only to a few people today), and broke into the prison at Acco, a veritable fortress. These operations were not directed against the British soldiers themselves and were meant exclusively to humiliate the Empire. Our aim was to expel them from the country, and in the end we were largely successful.

HISTORICAL BACKGROUND

The Jewish resettlement of Palestine began in the second half of the nineteenth century, and increased in pace and numbers under the auspices of the World Zionist Organization, founded by Theodor Herzl at the First Zionist Congress in 1896. By the beginning of World War I, the Jewish population of Palestine amounted to 85,000. Palestine at that time was part of the Turkish Empire, but Britain was determined to drive the Turks from the area. Seeking to obtain the support of world Jewry, the British issued the Balfour Doctrine in 1917, endorsing the idea of a "Jewish National Home" in Palestine. This was embodied in the Mandate over Palestine granted to Britain by the League of Nations after the war.

In the 1920s and 1930s, under the British Mandatory regime, the Palestinian Jewish community, generally referred to as the *Yishuv*, grew and flourished, reclaiming desert lands, building towns and farm settlements, and developing a set of autonomous communal institutions that constituted a kind of shadow government.

Throughout this period, differences in regard to tactics and overall goals steadily became more apparent. The Yishuv was controlled by secularists who wanted to establish a socialist society. Led by Z'ev Jabotinsky, a trend known as Revisionism developed, which favored free enterprise and religious tradition. In addition, it maintained that statehood should be obtained as quickly as possible, as opposed to giving first priority to the development of the Palestinian economy under a British umbrella, and insisted that the coming Jewish state would have to include the whole area of the Mandate, including the region east of the Jordan River.

Meanwhile, as the Yishuv increased in size, Arab hostility hardened. A full-scale Arab revolt broke out in 1936, and in order to secure its oil supply and its political relations with the Arab world, Britain began reneging on its commitment to incubate a Jewish state in Palestine. After the Arabs rejected a proposal to partition the country, Britain issued a White Paper, in 1939, restricting Jewish immigration and land purchases. European Jews fleeing the Nazis were thus deprived of their only sure place of refuge.

The Haganah, the Yishuv's self-defense militia, adopted a policy of self-restraint in the face of Arab provocations, but the

Revisionist fighting force, the Irgun, met the challenge with full-scale attacks. After the issuance of the White Paper, it also began an underground resistance against the British regime. The British responded with harsh police and military measures.

Early in World War II, the Irgun decided to refrain from fighting the British until the defeat of the Nazis was certain. Lehi, a group made up of militants unwilling to go along with this policy, broke off from the Irgun and began an underground war against the Mandatory government. Since the Irgun continued its organizational and propagandistic activities, British repression was directed against both organizations. The "national institutions" of the Yishuv also opposed them and sometimes cooperated with the British.

In 1944, under the leadership of Menachem Begin, the Irgun began an open revolt. The harsh British reprisals, the inspiring example set by the Irgun's courageous fighters, and Britain's refusal to permit Holocaust survivors to settle in Palestine, eventually sparked the spirit of revolt in wider circles.

※ ※ ※ ※ ※ ※

The Jewish Revolt Against the British in Historical Perspective

"There's nothing to worry about," a senior British police official is said to have remarked in early 1944, when informed that the Irgun Zvai Leumi had announced the launching of an armed revolt against the British forces in Mandatory Palestine.[1]

Indeed, the casual observer had little reason to expect that 600 badly-equipped Jewish guerrillas stood much chance of ousting a British occupation army of 80,000.

The Irgun's view, however, was forged from the perspective of a Jewish history rich with instances of the few overcoming the many. For the Jews to rise from the ashes of Auschwitz and re-establish a Jewish state, against the will of one of the mightiest nations on earth, would be no more surprising than, for example, the events celebrated by the holiday of Hanukkah.

Like the ancient Maccabees and countless other guerrilla armies before and since, the Irgunists made the most of advantages such as the element of surprise, their intimate knowledge of the terrain, and the protective sympathy of a significant part of the local population. Unlike their Maccabean counterparts, the Irgun also enjoyed an array of uniquely 20th-century advantages. With modern explosives, a handful of Jewish guerrillas could cause enormous damage to targets in urban areas. Mass communications technology enabled the Jewish militants

---

[1] Cited in J. Bowyer Bell, *Terror Out of Zion* (New York: St. Martin's, 1977), p.112.

1

to reach influential segments of foreign public opinion. The democratic systems of government in Great Britain and the United States by their very nature enabled the Irgun to mobilize sympathizers in parliament and congress to press for a British withdrawal from Palestine.

Much of the international sympathy that indirectly aided the Irgun derived not so much from admiration for the underground's war against the British, but from sorrow at the suffering of European Jewry under the Nazis. Western public consciousness of the Nazi genocide fueled Western public support for the goal of a Jewish state in Palestine. England's policy of preventing shiploads of European refugees from reaching Palestine further intensified American public sympathy for the Zionist cause. Savvy Irgun emissaries in the United States, well aware of America's own history of battling British colonial rulers, peppered their newspaper advertisements with references to 1776, the Boston Tea Party, and the midnight ride of Paul Revere.

The revolt itself was very much a product of its era. Although the Irgun had been established in the 1930s, prior to the onset of the Holocaust, it was the transformation of Nazi brutality from discrimination and sporadic violence to organized mass murder, combined with British immigration restrictionism, that were the decisive factors in igniting the rebellion. As Begin put it: "The blood of our people cried out to us from the foreign soil on which it had been shed, fired revolt in our hearts and gave the rebels strength."[2] The Holocaust created the atmosphere of urgency, even desperation, that drove legions of young Jews to the ranks of the underground.

The sight of the Jewish world going up in flames around them moved a generation of Jewish youth to shake off 20 centuries of powerlessness. "Out of blood and fire and tears and ashes," Begin wrote, "a new specimen of human being was born, a specimen completely unknown to the world for over 1800 years: the Fighting Jew."[3]

---

[2] Menachem Begin, *The Revolt* (Los Angeles: Nash, 1972), p.40.
[3] Ibid., p.xi.

Unbowed by the death sentence imposed upon him in 1947, Irgunist Meir Feinstein urged his comrades to always remember: "There is a life that is worse than death and a death greater than life."[4] It was this conviction which inspired Irgun militants to literally risk their lives each day. The relatively small units of front-line guerrillas were directly in the line of British fire every time they undertook an operation. But they were not the only ones who faced danger. Virtually everyone who participated in any aspect of the Irgun revolt risked imprisonment, harsh interrogation by their British captors, and sometimes even execution. Those who pasted up wall-posters explaining the Irgun's perspective or set off "pamphlet bombs" that scattered Irgun leaflets across a wide area —deeds crucial to facilitating public understanding of the underground's actions— could be shot on sight by a passing British patrol. Many were. Those who went door to door soliciting contributions for the militants' cause could be jailed indefinitely without charges or trial. Tzila Heller, whose stirring memoir of her Irgun years follows, spent long years in British detention and never faced a judge or jury. Yet far from being broken by the hardships they endured, she and her comrades were steeled by adversity.

The Jewish war against the British in Palestine was often more of a psychological contest of wills than a battlefield struggle. The Jews, after all, did not possess the necessary manpower or other resources to achieve a conventional military victory over the much larger and superior British armed forces. The British, for their part, could have eliminated the rebels only by using methods too harsh to be acceptable to British public opinion. As British Member of Parliament Richard Crossman put it: "We are not Nazis, and we are not prepared to take the step of liquidating the Jewish community [in Palestine], which would be necessary in order to crush the resistance movement."[5] Operating within the parameters created by their own weaknesses as well as those of the British, the Irgun took aim

---

[4] Ibid., p.42.
[5] Cited in Saul Zadka, *Blood in Zion* (Brassey's: London, 1997), p. 173.

at British pride as much as at British army bases, police stations, and government offices. Thus when the British, in June
1946, sentenced Irgun members Yosef Shimshon and Michael
Ashbel to death, their comrades responded by bursting into a
British officers' club in Tel Aviv in broad daylight, kidnapping
five officers, and threatening to hang them if the sentences
against Shimshon and Ashbel were carried out. Unable to
locate the kidnap victims or to put an end to ongoing attacks by
the Jewish underground, the desperate British decided to
intensify their pressure on the established Jewish leadership,
the Jewish Agency, to fight the Irgun. In a day-long mass
roundup on June 29, known as "Black Saturday," the British
jailed a number of Jewish Agency leaders as well as more than
2,000 other suspects. It was to no avail. The humiliated
Mandate authorities backed down and commuted the sentences. The officers' lives were saved, but the psychological
effect of the Jewish guerrillas' victory was inestimable.

A similar triumph for the Jewish guerrillas wounded the
British later that year. Two 17 year-olds convicted of Irgun
activity, Binyamin Kimche and Yehuda Katz, were sentenced to
lengthy prison terms plus 18 lashes. "These lashes would
wound the soul of Eretz Israel," Begin would later remark. "For
seventy generations, in seventy lands, we had suffered the
lashes of our oppressors. Was an oppressor now to whip us in
our own country?" Begin was determined not merely to
answer with a resounding "no" but to completely turn the
tables on the British. The next day's Irgun wall poster did not
mince words: "We warn the occupation Government not to
carry out this punishment...If it is put into effect—every officer
of the British occupation army in Eretz Israel will be able to be
punished in the same way: to get 18 whips." The British, refusing to knuckle under to the Irgun's threat, whipped Kimche.
The next day, four British soldiers were seized at gun point,
driven to remote locations along the coast, and given 18 lashes
each. Another Irgun warning followed: "If the oppressors dare
in the future to abuse the bodies and the human and national

honor of Jewish youths, we will shall no longer reply with the whip. We shall reply with fire." In one last attempt to avoid a complete surrender, the British pressed Katz to request mercy on the grounds that he was too weak to withstand a lashing. Katz defied the demand. The British granted him amnesty and abolished the practice of whipping. British officers in Palestine had been "kidnapped, killed, and even flogged," is how Lt.-General Evelyn Barker, commander of England's Palestine forces, put it. The humiliation for the British was almost unbearable. "Ridicule," Begin aptly noted, "can be more destructive than a high explosive bomb."[6]

Each successive Irgun attack seemed more audacious than its predecessors. In July 1946, Irgun bombers blew apart the southern wing of the King David Hotel in Jerusalem, which was used as the headquarters of the British military administration. Three months later, the Irgun demonstrated its ability to strike overseas as well, blowing up the British embassy in Rome. Scarcely a day passed without some new action by the Jewish underground. British airplanes were dynamited in their hangars. British troop trains were mined. British soldiers were gunned down in broad daylight. A brazen Irgun raid on the officers' club in Tel Aviv, Goldsmith House, left 17 dead. A British army intelligence report that month complained that "the illegal forces are going all out to 'thumb their noses' at the authorities."[7] And there was a limit to how much nose-thumbing the proud British empire could stand.

As the Palestine violence intensified, additional troops were brought in. The British "keep three to four times more soldiers [in Palestine] than in the whole of India," opposition leader Winston Churchill complained in one 1947 parliamentary debate.[8] Prisons camps were erected in the British East African territories of Eritrea and Sudan, and the Bethlehem prison for

---

[6] Bell, p.185; Begin, p.235.

[7] Zadka, p.163.

[8] Zadka, p.160

women was expanded to accommodate Tzila Heller and other female underground fighters. The contest of wills fought between the guerrillas and authorities all across the country was waged behind prison walls, as well. Tzila and her comrades understood that every tiny gesture of defiance constituted another chink in the occupier's armor. Every refusal to obey a warden's unfair order or follow an unjust prison routine struck another psychological blow against the authorities. The prisoner who escaped —and there more than a few— delivered the ultimate blow to the British jailer.

The most foreboding of the prisons in which the British jailed Jewish militants was situated in the ancient coastal citadel at Acre. Even Napoleon had failed in his attempt to storm the fortress-like structure during his 1799 invasion of the Holy Land. After the British hanged four Irgun members there in April 1947, the idea of assaulting that imposing symbol of foreign occupation assumed added significance. On May 4, a party of Irgun fighters dynamited their way through the prison's south wall, meeting up with imprisoned comrades who had, from within, blasted a series of heavy iron gates with explosives material that had been smuggled into the prison during the preceding weeks. The operation was a tremendous propaganda success for the Irgun, despite casualties suffered by the retreating raiders in shoot-outs with the British and the fact that only several dozen Jewish fighters actually escaped. The international media portrayed it as one of the most spectacular prison breaks of all time, emphasizing the presumed invulnerability of the Acre citadel, the sensational idea of the Irgun breaking into a prison to free its men, and the large number of escapees, thanks to the nearly 200 Arab criminals who fled in the confusion. The spectacular Acre raid, later immortalized in the film Exodus, dealt a shattering blow to British prestige and morale.

The final straw, however, was the battle of the gallows. The Irgun had won the first round handily, compelling the British to pardon two guerrillas on death row in the summer of 1946 by kidnapping five British officers and threatening to execute them in kind. In early 1947, the British sentenced four Irgun men to death. The Irgun kidnapped two Britons, an intelligence officer and a judge, and threatened retaliatory executions. The British suddenly announced that the death sentences would not yet be carried out, leading some in the Irgun to assume that the episode would conclude as had the gallows affair of the previous year. It was not to be. In mid-April, the British suddenly executed the four. Two other Jewish fighters, who in the meantime had also been sentenced to capitol punishment, cheated the hangman by blowing themselves up with explosives smuggled into the prison. While the Irgun was unsuccessfully seeking suitable British hostages, the authorities sentenced three more Irgun men to be hanged. The militants then managed to capture two British sergeants. The British, calling the Irgun's bluff, executed the three Jewish fighters; the Irgun responded by hanging the sergeants, in a grove near Netanya. That same afternoon, the S. S. Exodus, having been turned away from Palestine by the British authorities, arrived back in France with its pitiful cargo of Holocaust survivors. Their tragic journey provided the poignant backdrop to the Irgun's unprecedented action.

The hanging of the sergeants was the straw that broke the camel's back. The expense of the Palestine occupation, especially the cost in British lives, was wearing down the morale of the British public, exactly as the Irgun had expected. The accumulation of humiliations—the bold attacks on major British targets, the prison breaks, the retaliatory whippings, and now the hangings—was too much for the British government, and the British public, to stomach. Colonial Secretary Arthur Creech-Jones would later write that the hangings "struck a deadly blow against British patience and pride."[9] By the spring of 1947, England's patience had been exhausted, and its pride

---

[9] Zadka, p.85

✳ ✳ ✳ ✳ ✳ ✳

Chapter One

Arrest

Late evening, December 3, 1941. The sky was covered by a heavy, leaden cloud bank, and rain had been falling steadily for hours. Sheets of water attacked the few passers-by, striking them across the face and whipping their backs, turning the pavement beneath their feet into streams of uncertain depth. Fearing German attacks, the owners of the cafes had covered their windows with blackout curtains, and the dim light which filtered through did little to dispel the gloom on the rain-swept street.

On such a night people wanted only to stay at home and enjoy the warmth of a burning stove; nevertheless, the cinemas were full. The young people, having been brought up on self-restraint, were attracted to the movies and eager to enjoy the vicarious thrill of watching people performing acts of courage somewhere on the other side of the world. With bated breath they followed the deeds of underground fighters in faraway places as they fought to liberate their countries from the foreign powers which had enslaved them. There in the darkness, sitting in front of the silver screen, they found an outlet for the energy brewing inside them. Scarcely daring to breathe, they watched as the Yugoslav general Mihajlovic smote the Germans, as a young Norwegian freedom fighter went out into the snowy night to attack the enemy; with yearning they watched as a young Belgian overcame the foe; with fists clenched and grinding their teeth in helpless fury, they watched as a French resistance fighter was handed over to the Gestapo by a Nazi collaborator. They experienced the emotions——a nice substitute for taking action themselves!

It was strange that the British censors had not yet realized how dangerous it was to distribute such potentially explosive propaganda in Palestine, and that it might turn into a two-edged sword. Would it really be surprising if someone in the audience were to make the connection between Europe and his own homeland, stand up, and say, "If they can fight the invader, why can't we?"

A cinema! When was the last time I had been to the cinema? The thought almost made me laugh out loud. The last few months had been particularly onerous: I had been constantly busy, making fund-raising "house calls" to finance the Irgun's struggle. (The Irgun was the National Military Organization.[2] Its last commander was its most famous: Menachem Begin.[3]) I could rest between calls, but resting meant either a paramilitary training course or an operation against the British. There was no time to think about entertainment, much less to think about a cinema.

It began to rain harder. The puddles that usually formed in Tel Aviv's streets in the winter turned into coursing rivers. How wonderful it would be to sit at home with a hot cup of tea, to take off my wet shoes, to stretch out in bed. The house calls would still be waiting for me tomorrow, the Irgun didn't hold activities in the evening, and in any case I was far too tired to be persuasive. How hard it was to convince people that the time had come to fight for independence!

---

[2]The Irgun (in full, *Irgun Tz'vai L'umi*, also known by the acronym *Etzel*) was the military arm of the Revisionist movement.

[3]Menachem Begin (1913—1992), founder of the Herut Party and Israel's seventh Prime Minister (1977—83), became commander of the Irgun in 1943. He led the revolt against the British that began in 1944 and culminated in statehood in 1948.

I walked faster as I approached the building I lived in, the vision of the hot cup of tea dancing before my eyes. I could imagine Judith Gorenstein, my roommate, holding the cup out to me. With a sigh of relief I skipped up the stairs, walked along the hallway, and discovered to my amazement that the kitchen was dark. I turned on the light and had barely taken my coat off when someone knocked on the door.

My visitor was a stranger. His hat was pulled down to his eyebrows and the collar of his coat was turned up to his chin, so I could barely make out his eyes and nose. "He looks like a real Sherlock Holmes," I thought, and in a flash I realized that he was a policeman! The fated meeting, the one I had imagined in so many different forms, was finally taking place. I overcame my nervousness and asked him what he wanted.

"Are you Tzila Heller?"

"Yes."

"May I come in?"

"Certainly," I replied, as if he needed my permission. I didn't realize that I was extending the invitation to a whole regiment! He was followed in by half a dozen men as big as circus strongmen, each one taller and more muscular than the last, looking for all the world as though they had come to a boxing match.

In my mind's eye I saw the specter of the infamous women's prison at Bethlehem, near Rachel's Tomb. "Tzila," I said to myself, "that's where they'll send you."

I had no time to think: Sergeant Day came straight to the point:

"Officer Schiff wants to see you."

I said that I didn't understand English, although I had in fact understood. But the language barrier had been taken into consideration, and there was an interpreter with them.

Sergeant Day mumbled something, the gist of which was that a courtesy call in the kitchen was insufficient and he wanted to see my bedroom. I opened the door while pointing out patriotically that it would be best not to turn on the light since there were no blackout curtains on the windows.

Wartime secrecy must have been uppermost in their minds, because they contented themselves with a cursory look around, shining a flashlight briefly on the furniture. It was a very superficial search, because lying in plain view on top of the dresser was the receipt book I used in my fund-raising, and they never even touched it.

When they finished I asked them to leave the room, on the pretext that I wanted to change my clothing. As soon as I was alone I collected the receipt book and every slip of paper that might be suspect or incriminating, tore up everything, and threw it out the window, putting my faith in the wind and rain. Greatly relieved I returned to the kitchen, but my heart sank when I opened my purse. Among the papers in it I saw the article I had ready for the next issue of *Liberation*, the Irgun's illegal newspaper.

I began to check the contents of my purse out loud: "Face powder, lipstick——oh, dear, I forgot my mirror." I went back to the bedroom for my mirror and destroyed the article! Fortunately the regiment which had come to arrest me had forgotten to bring along a policewoman, which was usually standard operating procedure in such cases.

Just before we left the apartment I had a very strange sensation. As my gaze wandered along the kitchen walls I thought I saw the shadows of the Bethlehem prison, where I had visited Sarah a few months earlier. Silently I said goodbye to my room and its furnishings. Who knew when I would see them again? Nevertheless, I remembered to leave a note for Judith, asking her not to tell my mother anything.

I left the building flanked by my "honor guard," and only then did I notice the two small cars parked outside. I remembered that as I had hurried home, thinking only of my cup of tea, I had scarcely paid attention to them, whereas normally they would have aroused my suspicions.

I had been so eager to hide everything that might be incriminating that I only began thinking about my arrest and everything that might happen as a result of it when I was seated in the car. My family's fate worried me no end. My ex-husband was in a POW camp in Germany, having joined the British Army to fight the Nazis. He was one of the thousands of men who had volunteered to go to war against the enemies of the Jewish people, and it was a cruel jest of fate that officers of the same country on whose side he was fighting would now put his wife behind bars.

But my chief concern was for my mother: how would this blow affect her? I had always known that I might be arrested and had prepared her accordingly, but who knows what a devoted Jewish mother really thinks and feels? And what about my son, who was only four and a half years old? He was being looked after, of course. Aware I might be arrested at any moment, I had put him into a boarding school for soldiers' children so that he would have a roof over his head if anything happened to me. It wasn't his physical well-being that worried me, but how his young psyche would react to his mother's imprisonment. His father was far away, behind barbed wire, and now his mother would be, too.

My list of worries didn't end there. My roommate, Judith Gorenstein, might get in trouble because of me. She had her own problems to deal with: her husband, Isaac, had been arrested a few months earlier along with the other members of an officers' training course held at Mishmar Hayarden, a moshav in the north, and she had been left alone to take care of their daughter. The fact that I shared her apartment would go into her file and might be sufficient reason to send her to prison as well.

I turned to the Jewish policeman sitting next to me and said, "I want you to know that my roommate is not involved in this matter at all. She lets me live in her apartment out of the goodness of her heart, and there is no reason to punish her." There was nothing to be done about the trouble I was in, but I wanted to save Judith if I could. I even threatened him, saying that I would hold him personally responsible if she were arrested.

I was trying to remember whether there was anything else to worry about when we arrived at the Shachar police station. Sergeant Day skipped into the station house, almost dancing with joy at his victory, eager to tell Officer Schiff that they had hooked the big fish. Unable to restrain himself, he kept repeating, "This time it really *is* Tzila!" I understood why; they had already had their fingers burned with Tzilas. Seven months before, when they arrested Sarah, they had asked her if she was Tzila. When they arrested Ruth they had asked her the same question, and now, to their great joy, they had come face to face with the real Tzila.

I smiled wryly at the honor I was being accorded. All the officers in the station house came to look at me, each of them subjecting me to the closest scrutiny, and each of them terribly disappointed. They had pictured "Tzila the Terrorist" as a fire-breathing giantess with clenched fists, pursed lips, and flashing eyes, and before them stood an absolutely ordinary woman, obviously not about to devour them whole, but also obviously not expecting or wanting pity, and who, most important, although she had been arrested, was smiling. Not only was it disappointing, it was a little unnatural.

A telephone conversation led to my being brought out of the station house and ordered back into the car, which took me to the police station on Yehuda Halevi Street in southern Tel Aviv. They took me to a room in which a barefoot, disheveled woman was sitting. At that time women working in the world's oldest profession were being arrested quite frequently, and from her appearance I assumed she was one of them, so I tried to sit as far away from her as I could. For some reason the policeman who had brought me to the room ordered me to sit next to her, but I refused.

While we were in the midst of this argument, the reasons for which I understood only later, a whole troop of high-ranking officers came in to look me over, peering at me closely. Then I was hustled into another room where a group of police officers, headed by Schiff and Goldman, sat behind a small table. It was too small for all of them to sit side by side, so several had formed a second row, a kind of gallery.

Seeing all the trouble they had gone to, a wave of emotions passed over me. On the one hand, pride and satisfaction at being so important, and that because of me all the top policemen in the Tel Aviv area had been summoned in the middle of the night; on the other hand, terrible distress at having been uprooted from the firm ground of the resistance movement and cut off from the fighting front.

They finished shuffling their papers and instructed me to approach the table. Only then did I discover that my suspicions had been justified: the barefoot woman was none other than a policewoman of the Palestinian police force. Apparently they had summoned her so urgently (because of my arrest) that she hadn't even had time to put on her shoes.

I was ordered to empty the contents of my purse onto the table. As I took things out my heart stopped: there inside was a long, thin strip of paper. On it were "only" written the names of people who had been recommended to the Irgun as prospects to be contacted and recruited into the service as soldiers of the underground resistance movement. Turning their names over to the British would have decided their fate. I had only received the list a few hours earlier and was supposed to pass it on the next day.

Obviously I had to destroy the list, but how? I decided to exploit the fact that the policewoman was barefoot by moving my foot close to hers and treading on it. She would no doubt cry out and jump aside, and in the ensuing commotion I could hide the list in my dress. But it turned out that there was no need; in a flash I rolled the list tightly between my fingers and stuck the paper under my belt. The policewoman saw me but for some reason said nothing.

My troubles, however, were far from over. After I got rid of the list I noticed an envelope filled with photographs on I had written the telephone numbers of some people with whom I had talked about contributing to the Irgun. The list had been written with the kind of pencil we used then, and it was not indelible like the graphite pencils in use in 1956. Innocently wetting my thumb, I began to rub the numbers out. They noticed and ordered me to stop at once, asking angrily what I thought I was doing. I said that the envelope was dirty and offended my sense of aesthetics. In any case, I had managed to make the numbers illegible, because no one ever asked any questions about those people.

The interrogation began, and Schiff himself was the chief interrogator. He dispensed with formalities and got straight to the point.

"Do you engage in collecting money?" he asked.

"Yes," I answered.

He practically jumped out of his chair when I answered affirmatively, but he sat down again, furious. It turned out that we weren't talking about the same thing. I took a book of tickets out of my purse and showed it to him. They were tickets for a party which would be held in a few days, given by the National Labor Union. He threw another accusation at me.

"Do you engage in mailing letters?" he wanted to know.

"Yes," I answered again.

This time his reaction was more guarded, because he now knew what kind of answer to expect. From my purse I extracted a copy of a letter from the Social Services Department of the Tel Aviv municipality. I worked there, and of course part of my job was mailing letters. But what he had in mind was neither collecting money for the Histadrut nor working for Social Services, and after a few more questions he got up from the table and stood in back of me, spitting out his words furiously.

"She doesn't know anything, she's just one of the Irgun's policy makers, that's all!"

I turned around to face him and said, "If you know, why are you asking me all these questions?"

"She's a bloody fox," he said angrily. After a few more questions, he threw some of the most colorful expletives in the King's English in my direction and strode out of the room, slamming the door behind him.

I saw his outburst as a sign that I had passed the interrogation with flying colors. Soon the other officers left the room, until only one Jewish officer was left, who asked me to follow him. In the corridor he was joined by several English policemen, and I was again led to a waiting car. It was two o'clock in the morning. I had no idea where we were going, and none of the officers said anything. When the car stopped I recognized where we were: it was the Jaffa prison, where I used to visit Abrashka Stavsky, one of the men unjustly accused of Arlosoroff's murder[4]. I seemed to be following in his footsteps.

---

[4] Chaim Arlosoroff (1899—1933), a ranking member of Mapai and the head of the Jewish Agency's Political Department, was assassinated by unknown gunmen. Abrashka Stavsky and two Revisionist colleagues were charged with the crime. Stavsky was condemned to death in 1934, but the verdict was subsequently overturned.

✳ ✳ ✳ ✳ ✳ ✳

Chapter Two

The Jaffa Prison

That night the wind shrieked and waves broke angrily on the shore; rain beat down, accompanied by lightning and explosions of thunder: such was the backdrop against which my arrest was played. It was strange, but after the jolting car rides and the exhausting, nerve-wracking cross-examinations, I was actually looking forward to being able to rest in prison, even if it was a poor substitute for my one real desire: a hot cup of tea. However, the black iron portal that I had longed to see was not quick to admit me. After my guards had knocked again and again, a small narrow hatch opened and a sleepy Arab guard looked out at us. He was anxious lest some person unworthy of the honor might sneak into the prison, as though only the righteous could pass his gate; he opened it when he saw the policemen.

The "guest room" to which I was conducted was dark and gloomy despite the fact that a lamp had been lit. Joy shone from the guard's face (he had been awakened from a sound sleep in the middle of the night) when he realized that he was party to the arrest of a dangerous terrorist. A bell rang and awakened a woman guard, old enough to be my grandmother, and she came running. Squinting, she examined me from head to toe as though we were in a slave market and she was considering buying me and wanted to be sure I was worth the money. Then she led me to another room and searched my body and my clothing. My wallet and everything in it was confiscated, but "the law's the law," so the exact amount of money was written down, and my jewelry and watch were catalogued, and I received a promise that on my release everything would be returned to me. I also had to sign a form stating, not, of course, that I had been arrested, but that my possessions had been taken from me.

The full weight of my arrest struck me when my watch and pencil were taken away. Is there anything more symbolic of the confiscation of time than having one's watch impounded? What can make lack of freedom more tangible than being deprived of writing materials, the means of expression? But I had no time to reflect, I was again being ordered to move. My God, when would it end? My journey into the night seemed to last forever. The door opened again, and the police officer and the guard led me through the yard to a second gate, which a policewoman opened from the outside.

My journey was at an end. The policeman left, and I was alone with the guard. She was angrier than I at my arrest. I had disturbed her sleep, and for that reason she remained completely silent. We climbed a flight of steep, narrow stairs which led to a long narrow corridor. Realizing that I was about to reach my "sanctuary," I turned and said, "I hope you aren't going to put me into a cell with Arab women or criminals!"

She looked at me, shrugged her shoulders, and said nothing. I repeated what I had just said, this time less politely and in a louder voice. She stopped walking, turned, and asked, "Why not?"

"Because," I answered, "I am not a common criminal, I am a political prisoner, and therefore you have no right to put me in the same cell with them!"

When she saw that I was serious, she began to apologize for the shortage of rooms in the prison. "We only have three rooms," she said, "one is for the guards, one is for the prisoners, and the third is empty because the window is broken and the cold wind blows in."

"All right," I said, "I want the cell with the broken window."

She tried to convince me that sleeping there would be unhealthy; furthermore, she said, it was against the law for a prisoner to be alone in a cell. I refused to back down, however, so she finally gave in. As I passed the cell where the prisoners were kept, my nose was assailed by a revolting stench. They were lying on the floor, one next to the other——anything not to have to sleep in the cell with the broken window.

When I got there I asked to be allowed to choose my *bursh*. This was an Arabic word for a kind of mattress given to prisoners. They really weren't mattresses at all but thick blankets made by the prisoners themselves. The *burshes* were full of folds and seams; made of rags, they were ideal shelters for the prison's permanent guests: the lice and fleas and other assorted insects that infected the place. Every prisoner tried to get the *bursh* that looked the least awful. Every morning, when the prisoners were allowed into the yard, they hung the *burshes* out to air. In the late afternoon, when they returned to their cells, it was common to see them besiege the row of *burshes*, each trying to get the best one, or at least to get back her own, full of the lice and fleas she was used to.

Then I asked the guard to give me five blankets. She insisted that I couldn't have more than three. When I demanded a sheet and pillow, she couldn't believe her ears. For a minute I thought she would faint. Again she looked at me closely, as though trying to decide whether or not I was sane. Apparently she had been told the identity of the dangerous terrorist in her charge, so instead of venting her fury on me, she simply stood there helplessly. I helped her out of her predicament by pretending that I was worried about her. "You should rest," I said. "Go to sleep, and tomorrow I'll explain everything and it will be all right." Talking about sleep convinced her. I must have hit her Achilles' heel, because she brought me a sheet, swearing all the time that it was her own. As for a pillow: even she didn't have one.

After such an impressive list of victories, I smiled to myself and thought that if only Abba Achimeir, one of the founders of Brit ha-Biryonim, a Revisionist splinter group, could see me, he would be happy to know that his valiant campaign in prison had not been in vain.[5] I remember how as young girls we used to devour the stories about the group's members: how they fought in prison for the rights of political prisoners, how they rebelled against the humiliating, offensive, oppressive practices which robbed them of their dignity. Their struggle had been only partially successful, and those who came after them still had to fight for such elementary items as a sheet or another blanket.

It was almost dawn, but tired as I was I couldn't fall asleep on my regal pallet. Worries came thick and fast, and what distressed me above all was the question of what was going to happen next. Meanwhile, I was beginning to pay the price for choosing the only vacant cell: cold air came in through the broken window high in the wall, and the prison's permanent residents emerged from the interior of the *bursh* to visit the "invader." None of the stories I had heard about the prison's "house pets" had been exaggerated.

The cell was also invaded by the sound of waves breaking not far from the prison wall. Usually the sound of breaking waves is calming, but here it was quite the opposite. Everything, it would seem, depends on conditions and circumstances. The monotony of the breaking waves was enough to drive one mad; it was possible to predict to the second when the wave would break, when the water would recede, and when another wave would break and recede, with no variation in the rhythm.

---

[5]Brit ha-Biryonim was an underground activist group. One of its founders was Abba Achimeir (1898—1962), a ranking member of the Revisionist movement and of the Irgun. He was arrested several times and continued to foment resistance against the British while in prison.

But inside me waves were breaking too, and in the darkness of the cell, with no one to watch, I could release the emotions struggling within me. I kept seeing faces: first my poor son's, fatherless because my ex-husband was in a German prison camp, then my mother's. She would not only have the pleasure of seeing her daughter arrested, but would now be responsible for the welfare of the boy. One worry after another: who would replace me in the Irgun, especially now, when activists were so badly needed?

Suddenly I was thunderstruck! I remembered that I had arranged with Eitan Livni, the commander of the Irgun's military operations (and later one of those who broke into the prison at Acco),[6] that after he finished work he would come to my room with Chaim. We had to discuss plans for the party they wanted to give to celebrate their promotions. They belonged to a spirited group of commanders, all of whom were named Chaim, and when they spoke among themselves heaven only knew which Chaim they were referring to. Who knows, I thought, maybe a whole troop of Chaims had come to my room and fallen into the waiting arms of the CID. With this thought torturing me, I was barely able to doze off.

I was awakened by the cries of the prisoners in the next cell and by the clanking of heavy keys. The cell was separated from the corridor by a wall only a yard high and topped with iron bars which reached the ceiling. The door itself was made entirely of bars. In short, an overgrown chicken coop, inside which it was impossible to make the slightest movement without being seen by the guards in the corridor. Two women guards stood at the door. One was the guard it had been my privilege to meet the previous night, the other was her replacement. They spoke loudly in Arabic, confident that I couldn't

---

[6]On May 4, 1947, an Irgun unit attacked the maximum-security prison at Acco and freed the prisoners. The daring raid, described in a British newspaper as "the greatest jailbreak in history," was a serious blow to British prestige and morale.

understand them. I enjoyed listening to their conversation while innocently pretending that I couldn't understand. One of them said, "This new prisoner will be nothing but trouble. She thinks she's something special and has already made all kinds of demands."

The other one answered, "She's not going to get anything from me. I've seen plenty of her type already." She had worked there longer, and as I later found out, she had unlimited power over the prisoners and they thought of her as the queen. I was afraid that my face would give me away, so I turned my back to them.

It is a weird feeling to wake up in the morning after one's first night behind bars. At first I thought I'd had a nightmare and still wasn't fully awake, but the nightmare turned into reality only too soon. Things which in the outside world were taken for granted were missing here, and their lack brought the situation home to me quite forcefully. It was strange to get up in the morning without washing, changing clothes, or even brushing my teeth, and since the doors were only opened at eight o'clock in the morning, I had an hour of idleness before me.

Suddenly I heard a long, muted ringing and my heart stood still. The guard was being called, and the only reason to call her at such an early hour was to receive a new "guest."

A few minutes later I heard a man's footsteps. A British officer, no longer young, not bothering to conceal his anger, stood at my door. He raised his swagger stick and pointed it at the corner in which I sat. The sight of my sheet and all the blankets infuriated him. The guard could barely understand what he said, and gesturing wildly, her face piteously unhappy, she explained that she was not to blame. It wasn't she who had given me all the extra bedclothes, but rather I who had taken them. He began to shout and ordered her in no uncertain terms to take back the blankets. He was particularly angry at the "armchair" I had fashioned from them, but there was no chair and I had wanted to sit. "What," he yelled, "you don't have a chair?! Perhaps you would like me to bring you a piano as well?" I stood there feigning innocence, waiting for his anger to pass.

After he left it was the guard's turn to shout at me. "See what you have done! He yelled an me because of you and ordered me to take back all the blankets!" I let her shout until she ran out of breath and then said, "Don't be afraid that you will suffer because of me. I take full responsibility for all my actions. You can go to the prison office and tell them for me that I have no intention of obeying the officer's commands."

"Don't you know who that was?" she asked. "It was Hackett. He's the most important person here, and no one has ever refused to obey him before."

"In that case," I said, "I'll be the first."

Nervous and frightened, she went to the office. A few minutes later she came back with an Arab clerk who knew Hebrew. A long argument ensued in which he demanded that I return the blankets, and I answered that I hadn't been sentenced, only arrested, and therefore I had the rights of a political prisoner, and if they continued to treat me inappropriately, I would appeal to the regional governor. When he saw that arguing with me wouldn't get him anywhere he left, telling the guard to leave me alone, because otherwise I would make a lot of trouble for them.

From that moment on the guard saw me in a different light, and my prestige knew no bounds. She no longer viewed me as a nuisance sent to plague her, and when she understood that I would fight for my rights she changed both her tone of voice and the way she treated me—especially when she saw that I had succeeded in thwarting His Eminence, Officer Hackett.

Since I realized that my stay would be more or less extended, I decided to act like a house-proud homeowner. I asked for a pail of water and a rag, and began washing my "living room." After all the horror stories I had heard from prisoners about the filth of the Jaffa prison, I had to admit that except for the *burshes*, I was pleasantly surprised by the cleanliness of the

women's wing. It was due to the fact that the guards didn't
have to go to the Carmel market to hire cleaning women: all the
prisoners could be pressed into service.

It was almost noon. I knew this not because of the sun,
which I couldn't see, but because I was hungry. As a result of
my schedule as an Irgun worker, I often ate only one meal a
day, usually uncooked. Sometimes I ate nothing more than
falafel (fried chickpea balls) and pita (a flat kind of Arab bread).
But two days had passed since I had last eaten. While doing
Irgun work I was often so busy that I forgot to eat, but not here,
where I had nothing to do and the boredom was intolerable. I
sat on the steps of the little prison yard and looked around. The
only real scenery was the glorious roofs of the houses of the old
city of Jaffa. There was a chicken on one of them, and it
annoyed me no end as it scratched around, going in and out of
its coop whenever it pleased. I compared the two coops, the
chicken's and mine, and mine was quite obviously inferior. The
chicken could go wherever it wished, while I was locked in and
had no way out. Perhaps it was a good thing I had no writing
materials with me, otherwise, who knows what I might have
written, perhaps an article called "The Chicken and I."

The sound of someone knocking on the front gate woke me
out of my reverie. One of the prisoners had taught me the
meanings of the various knocks and rings. A knock on the door
meant a police officer from the men's wing had come, or someone from the main prison office. In fact, the new arrival was the
same clerk the guard had called that morning. This time he
wanted to fill out a form recording all my physical particulars,
lest I escape and the police have to search for me: the color of
my eyes and hair, scars on my face, any other identifying
marks.

When he finished, I demanded that he use the money which
had been confiscated from me to buy me food in Tel Aviv. This
too was something I had learned from one of the prisoners who
knew more than I about the ways things were done in this
"hotel." I couldn't possibly eat prison food, and while I was

arguing with him about buying me something, the guard came and whispered that someone had brought me food but I was forbidden to see the person. When she went to the door I took advantage of the opportunity, ran to the gate, and opened the hatch. There stood my friend Tzipora Gadanski. I only had time to say a few words. What was most important for me was to know who else had been arrested, but the guard sent Tzipora away and slammed the hatch shut. I angrily went back to my cell.

Opening the package almost made me weep. It smelled of home, and reminded me of life outside the prison walls. I could tell by the sandwiches that my friend Esther Raziel, the sister of David Raziel,[7] had prepared the ingredients. She was the only one who knew that I'd had an upset stomach for the past few days, and she had sent only suitable food. Tzipora, who knew a great deal about culinary matters, had made sure that the food was prepared aesthetically.

The guard locked my door, and once again I was alone with my thoughts. Then I had an idea: I would sing, and if a soldier of the Irgun was in the men's wing I would know immediately, since the window of my cell was on the same level as theirs, and they would certainly hear me. I was somewhat worried that Eitan might be there, because he didn't like my singing, and I was careful never to sing when he was in the vicinity. However, given the special circumstances, I was sure that he would forgive me. I sang the song by Jabotinsky[8] that we used to sing at Irgun functions:

> From the day I was called to the wonder
> Of Betar and Zion and Sinai,
> A brother's hand has imprisoned me

---

[7]David Raziel (1910—1941) became the Irgun's commander in 1938. In 1941 he was killed while conducting a covert operation, in cooperation with the British, against the pro-Nazi government of Iraq.
[8]Vladimir (Z'ev) Jabotinsky (1880—1940) was the founder and leader of the Revisionist Movement.

And my mother's house is closed to me . . .

I sang others as well, all of them appropriate to the circumstances I found myself in, but there was no answer. I felt much
better; perhaps no one had been arrested after all.

The day passed and was followed by a cold night in the cell
with the broken window, which was in turn followed by another morning, the morning of a long boring day which began
with the monotonal wail of the muezzin from the nearby
mosque: "There is no God but Allah." I was again plagued by
worries and distressing thoughts. If only I had a book to read,
to say nothing of a newspaper.

The only entertainment I had was talking to the guard. My
intransigence pleased her, and she became more friendly, and
even told me about her own nationalist views; she was happy
that I had gotten the best of Hackett. It turned out that we had
a few acquaintances in common. She asked me about my mother, and I told her that I had specifically asked people not to tell
her that I had been arrested. She began to smile, and I soon discovered why. While we were talking someone knocked on the
door, but not as loudly as the previous day. I ran to the hatch,
and when the guard opened it, there I saw my mother!

Much has been written about arrests and prisoners, suffering, bravery, and strength of character, but the story of the
heroism of the Hebrew mother has yet to be written, because
there is no power on earth that can describe it. It was the story
of the "Yiddishe Mama," the Jewish mother who, for the thousands of years of the Diaspora, knew, under the worst conditions imaginable, how to provide a sanctuary for her children.
With her inexhaustible love she protected them from all evil
and harm, and was always a symbol of tenderness and delica-
cy. Now she had suddenly taken on a new dimension: the
fighting nationalist. She herself could not fight on the front line,
but she knew how to make sure the fighters had a strong rear-
guard. She had to struggle ceaselessly with herself: on the one
hand, she didn't want her sons and daughters exposed to dan-

ger or involved in trouble; on the other, she understood their ambitions and their war, and she knew that she had to let them do what they had to for the good of the Jewish people. Sometimes, in a moment of weakness or pity, the first emotion would be uppermost, but it would be quickly conquered by the second. This terrible internal conflict was always camouflaged with external tranquility. Who could count the endless sleepless nights when a son or a daughter was away from home on an "outing," thinking that the mother had been fooled, that she didn't know these outings sometimes ended in death. The mother would sit with pounding heart, praying for the safety of the fighters, waiting for her child to come home. And here she was, on the other side of a barred hatch, smiling at me, hiding what she really felt.

"Who told you?" I blurted out. I had expressly asked that she be kept in the dark about my arrest.

"My child, my daughter! I knew about it before you did." She smiled her special smile, the one separated only by a hairline from tears, trying to hide the moisture at the corners of her eyes. "What I really want to know most is, what do you need? I brought you clothing, food, books, and a newspaper."

She had not received permission for the visit. While we were talking the guard stood there trembling with fear lest we be caught. If that happened, not only would she be punished, but I would be forbidden to receive packages. To keep that from happening she had closed the hatch, so that I had to speak to my mother through the cracks. Meanwhile, the guard waited outside to make sure no one came. If someone came, she would signal me and my mother to leave.

It was a very short visit. Before we parted she opened the hatch and I was able to clasp my mother's hand. Suddenly, although I didn't know how or why, the dam burst and I began to cry. It was as though all my pent-up distress had sought and found release: my anger at being arrested, at the collaborators who helped the alien regime to arrest underground fighters, at the fact that my work in the ranks of the Irgun, which I saw as the sole purpose of my life, had been stopped, and most of all, my worries about my son and my mother.

After she left I sat down to open the packages, and I was again made aware of what it meant to have a loving mother. What a gulf separated the packages from the gloomy prison walls and cell!

The guard came in and was amazed to see how emotional I was. "What happened?" she asked. "Until now you've been so brave and strong, and just seeing your mother makes your heart melt like wax!"

She told me that my mother had come to the prison the previous morning, but that there had been no way for her to get a package in. She had been afraid to tell me because she thought I would vent my anger on her. She had advised my mother to see the officer in charge of the prison, perhaps he would have pity on an old woman and authorize the visit. My mother, however, had preferred to return home with the packages of food rather than ask for favors from the prison commander. The struggle between the Yiddishe Mama, anxious about the welfare of her daughter, and the Hebrew mother of a fighting daughter was won by the latter. My eyes filled with tears again, but this time they were tears of pride. Happy is the nation which has such mothers!

Having suddenly become rich in food, I asked the guard to take some of it to the male prisoners. I was trying to find out whether any other Irgun soldiers had been arrested, and if so, who they were. However, the guard returned a few minutes later and told me that the sergeant refused to let her bring them food, claiming that the male prisoners had enough. That told me that there were, in fact, male prisoners, and I was annoyed by the fact that I didn't know who they were.

The packages of food, which had scant value outside the prison walls, were a treasure. Only someone who has been in prison and eaten prison food knows how sweet sugar is, and how good even dry bread can taste. Only such a person knows the worth of a clean towel, a toothbrush, and, strange as it may seem, a tin of sardines. I couldn't stop looking at the great riches I had received. But what made me happiest was the newspaper. It reported that a young girl had been arrested in connection with the kidnapping of a rich, influential Jew named Widenfeld. Until that minute I hadn't known that I was both the mother of a four-year-old son and a young girl. But it's an ill wind that blows no good, and thanks to my arrest I had received a compliment, and in public! The newspaper, incidentally, was wrong: I had nothing to do with Widenfeld's kidnapping.

Meanwhile I found a way, even in prison, to continue my underground work. I became friendly with the guards, shared what was in my packages with them, and tried to persuade them to join the Irgun. At night, when all the prisoners were in their cell, a guard would open my door and take me to their quarters, where, over a steaming cup of coffee which tasted ten times better than it could have in Brazil, the land of coffee, I lectured them on the role of the Jews in the liberation of their country from a foreign power. We also exercised all the usual underground precautions: if someone rang the bell at the outer gate, I had to return to my cell immediately and pretend to be fast asleep. My camouflage suit was perfect, because my mother had put pajamas in the package! On the third day I woke up happy, for I was able to wash and change my clothing. I was engrossed in reading *For Whom the Bell Tolls* when the bell at the main gate rang. A ring meant that an "event" of some kind was about to occur in the monotonous life of the Jaffa prison. The guard was called to the main office, and when she came back she told me that I had an invitation from Officer Schiff: he would be delighted if I would honor him with my presence. I was surprised, because he had already questioned me and had not learned anything. On the other hand, I was happy that I would be able to leave the prison even for a short while and see the city streets. It seemed like an eternity since I had last seen buildings and stores and people coming and going.

I was taken to the police station on Yehuda Halevi Street and

was amazed to see the two unlikely victims who had been captured by the police: Jacob T. and Isaac A. I had been afraid that
the "Chaims," all officers in the Irgun, had been arrested, but
where had police "intelligence" led it? They had arrested Jacob
while searching for Nissim Cohen, and since they hadn't found
him, they took a stand-in. Arbitrarily arresting other people
when those they were looking for couldn't be found was a
common occurrence in the chronicles of the British police in
Palestine. In one classic instance a short, dark-haired man was
arrested after the police had failed to find a tall man with blond
hair. Isaac was arrested because he worked for the National
Workers' Union and was in possession of tickets for a union
party. This was a labor union set up to provide work for people
whose political affiliations denied them entry into the leftist
Histadrut.

From there I was taken to Officer Schiff's office at the police
station on Shachar Street. Over his chair hung a picture of His
Majesty the King of England. Officer Schiff told Jacob and Isaac
that they were free to go, and then he turned to me and said,
"I'm very sorry to say that I am forced to release you as well."
I was amazed and didn't understand what he was talking
about. That he was sorry to release me I could understand: he
was a loyal servant of the British, and it was understandable
that he disliked me. But what did he mean by being forced?
Apparently something had happened in the meantime, and as
a result of whatever it was, he would have to release me.

The telephone rang and interrupted my train of thought.
From what Schiff said it became clear that he was being asked
what steps to take against a prisoner named Jacob T., who had
been released on the condition that he report to the police daily,
and who, for three days, had not presented himself at the station. It was obvious that as far as the police were concerned, the
left hand didn't know what the right hand was doing. The very
Jacob T. who had been arrested by one branch of the police and
was sitting in the same room with us was wanted by another
branch which didn't know that he couldn't report because he

was in prison! Schiff was obviously quite displeased by the whole matter and tried to gloss it over. Again he said to me, "I'm very sorry that I have to release you."

When I got back to the Jaffa prison, the two men told me that the sergeant had lied when he said that the male prisoners had enough food. The first thing I wanted to do was to make sure that they got my entire food supply.

Time passed slowly, and at four o'clock the guard said, "If you haven't been released by now, there's no chance you'll get out today. It's an unwritten law here that no one is released in the late afternoon, and certainly not in the evening. The gate only opens in one direction after dark: inward." I accepted the fact that I would have the pleasure of spending another night in prison. I planned to drink my traditional coffee with the guards, and in the meantime one of them gave me a cigarette as a down payment. I had barely entered their room when there was a sharp ring at the door. I ran back to my cell and pretended to be asleep.

Panting with excitement and amazement the guard came back. "What just happened now," she said, "has never happened before in all the time I've worked here. It's after six o'clock and outside the blackout is complete—and now they're going to release you!" I took a few minutes to remind them that from now on prisoners who belonged to the underground were not to be treated like the rest but were to get special treatment as political prisoners.

A car was waiting outside, and it took me to the police station on Yehuda Halevi Street. My friends Judith Gorenstein and Hannah Meir were waiting for me.

I walked out of the station and breathed the intoxicating air of freedom. I asked them to tell my mother immediately that I had been released, and also to relay the information to a certain address of the Irgun.

Only the next day did I learn the reason for my fantastic release. It was the result of negotiations between the Irgun and a Mr. Catling of the CID[8a]. They had reached the following

agreement: the Irgun would release Widenfeld, and the police
would announce that they had found him (this was vital for the
prestige of the police, which at that time was at an all-time low,
and Widenfeld was a very important man), and in return all the
men who had been captured at the officers' training course at
Mishmar Hayarden some months earlier would be let go. A
precondition for the negotiations was my release. The fact that
it was effected at night, prison customs notwithstanding, was
the result of an order direct from Jerusalem, instructing the
police to release me *immediately*, with no delay whatsoever, so
that the negotiations would not be delayed.

At six o'clock in the morning Jacob Yundoff, who had conducted the negotiations with Catling, went to my friend Judith
Gorenstein's house to tell her that her husband, who was one
of those arrested at Mishmar Hayarden, would be released
within a month's time. He recounted humorous and unflatter-
ing (to the British) details about the negotiations with the CID,
which were being conducted as if between equals.

The negotiations were held in an open field, with Catling of
the CID, the representative of the mighty British Empire on one
side, and on the other, a representative of the Irgun, a small
group of patriotic, militant dreamers, hounded by collaborators of their own nation. The Irgun was fighting to establish the
State of Israel, and by negotiating with its members it was as if
the British gave the State *de facto* recognition.

Equals they might have been, but the way each side
returned from the negotiations was not equal at all. The car
which carried the CID man got back safely to its base, while the
broken-down jalopy in which the Irgun fighters were riding
got stuck in the mud, and it took a wagon and horses to get it
out.

When I heard about the negotiations that had preceded my
release I said that in my opinion Officer Schiff wouldn't have to
be sorry about letting me go for long, and that I would soon be

---

[8a] British Central Intelligence Department.

rearrested on another pretext. Jacob, however, insisted that he had received the promise of a gentleman from both Catling and Wilkins (a notorious member of the CID) that I would not be arrested again. Blessed is he who has faith.

The first thing I did was go to my mother, who told me the amazing, mystery-like story about how she had found out about my arrest.

In the afternoon on the December 3, 1941, that is to say, on the day I was arrested, a stranger (who later turned out to be a detective) arrived at the kiosk owned by my stepfather and asked him where his daughter Tzila lived. Since my stepfather had a daughter named Tzila by his first wife, the question did not arouse his suspicions, and he gave the man her address.

That same day police officers went to Tzila's house with a warrant for her arrest. Again and again she swore that she had no connection with any illegal organization or activity, but they refused to believe her. She tried to contact her husband, Aharon Becker,[9] who is now the general secretary of the Histadrut, but her attempts were unsuccessful. They searched her closet and saw that the descriptions they had been given of my clothing didn't match the dresses they found. As they were walking down the stairs after they had formally arrested her, it occurred to Sergeant Day to ask if her mother was still alive. When she answered that her mother was dead, they asked if her father had remarried, and if his wife had a daughter named Tzila, and thus they discovered their mistake.

Since she didn't know my address, they asked for my mother's. When the police went to my mother's house, she wasn't there. After she came home the neighbors told her about the "guests" who had come visiting. Immediately realizing that they were looking for me, she ran to my house and took everything she found that she felt might incriminate me. And in fact,

---

[9]Aharon Becker (1906), a Mapai member, was secretary general of Histadrut from 1961 to 1969. In 1941 he was managing director of the industrial department of the Cooperative Wholesale Society.

when I was arrested I noticed that several things were missing and I was quite surprised.

Only after she had "cleaned" my room as best she could did my mother go to 4 Herzl Street, the headquarters of the National Workers' Union, to tell them that I was about to be arrested. From there she went to the home of one of my friends and gave her everything she had taken from my room. After running these errands she went home and, as she had suspected, found the police waiting. She gave them my address with a heavy heart, and consoled herself with the knowledge that she had removed everything that might be suspicious. She had in fact also saved the Chaims from arrest, because they were supposed to come to my house that evening.

In the meantime I also discovered how the police had managed to find the link between me and the kiosk. During one of my house calls to the owners of a certain factory, who were waiting for a messenger from the Irgun to come about fundraising, some police officers had been stationed near the factory. There was a doorkeeper downstairs, and he had been given orders to let people in but not to let anyone out on any condition unless specifically told to by the owners of the factory. Regardless, I went to the second floor, and after some heavy hints to the owners that it would be better for them if they did not notify the police, they allowed me to leave. To my great misfortune there was a woman who knew me standing next to the doorkeeper, and she asked how I was. He asked her what my name was, and she answered, "Tzila." That was the first time the police heard my name. Eight months later I visited the owner of a different factory, and despite the fact that nothing had been done against him, he gave my name to the police. He knew that there was a connection between me and the kiosk, and thus eight months passed between the time the Sherlocks of the Palestinian police first heard my name and my arrest. Two women had been arrested before me, and the first thing the police asked them was whether by any chance they happened to be named Tzila.

Chapter Three

The Road to Bethlehem

I had not been released unconditionally. My "freedom" was very limited, and it was clear that I had only been released because the British had no choice. I had to present myself at the police station three times a day, in the morning, at noon, and in the evening, somewhat like an observant Jew who had to pray in the synagogue three times a day—but only somewhat. Every morning I had to sign in, lest someone else appear in my place, and from dusk to dawn I was forbidden to leave my house. The first evening, however, after signing in I ran from the police station straight to the cinema, where *Gone with the Wind* was playing. The line waiting to buy tickets was very long, and I didn't see any point in asking anyone to let me in first just because they could see the movie whenever they wanted to during the following weeks, whereas my freedom might easily "go with the wind." Since there was no way I could get a ticket to the cinema, I went to the theater instead, but the play, a comedy, seemed faraway and alien, as though I were watching it through a fog. I couldn't concentrate on the play because far more pressing matters kept intruding on my thoughts, and it was difficult for me to laugh. The threat of arrest and imprisonment cast its shadow on me, and I couldn't enjoy the show.

Like a good girl, I reported to the police station three times the following day. On the third day, as I went to sign in at noon, I decided to try to trick them. I would sign twice and thus save myself the bother of having to go again in the evening. I was almost at the station house when I met Esther Raziel. She asked me a few questions and then said, incidentally, that a surprise was waiting for me: Officer Schiff wanted to see me. "Apparently," she said, "he decided to stop being sorry and wants to arrest you again. We are in contact with some of the police there, and they told us about it. The decision is up to you, Tzila; you can either go underground, where the police won't find you, or be prepared to go to prison."

In point of fact, there was no decision to make. I knew how hard things were for the Irgun, and going underground would have been too much of a financial burden, especially since I would no longer be able to work and earn my keep. Not only that, but the mother of a child would have a hard time keeping underground, and in addition, as a senior member of Betar.[10] Since I was well known to several members of the Haganah who were collaborating with the CID, it would have been difficult for me to hide. Going underground would probably have been more pleasant and even more heroic, but logic and clear thinking warned against taking such a step.

The few minutes I stood on the street deciding my fate seemed like an eternity. It was a hard decision to make. Perhaps in other organizations decisions of this kind would have been made by the people at the top. That would have made the situation much easier: an order is received and followed. But therein lay the essence of the Irgun spirit. The Irgun's soldiers were not automata who simply followed orders. They were reliable and worthy of trust; their decisions were not made selfishly, but first and foremost took into consideration what was best for the whole organization.

---

[10]Betar is the Hebrew acronym for Beit Yosef Trumpeldor, the name of the youth movement founded in 1925 by Vladimir Jabotinsky. Its goals were nationalist education and self-defense. Joseph Trumpeldor was the hero of Tel Hai.

"I'm going to the police station," I told Esther.

"Is that your final decision?" she asked.

"Yes," I said. "Who knows better than I what difficult financial straits the Irgun is in. I don't want to be an additional burden." Both of us were sad, she because she couldn't help me, and I because I was sentencing myself to prison. I asked her to take care of some things for me, to tell my mother, and insofar as possible, to make sure the child, orphaned again, would be all right. Esther shook my hand and we parted without saying anything further, although the expression on her face said it all.

When I entered the police station, the duty officer asked me to step inside the low railing that stood before his raised desk. Ordinarily I would sign in from the outer side of the railing, and I asked why I was required to come in, but no answer was forthcoming. When the two of us were alone for a moment, he showed me his log book, in which it was clearly written that he was forbidden to speak to me. My name was underlined in red to emphasize how strict the regulation was.

An officer named Bendel came into the station house and I asked him why I had been arrested. The question caused him great uneasiness, and he was quick to reply that it was not he who was responsible. When I told him that I was due back in two hours to sign in again, he said that it wouldn't be necessary, because I had to stay. He also said that he couldn't let me inform my mother, since he was not authorized to do so.

One by one the policemen left the station house. Only the duty officer, another policeman, and I were left. The duty officer woke a policeman who had been sleeping somewhere in the station and told him that I could give him a note listing the things I wanted brought from home. I was sure that Esther would take care of everything, but this was a good way to tell them that I had been arrested again. I wrote the note and the officer took it with him.

My second arrival at the Jaffa prison was a good deal more prosaic than the first. No more examinations, no more being ordered around, no more officers coming to interrogate me. So much the better! The first time they hadn't stopped talking, and this time, utter silence. Everyone had been forbidden to speak to me.

I entered the prison like someone returning to a house left only yesterday. The guard knew I was coming, so she wasn't in the least bit surprised to see me. There had been a change in orders. The first time I was arrested they had wanted to put me in the same cell as the other prisoners, and I had fought for my right to be by myself, whereas this time the CID demanded that I be put in my former cell, and I was assigned a special "honor guard" as well, who was to be stationed at my door with orders to take note of everything I did and not leave me alone for an instant. The guard didn't bother me in the least. She and I quickly became friends, and our nightly cups of coffee were drunk by one prisoner and three, not two, guards. The number of people listening to my "lectures" therefore increased by 50 percent.

One of the guards was the daughter of the guard who had received me on my first night at the prison. They knew by now that I understood Arabic, and they laughed when I repeated the conversation I had overheard that first morning. They apologized, saying that they were used to only one kind of political prisoner: Communists. Other political prisoners had passed through but had only stayed for a few hours, and they had not had the chance to speak to them.

This time I was more experienced and managed to smuggle in a pencil, money, cigarettes, and other small objects. The search conducted by the policewomen was quite superficial, and I had no problem about smuggling in what I wanted. When the Arab prisoners saw me in the corridor they cried out in sympathy, "You poor thing, are you here again? You just left and they've caught you again!" I returned to my cell and found it just as I had left it: everything that had been broken was still broken, there was still no glass in the window. Since this time I had been ordered to stay there, I immediately demanded that the window be fixed.

Again I was tormented by my thoughts: had I done the right thing? I had only been with my child for three days. I had brought everything he needed, and the head of the boarding school knew that I was going to prison again, possibly for a long time. In spite of the fact that she and her husband were members of Hashomer Hatzair, a leftist organization, they were fond of him and treated him well. I had even told them that I might not be able to pay for his room and board, but as directors of an institution for children of soldiers, they displayed exceptional understanding, our political differences notwithstanding. That was the one bright spot during those dark days.

At last I fell into a deep sleep which rescued me from the dilemmas and problems which had been tormenting me. The next morning I had to face the Arab women's expressions of condolence again. They wrung their hands and even tore their hair when they met me in the corridor. I was quite touched by their display of sorrow, which was so great that I found myself consoling them.

That morning a prison official came to pay me a courtesy call. "You're a very dangerous prisoner," he told me, "and therefore we are going to keep you in solitary confinement under special guard. You pose a grave danger to the British Empire!" It was only then that I understood the meaning of the red lines under my name in the station log book.

I was privileged more than once to hear about what a great danger I posed to the British Empire. It would be hard to say that I didn't find it all very complimentary.

When the official left, the guards approached me, astounded. They looked at me closely again, pleased by the status accorded me as "an enemy of the Empire," and asked me if it was true. I told them to ask the official for more information if they were really interested. One of them was so impressed that she clasped my hand warmly.

The Irgun sent a lawyer named Lebell to call on me, and I will never forget his visit. I cannot deny that this time imprisonment came as quite a blow, especially in view of the definite promises given to me by senior police officials. He told me that he was going to demand that I either be released immediately or stand trial. If I stood trial he was sure I would be found innocent, since there was no evidence against me whatsoever. I told him that I didn't think he would succeed, since the British would rely upon the laws governing emergency situations, according to which they could arrest anyone without giving him or her a trial. I asked him to bring me books and newspapers, but he laughed and said there was no need, since I would soon be released. I also asked him to refrain from sending food packages, because I knew how hard-pressed the Irgun was for money. His response was quite original. He bought candy, fruit, and cake with his own money; from then on the guards would eagerly look forward to his visits.

The same day a Jewish woman who was mentally ill was brought to the prison. It is hard to describe how filthy she was. She was put into the cell with the Arab prisoners, and they treated her with great cruelty and sadism. I appealed to a guard and told her to move the woman into my cell. She was sure that I had lost my mind, and told me that the woman was dangerous and attacked people, and that the other prisoners were only protecting themselves. When she saw that I was not about to change my mind, she agreed and brought the woman into my cell. I gave her food, made her lie down, and covered her. She slept soundly, but I didn't close an eye all night long, afraid that she would strangle me if I fell asleep. The next morning, when my friend Grunia Kimchi came to visit me, she was horrified by the way I looked and asked what had happened. I told her that I hadn't slept a wink all night.

The night, however, was nothing compared to the morning, when the same clerk told me that I would soon be transferred to Bethlehem Women's Prison. Grunia said that I must have been infected by the woman's madness, and that "we are all waiting for you to come home, and here you are talking about Bethlehem!" Only when I told her the source of my information did she begin to believe me. I asked her to tell my mother to come to visit me and to bring my son so that I could say good-bye to him.

That same day my mother did come to see me, although of course it was not an official visit. During my previous incarceration she had been brave, but this time she choked on her tears. "They said you had been released, they promised," was all she managed to say.

In fact, among all the terrible, sadistic practices instituted by the police and the CID, one of the worst was the way they behaved with the families of those who had been arrested. They hoped in this way to weaken the spirit of the underground resistance movement and frighten young people away from joining it. They promised to release prisoners and instead sent them to Bethlehem or Acco, and later to Eritrea, Sudan, or Kenya.

Hovering between the hope of release and the despair of imprisonment was the worst torture imaginable for both the prisoners and their families. I asked my mother to bring my son the next day, and we said goodbye through the small barred window. The burning tear that fell from her eye onto my hand spoke more than words could. Our leave-taking was rushed, since the police saw no need for a mother to say good-bye to her daughter before she was taken to a remote prison.

On my way back to my cell I decided that the guard would never again see me in a moment of weakness, as she had after my mother's first visit. It took every ounce of strength I possessed to stand firm. I took a book and pretended to read, but all I saw was a gray blur. Sometimes I saw the face of my mother, sometimes the face of my son, but always before my eyes were the walls of the prison at Bethlehem.

A bell rang and the guard hastened to the prison office, returning with a new visitor. It was a blonde woman, a Communist who was supposed to report to the police station every day but for several days had not done so. Needless to say, the guard was planning to put her into the cell which housed the common criminals. When the woman saw how much influence I had, she asked me to put in a good word for her with the guards. I managed to arrange that instead of the cell where they would ordinarily have put her, she was instead given a small area between the bed of the guard who slept outside my door and the end of the corridor. When the bell rang, however, she had to get up and go into the cell with the other prisoners.

At the time I didn't know about the barbaric treatment the Jewish Communist prisoners had given an immigrant who had been caught and brought to the prison in Bethlehem along with her infant. Her only crime had been to enter the country illegally. They had plenty of food and shared it with the Arab women who had been arrested for robbing Jewish homes during the riots, but they wouldn't give so much as a crust of bread to the infant, to say nothing of its mother. I treated this woman well out of a feeling of female solidarity, but had I known then what I later found out, I would not have helped her at all.

The next morning I was told to prepare myself for a journey. I would not have a chance to say goodbye to my son. I asked that at least my mother be told not to make the effort to come to see me at the Jaffa prison. I gave the food I had to the other prisoners, and the small amount of money which had been confiscated from me and kept in the office I gave to the guards. "I'm not trying to bribe you by giving you this money before I leave," I said. But I was sure that they were now on my side, and I only hoped that if any other women resistance fighters happened to be brought there, they would be well treated.

I left the prison at Jaffa; it had been merely the foyer to be passed through before I entered the main hall, the women's prison at Bethlehem.

✳ ✳ ✳ ✳ ✳ ✳

Chapter Four

The Prison at Bethlehem

The women's prison at Bethlehem was infamous and had the reputation of being a terrifying place, something along the lines of Sing Sing. Needless to say, women underground resistance fighters, all of whom were earmarked as potential guests, were especially interested in the place, and it had been the main topic of conversation more than once. But my knowledge of the prison did not come only from the stories I had heard.

I had been so interested that, despite the great danger to which I was exposing myself, I once went to visit and see for myself what it was like. It was in 1940, during the days between Rosh Hashanah and Yom Kippur. One of my duties in the Irgun was to distribute food to prisoners, men and women alike, in the jails and detainment camps. I had been to all of them except Bethlehem, where I avoided going lest I tempt fate. The CID paid special attention to everyone who visited the women there because they had come to the logical conclusion that the visitors probably belonged to the underground resistance movement.

Despite my doubts, hesitations, and misgivings, I was overcome by curiosity and wanted to see the place where I would one day certainly be incarcerated. I went to Jerusalem, and ordered a meal in a kosher restaurant in honor of Yom Kippur, buying enough food for the four women imprisoned in Bethlehem. Then I disguised myself in an elegant hat (which even boasted a feather on its brim!), put on my best dress, and took a taxi to the prison. On my way there I debated whether or not to use my real name, and decided to call myself Gila. It sounded enough like Tzila so that if I happened to be recognized, I could always say that they hadn't understood me when I gave my name.

At the prison I visited Sarah Wasserzug, who told me that the first question, when she was arrested, was whether her name was Tzila. I gave them the food and told them in what order to eat the different courses, which was a coded way of giving them instructions and messages, and by their answers I knew what to tell the Irgun.

And now I was going to Bethlehem again, without a taxi, without a feather, without an elegant dress, and for who knew how long?

To my surprise, when I left the Jaffa prison I was ordered into a closed van called a *zinzaneh*, Arabic for "punishment cell," the kind that was usually cold, underground, not well lit, and with barely enough room to sit on the floor—-and sometimes not even that. The *zinzaneh* was black and did look like a cell. It had no windows, just narrow, barred slits which barely admitted light and air. Going to Jerusalem as the only passenger in such a vehicle would have been torture enough, but at Ramallah I was joined by a group of Arab criminals bound hand and foot, all of them filthy and drunk. They threw up during the entire journey, and when the pails were full they vomited up directly onto the floor. The ride took two ghastly hours, and I just kept praying that we would reach Jerusalem, where I could be rid of all the filth. Every now and then I tried to look out through the slits to see what was going on outside. I could see passers-by hurrying on their way, some of them no doubt going to work, pressed for time. I, thank heaven, had all the time in the world.

Eventually my deliverance came: we arrived at the courtyard of the prison in Jerusalem, and it looked like a fairy-tale castle after the trip in the *zinzaneh*. I jumped out, and the hope

I had toyed with during the journey, that once in Jerusalem I would be able to meet friends who had been arrested, was realized. The men in the prisons were always eager for the *zinzaneh*'s arrival, since it meant that they could get news from and send regards to people in other prisons: the *zinzaneh* was like a kind of mobile post office. The first person I saw was a man named Raphael Saban, and he acted as if we were meeting at a party somewhere in Tel Aviv. From a short distance away some men waved and asked me to give their regards to four women in the Bethlehem prison.

I had different company for the rest of my journey: a criminal Arab woman, deaf and dumb, and suffering from epilepsy as well. She too was on her way to Bethlehem.

We passed the Tomb of Rachel the Matriarch, which stood alone and isolated at the side of the road. I remembered the passage from the Book of Jeremiah, repeated in prayers on Rosh Hashanah and Yom Kippur:

> A voice is heard in Ramah,
> Lamentation, and bitter weeping,
> Rachel weeping for her children;
> She refuseth to be comforted for her children,
> Because they are not.

> Thus saith the Lord:
> Refrain thy voice from weeping,
> And thine eyes from tears;
> For thy work shall be rewarded, saith the Lord;
> And they shall come from the land of the enemy.
> And there is hope for thy future, saith the Lord;
> And thy children shall return to their own border.

The site of Rachel's Tomb was symbolic, as though a divine hand had set it close by the women's prison. The Tomb had become a stopping place for those on their way to visit the prison. Mothers going to see their daughters would stop there first to pray for the release of the imprisoned underground fighters, for the health and safety of their children and of the nation, pouring their hearts out and finding strength, inspiration, and hope, and then would continue on their way. On my previous visit I too had stopped there to pray, but now I could only say a silent prayer from afar, looking at the Tomb through barred slits.

Just after the Tomb there was a fork in the road: right to Hebron, left to Bethlehem.

The prison was situated on a hill, and a winding road led up to it. On the right-hand side of the road was a large monastery with a bell tower, and its bell played an important role in our lives. It tolled the hours, and thus we knew the time, and when on occasion it broke down, it seemed to us as though time itself had stopped.

On the left-hand side of the road was a large building which looked like a castle from the Middle Ages. The road meandering around it looked from afar like a river and made the building seem as though it were a knight's stronghold, surrounded by a moat. A high stone wall topped with barbed wire encircled the building, and at its entrance was an enormous rusty iron gate.

Getting into the building was a complicated procedure. One had to pull at an iron rod hung to the right of the gate, causing a bell to ring in the office, the sound muffled but still audible. A prison guard, dressed for some reason like a nun and carrying a huge key (a foot and a half in length, and more than an inch in diameter) would leave the office, come to the gate, and open a small window to see who was there. Through this window she would negotiate about permission to enter. The visitor would pass whatever documents were in his or her possession through the window, and the guard would return to the office for further instructions. This was the procedure for visitors, but if the guard saw that there was a new inmate to be admitted, formalities would be dispensed with and she would open the gate immediately. The gate had its own character, one admirably suited to where it had been installed. It refused to swing open easily, and when coerced it would screech on its hinges and groan as if to say, "I did what I could not to open, and if in the end I did, it was only because I was forced to." And one would have liked to answer, "You are forgiven. The women's desire not to enter is far greater than your desire not to admit them."

The prison building was two or three stories high and enclosed a beautiful garden, which was not, however, for the pleasure of the prisoners, but rather for the exclusive use of the staff. Seeing the lovely scenery and garden made one think that when the State of Israel was established the best thing to do would be to take down the walls and destroy the bars and turn the prison into a resort where every year former inmates could meet and remember their days here. (Who imagined then that Bethlehem, the birthplace of David, cradle of the Kingdom of Israel, would be outside the borders of the Jewish state?) As soon as one entered the building, however, the idea of turning it into a resort was instantly replaced by the desire to see it totally and immediately destroyed—razed to its very foundations; the walls which had absorbed such endless sorrow and grief ground into dust, and its hellish memory erased forever.

Once inside the new prisoner was overcome by a longing to find a quiet corner in which to rest after her arduous journey, but no such thing was forthcoming. The "Via Dolorosa" was far from over. She was first taken to the prison office, where a guard sat in front of a log book and the policemen accompanying her would hand over the papers necessary to arrange for the transfer of the human cargo. The guard would sign a receipt for the "merchandise" and the policemen would leave. Then the guard herself would examine the merchandise and hand it over to a second guard, who would roll up her sleeves and begin her "holy work."

At this point the prisoner ceased to be a human being and lost her rights. The guard began by stripping her of all her possessions. A watch? Forbidden. Cigarettes? Forbidden.

Matches? Forbidden. Paper, pencil? Sometimes permitted, depending on the guard's mood. Jewelry? It had to come off. Mirror? Out of the question——what for, to be able to see one-self aging behind prison walls? We had a terrible argument about my wedding ring because my fingers had become enlarged and I couldn't remove it. I must admit that I was for-tunate, since unlike a gangster who would have cut my finger off to take the ring, the guard let me keep both the ring and the finger. All this was written down in the day book and duly signed, and when I was fortunate enough to leave this hell-hole, everything would be returned——except for the time that had been stolen from me.

I wanted to believe that the worst was over, but I was wrong: the worst was yet to come. The guard dragged me into a room that was something between a storeroom and the den of a wild animal. A faint light burned day and night, and it was there that they searched the prisoners' clothing, and posses-sions, and body. . . I was humiliated, filled with disgust and revulsion.

The expression on the face of the guard was repellent and reminded me of the Hunchback of Notre Dame, except for the fact that she was taller than he. She even had a pretty name, "Blossom," and she was quite a flower! She did not ask me to remove my clothes but began to remove them herself in the most offensive way possible, and thus we started struggling as she pulled my clothes in one direction and I pulled them in the other. This made her angry and she swore at me, using the foulest Arabic curse words she knew.

In time we taught Blossom how to treat Jewish prisoners, but meanwhile she ruled by brute force, and her body searches were deeply humiliating and insulting. There was no doubt in my mind that she had received special orders to deal particu-larly harshly with "terrorists," but in addition she was trying to make up for her failure to prevent two Communists (whom she had been guarding) from escaping. It was especially important to her since there were people who said that she had helped them, and she was trying to demonstrate her loyalty and devotion to the job. Like the other guards, she had a particular hatred for Jews, and having Jewish prisoners in her charge gave her a way to vent that hatred. Eventually we managed to teach her a lesson, and the prisoners who were brought to Bethlehem during the years 1945—1946 suffered far less at her hands.

From there I marched in the wake of the guard, who kept clanking her key ring, a sound which reminded me of the clanking of chains, and I could imagine them on my legs.

The two of us walked through long rooms smelling of mold. My nose was assailed by the harsh, unpleasant odors of Arabic food as it cooked, and the closer we got to the kitchen, which was on the first floor of the prison, the stronger the smell became. The food was cooked on a wood-burning stove; the kitchen was always full of smoke, and the walls were covered with soot.

Having passed through rooms in which food, utensils, disinfectants, laundry, and other things were stored, we went along a corridor on one of whose sides was a kind of cave: this was the prisoners' kitchen. Just looking at the women there made me shudder, for most of them were murderesses and criminals of the worst sort. For an instant I felt that I must be at the cinema, and that soon the film would end and the lights would go up, and then I would leave the theater and go home. It was impossible to believe that what I saw was real, and that there was no way out, nothing and no one to save me.

On the right of the kitchen were stairs leading to the second floor. At the top of the stairs was a gate with iron bars reaching to the ceiling. For the sake of security the keys were kept by the guard who was on duty on the top floor, and a guard who wanted to enter had to call her and ask her to unlock the gate. The stone steps were worn smooth from the passage of many feet, and if one weren't careful a nasty fall would ensue, as often happened to the prisoners.

The gate opened, but the trek wasn't over. There were more narrow stairs and another gate, but this one did not open: it was the gate at which visits with prisoners were held. I too had once visited here, but from the other side, and it was quite a different feeling. Opposite the stairs was a long corridor with doors on both sides. The stench in the corridor was unbearable, and was accompanied by the screams and screeches of women who had been cursed by fate, for the building also housed the indigent mentally ill, who were held for unlimited terms, "until the High Commissioner decided to release them." Most of them were released by the Angel of Death. Almost all of them were Jewish, and the great iron key had been systematically wielded on their backs, the beatings punctuated with kicks and blows. These poor wretches received no medical treatment and almost no food, and their sanitary facilities were appalling. The devil himself could not have devised such conditions, yet they had been knowingly imposed by people belonging to a nation whose citizens were concerned about sick cats and dogs, and who were proud of their Royal Society for the Prevention of Cruelty to Animals.

I climbed more stairs. Between the stories there were two rooms. The one on the right was immaculately clean, a bit of paradise in this hell. A heroine of the Jewish people named Rachel Havshush Ohevet-Ami worked there, passing her time in prison by ironing for the prison staff.[11] The room on the left was the prison superintendent's office. I kept climbing stairs, asking myself how much farther up I would have to go in my descent into this pit. We came to another corridor, which ended in a large window.

It was cleaner here, and there was more light. We were in a typical Arab house: marble, pictures, vaulted roofs, and corridors. On the left were the rooms of the Jewish prisoners, on the right, those of the Arab prisoners, and in the midst of it all, Rachel. Sometimes, when the door to one of the Arab prison-

---

[11]The story of her heroism is the subject of the next chapter.

ers' rooms opened a wave of foul air escaped, as though a gas jet had been released. Most of these Arab women were homeless peasants used to sleeping on the floor, and they were permitted to bring their children with them, for whom orange crates served as cradles. The doors were typically Arab, that is to say, double-leafed doors that fastened in the middle with a bolt and were locked from the outside, with a small barred window set into one of the leaves through which a guard could see into the room.

Only after this long trek did I reach "safety and security"—-my sisters, the underground fighters incarcerated in the Bethlehem prison.

So, Tzila, I said to myself, it has finally come to pass. The nightmare threat of Bethlehem which hovered over you, consciously and subconsciously, like the double-edged sword which hovered over Adam and Eve, has vanished. You are secure now——free of the fear of arrest and all the worries that accompany it.

Strange to say, the feeling a prisoner has after the crisis of his or her first imprisonment has passed is peace of mind: "How good it is that the worst is behind me." Only then comes the realization of how heavy the burden of fear was. But this was my second incarceration, and it was quite unlike my first experience with the world behind bars and barbed wire, nor was the prison in Jaffa anything like the one in Bethlehem. Jaffa had an air of impermanence, like the booths erected during Sukkot (the Feast of Tabernacles) and dismantled after seven days. Here the prisoner felt she had moved in permanently.

Moreover, the situation of those arrested in accordance with the arbitrary administrative law was far worse than that of the convicted criminals who had been given long sentences, in that they knew exactly what crime they had been arrested for and were entitled to a trial and a defense attorney. Most important, they knew exactly how long they would stay behind bars and could state with certainty the date on which they would be released, and every day that passed brought them closer to it.

But here? The slightest suspicion was enough to rob you of your liberty without your being able to defend yourself in court, the natural right of every arrested person, and without knowing how long you would be looking at the world through bars and barbed wire: a month, a year, an endless number of years.

An arbitrary decision of the CID had sentenced you to what was virtually life imprisonment. In addition, a convicted criminal who had served part of his sentence had paid for part of his crime, but this was not the case for someone who had merely been arrested and detained. The longer such people stayed behind bars, the more important they became to the CID. More than once, when newly appointed CID officers appeared on the scene or a show investigation committee was appointed, the files of the detainees would be examined. When it was seen that someone had been under arrest for a long time, the natural conclusion would be reached that if the detention had been so long, the detainee was particularly dangerous, and had, of course, to remain in custody.

However, the heartfelt reception I received from the women who had been arrested for underground activities made me forget everything for a moment. After the awful experience of the Via Dolorosa to Bethlehem, and of the prison itself, where I would have to remain until I was released by the authorities, all was forgotten and my spirit was uplifted. I met friends I had suffered and fought with, women who had proved themselves valorous on both fronts: in the field, and here, captured and imprisoned by the enemy. They were anxious about me and about how I felt, and tried to make things easier for me.

Seeing the way they behaved filled my heart with warmth and pride. Happy is the nation which is mother to such daughters! They surrounded me, asking endless questions about what was happening in the outside world. They were not interested in which movies were showing or what the latest fashion in dresses was, but only about the fight to liberate the homeland. Open-mouthed, eyes shining, they listened to stories about military actions and operations, and about how we would fight on to the final victory. Self and place were forgotten, and as I was carried aloft on the strength of their enthusiasm, the prison walls disappeared, the bars faded, and Bethlehem once again became the cradle of the Kingdom of Israel.

✳ ✳ ✳ ✳ ✳ ✳

Chapter Five

Rachel Ohevet-Ami, Heroine

The prison at Bethlehem was the Hall of Fame for the young Jewish women who sacrificed the years of their youth on the altar of the war of resistance and resurrection. However, its story cannot be written without special reference to the girl who symbolized par excellence the spirit of the fearless Hebrew fighter. Every temple has its priest or priestess, and in the temple of valor called the Bethlehem Women's Prison, the high priestess was an exceptional young woman named Rachel Havshush Ohevet-Ami.[12] She was like the girl in Bialik's[12a] poem,

> Oh, that I might be like you, silent-souled, humble,
> Weaving your lives unseen, modest in thought and action;
> Hidden dreamers, speaking but little, great in glory.
> Within you, the beauty of the soul is concealed, like a pearl
> in the depths of the sea.
> Your virtues are like the berries of the forest, growing in
> the dark of the shadows.

---

[12]Rachel's family name was Havshush. Ohevet-Ami, meaning "Lover of my people" in Hebrew, was the name she took for herself after her heroic attempt failed.

[12a]Haim Nachman Bialik was one of Israels most famous authors and poets.

Your hearts—a sacred temple; your closed lips—its portals.
Noble you are, unknown and unknowing . . .

Much has been written about the young Jewish women who risked their lives fighting for the freedom of their country, but as of this writing people of perverse intentions, unaware of their folly, are trying to erase some of the most glorious chapters of the annals of Israel's War of Independence, and among them is the story of Rachel.

The time was 1939, shameful days of bloody riots, when murdering bands of Arabs sowed death and mourning in the houses of Israel, and Jewish blood was shed unavenged. Every day saw a new massacre in the cities, on the roads, in the settlements. The only officially sanctioned response to the tidal wave of bloodshed was a wall of Jewish stupidity, called "self-restraint" by its proponents.[13]

Today, when we take our state and our army for granted, it seems unbelievable that such foolishness could have prevailed. Then, however, it was no more than bitter reality. Who would believe today that there was a time when defensive weapons which would only have rescued Jews were considered tainted by the same people who proudly sell Israeli weapons to Germany, the country which butchered the Jewish people? Who would believe that using sports to train young people to defend themselves was libeled by the same people as unclean, as militarism, as chauvinism? Who would believe that every act of revenge on the enemy, designed to make him desist and withdraw, would be considered a crime bordering on treason, for which there was no atonement, and that the national order

---

[13]During the Arab uprising of 1936—39, the leaders of the *Yishuv* and the Haganah adopted a policy known as "self-restraint" (*havlagah*) in order to avoid provoking the British. Jewish military activities were limited to self-defense. The Irgun bitterly opposed this policy, both advocating and engaging in retaliatory attacks.

of the day would be to prove to the enlightened world that we were morally and culturally superior to the Arabs who murdered us in cold blood?

The Arabs ridiculed our self-restraint and were only too happy to exploit it by continuing to slaughter us without fear of reprisals. Their boldness was so great that they even began to come into metropolitan Jewish centers to assault people. Every day the city streets turned into theaters, and funereal dramas were played out as they had been in the days of the ghettos, in the days of the pogroms against the Jews of the Ukraine; and the orators of the "national institutions" gave their customary speeches about not demeaning ourselves by using the same tactics as the Arabs. "For every tree that is uprooted," they would proclaim, "we will plant ten more."

The Arabs, laughing up their sleeves and feeling secure in the knowledge that they could continue the massacres without interference, called the Jews "children of death." That was the nickname the Arabs had given to the first Jewish settlers in Petach Tikvah, and they continuing using it until the day Abraham Shapira[14] and his comrades rose up, and with their acts of heroism taught the Arabs that they were not children of death, but rather the sons of the Maccabees, who knew how to repay murderers. It was as though the clock had been turned back fifty years.

At that time David Raziel was the Irgun's commander, and the decision was taken to put an end to the disgraceful self-restraint and to the slaughter of Jews in their own homeland. In direct contradiction to the will of the "leaders," the Irgun abandoned the policy of self-restraint. On the day that would be remembered by the Arabs as Black Friday, the Irgun's soldiers in Jerusalem smote a terrible blow which sent shock waves through the Arab community.

---

[14]Abraham Shapira (1870—1965), a colorful figure much admired both by Jews and Arabs, founded the Shomerim, the Yishuv's first self-defense force, at Petach Tikvah in 1890.

In the Arab market in Haifa (a well-known meeting place for those plotting to murder Jews), a bomb exploded killing dozens of people and wounding many more. All at once, as though someone had waved a magic wand, the situation of the Yishuv, the Jewish settlement in what was then Palestine, changed radically. The Arabs were terrified, and attacking Jews became less important than preserving their own safety. The Yishuv gained the respect of the international community: previously, other nations had seen the Yishuv as a nuisance, a source of trouble, a weak, artificial entity which could not defend itself and needed outside help—that is to say, foreign soldiers whose blood would be shed in its defense, something no politician was willing to commit himself to—but now they had to revise their opinion.

The war was being fought for the soul and honor of the Yishuv in Palestine, and the Irgun fought it on three fronts simultaneously. The first was the homefront, and it was the most difficult; the members of the Irgun were reviled as unbridled terrorists, defilers of the pure Jewish sense of morality, and were damned and ostracized. The bitter anger and fratricidal hatred directed toward the Irgun were diametrically (and cynically) opposed to the policy of self-restraint taken toward the Arab murderers, and exemplified the infernal stupidity which characterized the leaders of the Yishuv. Before a Hebrew fighter could go out to do battle with the murderers of his brothers and sisters, he had first to overcome the barriers placed in his path by his own people.

The second front they faced was the British, and the third was the Arabs. Only the spirit of valor and courage found in the hearts of the Irgun soldiers could overcome these opposing factors.

During this time an Irgun fighter named Jacob Raz was taken prisoner by the enemy. Caught trying to plant a bomb in the Arab market in Jerusalem, he was captured by Arabs who hurt him badly and then turned him over to the CID. They in turn took him to the hospital, his body riddled with knife wounds. Lying in a hospital bed, writhing in agony, he feared that his captors would torture him into revealing Irgun secrets, and he decided to foil them. In an unprecedented act of courage, he tore his bandages off and lay there bleeding until his brave, pure soul returned to its Maker.

Another of the anonymous fighters who challenged the policy of self-restraint was Rachel Havshush Ohevet-Ami. She was arrested in 1939 when she tried to plant a bomb near the prison in Jerusalem that would have detonated as Arab family members came to visit their murdering relatives whose hands dripped with Jewish blood. She was only seventeen years old, and the Irgun had refused to allow her to go on such a dangerous mission, but she would not back down and eventually convinced them. Dressed as an Arab, she carried a basket of vegetables in which she had placed a powerful bomb. Since the basket was heavy, she asked a young Arab man to carry it for her. Its weight aroused his suspicions and the bomb was discovered. The Arabs would have killed her on the spot if a policeman hadn't chanced by and rescued her from the crowd, although they did manage to beat her severely.

When brought before the CID she refused to speak at all. She wouldn't answer their questions and was even prepared to be tortured. She later related that they had not actually tortured her, but had refused to let her sit, and had forced her to stand without moving, her hands raised above her head. She was too modest to consider such treatment torture, but it was certainly more than merely extreme punishment if one takes into account the fact that she had been beaten by the crowd.

At that time there was a prison for women in Bethlehem, but Jewish women were not sent there because of the Arab riots. There were four Irgun fighters in the prison in Jerusalem: Rachel Broshi, Rachel Hoenigman, Esther Cohen, and Tovah Reichman. They knew that Rachel had been arrested, but she had not been brought to their cell, since the CID did not consider it secure enough for such a dangerous prisoner. The women prisoners learned through the grapevine that a special

cell with reinforced bars and windows was being prepared for
a special prisoner. And that was where she was locked up after
her trial, in which she was sentenced to life imprisonment (her
youth saved her from the death penalty). She was, incidentally,
the first Jewish woman given a life sentence.

The prison had once been a maternity hospital and was
located behind the Italian school in the heart of Jerusalem.
Rachel had no contact with the other prisoners, and when
taken to the yard for exercise was accompanied by the prison
superintendent and a policewoman. Rachel Broshi finally succeeded in making contact with her in the bathroom, and they
communicated regularly until they were both transferred to the
prison in Bethlehem. There too they were separated, but they
were able to contact each other during prayer services and on
holidays, although the right to hold services was only granted
after long negotiations with Miss Graham, the prison superintendent. Food could also be given to her, since the four young
women had been arrested, not sentenced, and were permitted
to receive food from outside the prison. Thus it turned out that
almost from the first moment of her arrest Rachel was not
alone, and that made her imprisonment easier to bear.

From the day of her arrest to her release, Rachel was the
princess of the prison. She was respected and admired by
everyone, even by the administration. That was because of her
bravery and courage during her arrest, trial, and sentencing. As
previously mentioned, she was seventeen years old, the only
girl in a family of four children. It was easy to understand how
her parents felt when they saw their only daughter standing in
the shadow of death, sentenced to life imprisonment. Her
father was so devastated that during his first visit to Bethlehem
he couldn't come to where the prisoners met their visitors, but
could only sit and groan and weep. Her mother did come,
weeping and wiping away her tears. Rachel was the only one
to stand firm, and even tried to lift her parents' spirits and comfort them, promising them again and again that everything
would be all right. "Don't worry about me," she would say, "I

am not suffering and I lack nothing. My only worry is for you, that you be strong!" That was what she told them the first time they came to see her.

All the other prisoners were amazed at the courage of such a child, and thus from the beginning her standing at the prison was high. The Jewish prisoners, even the convicted criminals, considered it an honor to be in her company and to serve her. The Arab prisoners really complimented her; they used to call her Rachel the Bomb!

Ironing was her assigned work. Standing in the same place for eight hours each day, ironing the starched clothing of the prison staff, was not a pleasant or an easy task by any means. Eventually they brought her all the uniforms of the high-ranking officers of the prison and even uniforms from Jerusalem.

The conditions of her incarceration were severe because no special recommendations had been made. She had to eat regular prison food, wear regular prison clothing, and sleep on the floor without a bed. She was permitted one bimonthly visit, had to work long hours, and wasn't allowed to study. In spite of those hardships, she managed to learn French, Arabic, and English. She did all kinds of handiwork, knitting, and embroidery, and all of it sitting on a mattress on the floor with only a small black crate in which to keep her things.

Efforts to obtain some kind of special status for Rachel were in vain, not only because the regime was hard-hearted, but because the institutions of the Yishuv were indifferent to her. Some public-spirited women[15] tried to awaken popular opinion in order to improve the conditions of her imprisonment. They appealed to important people and women's organizations, asking them to sign a petition, and although the people they approached had been willing to sign the same sort of petition for Communists, they were unwilling to sign one for Rachel.

Various charitable organizations, such as the Organization

---

[15]Dr. Danziger, Mrs. Gensia Herzog, Mrs. Plotkin, Mrs. Recanati, and Mrs. Nevisky.

of Working Mothers and WIZO (the Women's International Zionist Organization), also refused, but the members of the National Union of Women, headed by Dr. Giladi, an active worker in the community and herself a former political prisoner (arrested in 1936), would not give up. Mrs. Recanati contacted Dr. Oplatka and asked him to involve a doctor in the employ of the British government who would attest to the fact that Rachel's health required special consideration, but her efforts were unsuccessful, because at that time Rachel was healthy and he was unwilling to cooperate. The late Mrs. Herzog[16] knocked on every door, followed all the stages of Rachel's incarceration, and kept in touch with her even after her release. They also appealed to the Chief Rabbis. Dr. Danziger succeeded in interesting the late Professor Magnes[17] in Rachel's situation, and after her daughter married his son she even took the young couple to visit her in prison.

The ice cracked slightly but did not melt. When I was released I vowed not to rest until Rachel was awarded special treatment, and I worked alongside those women and the heads of the Revisionist movement. Tzvi Kulich joined our struggle, as did others, and finally we were successful, although only partially. Rachel was given a bed, her work-day was shortened, and she received one or two other small privileges. The problem of food became less critical because as long as we older women were there she ate with us, and we did everything we could to make her time in prison more pleasant.

In 1940 four resistance fighters were released, and a few months later four new prisoners, women who had been among the forty people arrested at the training course at Mishmar

---

[16]Mrs. Herzog came from a family of rabbis and was not related to Chaim Herzog, President of Israel from 1983 to 1992.

[17]Rabbi Judah Magnes (1877—1948), an ardent Zionist, served as chancellor, and then as president, of the Hebrew University from its founding until his death.

Hayarden, arrived. They were Bella Atara Heitin, Eve Kafka Amrami, Ruth Halevi, and Rivka Neuman Ben Meir. When they were arrested a delegation of women went to the late Rabbi Uziel[18] to ask him to use his influence to gain their release. One of the women said, "They are young girls and don't know what they are doing." He answered, "They knew exactly what they were doing, and they are heroines! If I were only younger, I would do exactly the same thing!"

A few months later, they were released. Meanwhile, Miriam Robowitz, Naomi Orenstein, Sarah Wasserzug, Miriam Shuchman, Ruth Halevi (for the second time), and I were arrested.

We were all older than Rachel and indulged her whims, accepting her with love and understanding and goodwill. Our fight to be transferred to a special camp was only a matter of lip service, a demonstration to show that we refused to accept our imprisonment: we didn't want to leave her alone with the convicted prisoners, even if they were Jewish.

The story of the visitors she received deserves special mention. Before 1941 members of Betar, usually from Jerusalem, used to make a pilgrimage to bring her gifts on every holiday. From 1941 on, the authorities began increasing their pressure on the organization, and when arrests became a daily occurrence fewer people visited her, although some still did. Even Menachem Begin went to see her in prison when he arrived in the country. It was only in 1943 that the visits from members of Betar stopped completely, because people were afraid of the CID, and only family members came.

As previously mentioned, Rachel's parents went to see her every two months, and on holidays parents and friends could come. During each visit someone from the CID had to be present, and only one of three languages could be spoken:

---

[18]Ben-Zion Meir Uziel (1880—1953), a committed Zionist and leader of Mizrachi, was Rishon le-Zion, or Sephardic Chief Rabbi of Israel, from 1939 until his death.

Hebrew, Arabic, or English. Needless to say, we spoke only Hebrew with Rachel. Once, when her parents arrived, no one from the CID was available, and Rachel was told that the visit would not be permitted unless they spoke in Arabic. She decided that it was better not to see them than have to speak Arabic. The warden of the prison turned on her and in a voice full of venom said, "At home you speak Arabic, and your father's Arabic is better than his Hebrew." Rachel answered, "I have many things at home that I don't have here, and vice versa. Here I am willing to speak——and will speak!——only one language: Hebrew." The warden then went to speak to her parents, and their answer was the same. She gnashed her teeth in fury.

It should be noted that except for the first visit, when her father's pain and sorrow were too much for him to bear, the parents were as strong as the daughter and were not about to give up one ounce of their pride as Jews. They came to every visit holding their heads high, never complained or wept, asked after each one of us by name, and demanded to know what they could do to help us. It was a matter of honor for each woman who was released to visit Rachel's parents at their home. Their house turned into a meeting place for former prisoners and detainees.

Rachel spent the best years of her life serving a life sentence; seven years, from 1939 to 1946. She was only pardoned and released at the end of the Second World War.

✳ ✳ ✳ ✳ ✳ ✳

Chapter Six

Fire . . .

A whole new world opened before me, squeezed behind the walls of the prison. Someone who has never been incarcerated can never understand how many problems arise every hour of every day, all of them demanding solutions. Serving time in prison is something static, monotone, unchanging. When someone is put in prison, all of his daily worries become the charge of the prison administration, and his main worry is that his freedom has been taken away from him. That's how it is for regular criminal prisoners, but the situation of political prisoners and detainees was completely different. To their credit, it must be said that they knew how to turn the darkness of incarceration into light, to forge themselves on the anvil of their afflictions and blunt the weapon of imprisonment with faith and hope.

Administrative detention was not designed to prevent "terrorists" from taking action, but to turn their imprisonment into a nightmare for every young person in the country and thus make them afraid to join the fighting underground resistance movement. The names of Bethlehem, Acco, Latrun, Jerusalem, and later Eritrea, Sudan, and Kenya were intended to become a kind of sword of Damocles hanging over the heads of those who sought freedom for the homeland, preventing them from even thinking the dangerous thought of freedom for their people.

The prisoners themselves were to be broken physically and morally as a warning to potential rebels. Their families—mothers, fathers, wives, children—were an important part of the plan. No one was more surprised than the authorities to discover that they were up against a brick wall, and that the prisoners and their families frustrated the plan. The prisons and the detention camps turned into schools for the underground in every sense of the word, and inmates who happened to be in prison but were innocent of political thought left as enthusiastic converts to the cause. Eliezer Kashnai was not a member of the underground when he was arrested and exiled, but when he was released and returned to the country, he joined the fighters, made the supreme sacrifice, and was hanged for his beliefs.

The prisoners fought a hard, bitter fight to win elementary human rights, but the Jewish women prisoners had to fight ten times harder. The male prisoners were put into detention camps, but the women at Bethlehem lived under real prison conditions, even after they were moved to the "villa" near the prison. It was in regard to the issue of incarcerated women that the British "gentlemen" revealed their hypocrisy toward the "weaker" sex. The English expression "ladies first" here meant "first to suffer." Many of the myths about the British, who called themselves the people of the Bible, were proved to be just that, myths. For instance, the English were usually thought to be have a certain *sangfroid*, but we discovered the truth: they kept their tempers so long as no one annoyed them, but as soon as someone did annoy them, they completely lost their self-control. They liked to wrap themselves in a cloak of compassion, seeing themselves as kind to all living creatures, whether a mangy dog or a wounded horse, but their hearts were devoid of mercy when confronted with wounded resistance fighters.

The very fact of confining young women in the Bethlehem prison with its gruesome conditions was an act of sadism and a constant torment. It is difficult to understand why a detention camp for women wasn't established, since there were such camps for men. Perhaps that was their way of getting revenge on members of the weaker sex who dared to fight against them. They could understand taking blows from men, but not from women.

My first experience with prison life was in the kitchen, if the cave that bore that name might be so called. If there are exactly seven circles in hell, something that has yet to be proved by reliable witnesses, then the kitchen was definitely the seventh circle of the Bethlehem hell. It had all sorts of "good qualities":

1. Its windows faced the prison yard, and the freedom that was so near and yet so far. We used to look at the scenery, so enchanting, so appealing that one's heart would thrill and one's breast would be flooded with hidden waves of yearning. Accursed bars separated us from it, and we kept peeling potatoes, our hearts aching.

2. The smells emanating from the food of the Arab prisoners as it cooked were so bad as to cause dizziness and nausea. Heaven alone knew what ingredients they used!

3. To the really astonishing smells of cooking was added the stench coming from the rooms of the mentally ill women, which was enough to drive a normal person mad. And as if that weren't sufficient, the Arab women often fought among themselves, the expressions on their faces making them look like witches in stories meant to frighten children. Every squabble might end in someone being stabbed with a knife or having boiling water or oil thrown over her, and they demanded that the neutral Jewish prisoner be the judge and angel of peace. Keeping the peace was extremely dangerous, since only a hair's-breadth separated judge and victim.

In the midst of all of this, one had to remember why one was in the kitchen in the first place, and that was to prepare food from almost nothing, and sometimes even from what was really garbage. There were only two things wrong with the provisions brought to the kitchen: quantity and quality. The amount of food was small and not suitable for European cuisine, but rather for the nutritional level of the Arab peasant. Every one of us who worked in the kitchen had to cope with this painful problem. The unfortunate prisoner whose turn it was to cook would do her utmost to prepare food that was nourishing and tasty, and her disappointment was immense when she saw the fruit of her labors thrown into the garbage can. It should be noted that the prisoners of Eastern Jewish origin knew about cooking vegetables, but the women who did not know what to do with them cursed their fate and would have been only too willing to throw them into the garbage if only they had something to use in their place. Having no other choice, the cooks would throw the vegetables into the pot, and it is not difficult to imagine what the outcome would be. In time we all learned to make something out of nothing, and that, along with our fight for a change of diet, changed our culinary situation.

The Arab prisoners knew nothing about taking turns and were not organized. They received their orders from the prison administration, and the prisoner in charge of the kitchen remained in charge until she was replaced or released. At this time she was a woman named Fatima. The crime for which she had been imprisoned was throwing her husband into a well, neither more nor less. He had been blind, which was easily understood, since only a blind man would have married a monster like Fatima. She looked like the Hunchback of Notre Dame, both in size and shape; she really did have a humped back.

One day Fatima insulted the daughter of the sheik of a village called Lifta (she too was named Fatima), who had been sentenced to prison for having murdered someone who had insulted her. She dared to call the sheik's daughter a whore, and the latter, without a moment's hesitation, was quite prepared to answer her by sinking a knife into her back. Fortunately for Fatima of Notre Dame, I caught hold of the other woman's hand, an instinctive reaction on my part to prevent a murder. I was lucky because a guard happened by and called for help. Both Fatimas were bound and handcuffed, and they flopped around on the floor like fish in a net, each one eager to be free to kill the other. As a direct result of this incident, the prisoners had nothing to eat that day. The warden of the prison was called, and she calmed them down with a few hard slaps and additional punishments; I ran out of the kitchen as fast as my legs could carry me.

As time went by I witnessed many such quarrels in the kitchen, and while most of them were not as serious, they were terribly nerve-wracking. Prison conditions were intolerable, and one reason for this was the behavior of our neighbors, the women (with their children) whose rooms were on our corridor. Their lack of morality and culture revolted and repelled us. Between us lay a gulf of customs, culture, and way of life. Two worlds met here, and the meeting was unsuccessful.

The affair of the kitchen utensils deserves special mention. The utensils in question were deep tin bowls whose very form was disgusting, and spoons. We weren't allowed knives and forks, which were considered dangerous, since we might use them to kill each other, or worse, the guards, thus the spoons had to do triple duty. In addition, the pots were made of cast iron and very heavy; they certainly could have been used to kill someone. All the utensils were ugly, as if they had been fashioned deliberately to turn preparing food into something hateful.

Our first fight was not only for decent utensils, but for separate ones for meat and milk, and we wanted plates instead of bowls. We weren't asking for ceramic ware, which was forbidden in prison, just regular tin plates, and better cooking equipment. The cast-iron pots were never replaced.

Even bringing the food from the kitchen to the rooms was painful and humiliating. While we were locked in our rooms the women on duty, usually two in number, brought the food up from the kitchen. The doors were unlocked, the food was distributed, and the doors were relocked till the morning. The meal in question was dinner, served at four o'clock in the afternoon.

More than once the women on kitchen duty fell on the steep,

slippery stairs and arrived at our rooms bruised and with empty pots. The punishment was double: hunger, and what was worse, the pain and suffering of the women who had fallen. Storing food in our rooms was not permitted, but we always managed to have a small supply on hand.

Cigarettes were another problem, and very important for those who smoked. We were, of course, forbidden to have matches, but how could food be cooked without lighting a fire? For that we had a "shabbes goy"[19] who even worked on weekdays, a policewoman who lit the stove for us. The prison officials were afraid that if we got our hands on matches we would set fire to the prison.

We were forbidden to smoke in our rooms for the same reason, but we were allowed two hours for smoking on the exercise roof (exercise which will be discussed later). A policewoman would go up onto the roof with us and distribute cigarettes and matches (one or two cigarettes, as I recall). When we had finished exercising we had to give her the cigarette butts as proof that we had smoked and used the matches. It should come as no surprise that we managed to fool the policewoman and used to smoke in our rooms, but for that we had to go underground, because if we had been caught we would have been punished and forbidden to smoke at all. When cigarettes were scarce, one cigarette would make the rounds, everyone getting a puff. We always tried to make the cigarettes we had last till the next visiting day.

I was not the first woman to be incarcerated in Bethlehem. There were Sarah Wasserzug, Miriam Robowitz-Goldman, Naomi Orenstein, Miriam Shuchman, and Ruth Halevi (arrested for the second time, having already been in prison once with the women from the training course at Mishmar Hayarden). When I got there, Sarah and Miriam had already been released. Therefore we were four, and we were all in the same room.

---

[19]A *shabbes goy* is a non-Jewish person who lights the fire on Saturday, since this is forbidden to observant Jews.

Rachel was in the room with the convicted criminals. Shortly afterwards four women from Netanya were arrested: Haya Serolowitz, Ully Deutsch, Gerti Shechter, and Gertel Herzl. They were brought at an hour when we had all been locked in our room, and fortunately they were put next door to us. We contacted them immediately and, with the help of a guard, passed them food and other important items. Hassidah Lifschitz was imprisoned after them, and Julie Elazar shortly after her. All of them belonged to (or were suspected of belonging to) Lehi[20] (Fighters for the Freedom of Israel). Julie, who was a high-ranking Lehi officer, was brought in the afternoon, and we didn't have the time to bring her the bedclothes she needed, so we had to take our mattresses off the beds and put them on the floor so that we could all go to sleep. It wouldn't have done us any good to push the beds together, since each one was a different model and of a different height.

After Abraham Stern (whose pseudonym was Yair) was foully murdered by the British,[21] Bella Shechter and Tovah Savorai were brought to Bethlehem. Stern had lived in Tovah's house and she was with him at the end. In unbroken silence we listened as she told us the details of the awful tragedy that had taken place on Mizrachi Street, where a bold Hebrew leader, a dreamer and a fighter for the liberty of Israel, was murdered in cold blood. This is Tovah's story:

"At about nine-thirty there was a knock at the door, too gentle a tapping to signal the presence of the police. Yair, as was his wont, went into the closet, and only then did I open the door.

---

[20]A radical group of former members of the Irgun. The split came at the beginning of the Second World War, when the Irgun decided that it was more important to fight the Nazis than the English, and the Lehi disagreed. There was no love lost between the two groups.
[21]Abraham Stern (1907—1942) left the Irgun early in World War II when it decided to suspend its campaign against the British until the Nazis were defeated. As leader of Lehi, sometimes referred to as the Stern Group, he conducted an underground war against the British but was eventually killed by the police.

"At the door stood the `good' detective Wilkins with two men behind him. Wilkins was always very polite, too polite perhaps. He asked me why I hadn't gone to visit my husband Moshe and if I weren't worried about him. I told him that if I had gone to the hospital I would have been arrested immediately.

"They searched my room, but very slowly, looking at every book and piece of paper. Then they went downstairs and brought two neighbors, women, so that they might have witnesses. After they searched the whole room they went over to the closet. I was standing next to the sofa, facing the closet door. One of the policemen opened it. Yair was nowhere to be seen. The policeman thrust his left hand into the closet and began searching, and when his hand came upon Yair he pulled him out. At the same time he put his right hand into his back pants pocket and took out his gun. I ran between him and Yair and said, `Don't shoot! If you shoot, you shoot me.' Wilkins went over to the policeman, `gently' pushed his arm down, and said something I couldn't hear. In my innocence I thought I had saved Yair's life, and that only in a moment of temporary loss of self-control would they shoot Yair without a trial. How wrong I was!

"They made him sit on the sofa, which was at the right of the door. Across from him sat the detective, his gun pointed at Yair. A few minutes later more detectives appeared; they had handcuffs, and used them to bind Yair's hands behind his back. At the same time the other detectives were busy inspecting my dresses and underwear, and made all sorts of `complimentary' comments about them. Wilkins tried to convince the two neighbors from downstairs that the man who had been captured was a murderer, and showed them pictures of him which had appeared in the newspapers. But the pictures were unclear, and reality was different, the man in front of them had a noble visage. I told them who he really was, and that what the British said was untrue. A few minutes after Yair was found the house was full of tall, strong, English detectives. An unknown person suddenly appeared, tall, dark, and with a lean face. He looked at Yair, and then he looked around the room. Unlike the other people in the room, he was silent, and after a few moments he left. I recognized him: he had been hanging around the house a few days earlier. They told me to get dressed and go down-stairs. When I was in the street I was surprised to see that they were rudely pushing the women out of the house.

"I got into a small car that was waiting near the entrance to the house. Across from it was a van. The officer who had come down the stairs with me did not get into the car but stood out-side, looking up. I thought that he too was waiting for Yair to come downstairs and be put into the waiting van. Suddenly I heard three shots . . ."

Tovah had nothing else to say, and we all sat without mov-ing or saying anything. The pain and sorrow we felt were immense. Another victim had been sacrificed on the altar of Jewish resistance, one of our best fighters, who had given his life for the rebirth of Hebrew independence.

Tovah's arrest, and that of Bella Shechter ("Putzi"), and their arrival at Bethlehem, were greatly discussed by the women in prison. The CID had been looking for Putzi for a long time, and we didn't know that they had found her until we saw her. Her sister Ruth ("Gerti") had been in prison for several months, and now both of them were here together. Putzi had asthma, and she was afraid that incarceration would worsen her condi-tion.

The meeting between the two sisters was hard. They tried to remain strong for each other, but it was a very emotional moment. We found their "family reunion" deeply shocking. Gerti was quite open about the fact that she was glad that an end had come to her being hunted and to Bella's voluntary incarceration—life in the underground was sometimes worse than being in prison. Here, at least, they could be together.

We had been expecting Tovah because we knew from the newspapers that Yair had been killed in her house. When she arrived our hearts almost stopped beating with excitement, because we knew that here before us was the only living witness to the tragedy. Ruth Halevi and I tried to leave the Lehi women together, knowing that they preferred to be alone. The situation was sad because of the events on the outside, and in addition, Frieda Friedman-Yellin arrived.

Bella was particularly affected by Frieda's incarceration, because she had lived in Frieda's house and had always been worried that she and her husband might be put in prison because of her.

Every new arrest, every new woman brought to prison was an additional source of sorrow, and even of suffering when the reasons for her imprisonment and its history became known. But people are naturally egoistical, especially in situations in which they are cut off from the outside world, and the only thing that blows a breath of life into the surroundings is a new arrest, bringing with it news and regards from people in the outside world. Then sorrow is pushed aside and replaced by curiosity. So it was with us, and only after a few days, when all the new topics of conversation had been exhausted, did we begin to take stock of the situation surrounding each arrest and its possible consequences, and then we became gloomy and unhappy again.

There were twelve of us, thirteen with Rachel, and we had three rooms at our disposal. The left-hand side of the corridor was ours, and the right-hand side belonged to those convicted of criminal offenses, including some Jewish women with whom we had almost no contact. They felt better with convicted Arab criminals than they did with us, and we ourselves were not sorry about it.

It should be noted that our rooms were well-aired. The room I was in was particularly good, its windows facing southeast. We were forced to spend most of our time in our rooms and were only allowed on the roof twice a day, an hour in the morning and an hour in the afternoon. In prison language this was known as "exercise." We couldn't really exercise, not even calisthenics, because there wasn't enough room, but we walked around and around the roof, and it wasn't always pleasant to walk in circles. Most of the time Julie was my companion, and we used to talk about the past and a bit about the future. We never spoke about the present; it was too close.

I had met Julie in the outside world before the split between the Irgun and the Lehi, but then we lost contact. We had only worked together for a short time and had no special relationship, but here, enclosed by prison walls, we found that we had more and more to talk about and became close friends.

Soon after our number increased from four to twelve, Nelly Fisher arrived. We had to institute a system of taking turns to do all the work: cleaning the rooms, cooking, cleaning the toilets, appealing to the prison administration, carrying water. Cleaning the individual rooms and doing the laundry was the duty of whoever lived in any particular room, but the other chores were done by one and all. There were two pressing problems for which we had to find immediate solutions: (1) the inhuman conditions and hard work in the kitchen; and (2) the problem of water, or rather the lack of water, and hauling it up from the ground floor. This will be the subject of the next chapter.

✳ ✳ ✳ ✳ ✳ ✳

Chapter Seven

. . . and Water

Lack of water was one of our most serious problems. It caused us great bitterness and suffering, first in the prison itself and later in the detention camp set up in the "villa," and our health suffered because of it. The area around Bethlehem was not well supplied with water, at least not during the years 1937—1947. In normal circumstances a person can calculate the amount of water he needs and ration himself accordingly, but the situation in prison is very different, because one cannot make one's own decisions. With regard to water as with to everything else, one is forced either to accept things the way they are, rules and regulations included, or to revolt.

There was a large number of Arab prisoners in Bethlehem, and the few Jewish prisoners had been cast from a different mold. Convicted criminals can also revolt, but the Arab women were incapable of it. During those years the Grahams ruled the prison: husband, wife, and the dogs they kept instead of having children. Actually, the wife was in charge, and she ruled the prisoners with the use of force untempered by human emotion or feeling, treating them far worse than she treated her dogs. Her attitude manifested itself in the long list of rules and regulations established in that accursed building before our arrival. Needless to say, it was difficult to change everything at once, but it was equally difficult for us to sit patiently and wait for drastic changes to take place, meanwhile contenting ourselves with a few minor improvements.

With regard to matters concerning water, our "castle" might just as well have really been in the Middle Ages. Water was hauled in heavy vessels called tanks too heavy for even a healthy man to carry by himself. We had to use them to bring water from the kitchen on the ground floor to our rooms on the second floor. Because of the way buildings were built in those days, that meant climbing two very steep flights of stone stairs. The steps themselves were worn and slippery, and it was a dangerous enough business to go up and down them empty-handed; we had to be particularly careful not to slip and fall.

We needed large amounts of water because it was important that everything be as clean as possible. We had to wash in our rooms and also do the laundry, and as a result vast amounts of water had to be carried up to the second floor. With the exception of a few women from Jerusalem, most of the prisoners were from Tel Aviv and the coastal plain, places where there was plenty of water and it had never been a problem. We were bitterly opposed to hauling water and demanded that the prison install plumbing to pipe water up to the second floor, and also insisted that water supplies be sufficient for all the inmates.

As a compromise, the prison administration suggested that the Arab women haul the water for us, but we objected for two reasons. First, the water vessels were so constructed that who-ever carried them had to put her hands into the water to be able to hold the vessel, meaning that Fatima and Hadijeh would be washing their hands in the water. Second, and this was our main reason for opposing the proposal, we didn't want to cre-ate a situation in which the Arab prisoners would see them-selves as our servants. This would only have made them hate us more and would have led to a deterioration of relations. Such a situation would have been dangerous even outside the prison walls, but here inside it was ten times worse, since the administration was anxious to divide and conquer, and to have the Jews and Arabs at each other's throats.

It was very difficult for the White Angel, as we called Mrs. Graham, to yield even when justice was so obviously on our side. However, she was facing a body of twelve women, small in number but strong in spirit and firm in its decisions. She looked for a way to retreat with honor, but we had no interest in her retreat being honorable because we wanted to undermine and destroy her authority, and thus to force her to treat our future demands with consideration.

The matter reached the attention of people in higher places, and a committee headed by Mr. Scott, director of prisons in Palestine, came to visit. At one of the meetings between the committee and the camp commission, Ruth Halevi and Naomi Orenstein, who spoke English, presented our demands to be moved from the prison to the detention camp. However, this was only done as a matter of form to force them to improve conditions in the prison. An important factor mitigating our fight to move to the camp was, as previously mentioned, the plight of Rachel Ohevet-Ami, who would have remained alone if we had gone.

It was hard to establish detention-camp conditions in the prison because of the nature of the building and also because of all the prison regulations, which were quite the opposite of what camp regulations would have been. Nevertheless, our struggle did bear some fruit in the end, and we won the right to do our laundry on the porch of the kitchen, and thus we no longer had to haul water upstairs for that purpose. The plumbing was eventually installed, but by Anton the "expert" plumber, and it broke down more often than it worked.

Anton used to come to work accompanied by his helper, an eight-year-old boy. Actually, he and the child had about the same degree of expertise, but we felt that the very fact that he put in an appearance, carrying his primitive tools, was something to be happy about, since several days usually passed between the time he was called and the time he came. As for the actual repair, the most we could hope for was that it would hold out until Anton left.

As a result of his expert ministrations, we often had to haul water in the tank. The word "tank" had bitter connotations for us, and without being aware of it, when I saw the first real tanks belonging to the defense forces of the State of Israel, I could not help but make the connection between the hateful tanks of Bethlehem and the tanks of the Israeli army, and think how lucky I was to see my son as an officer in the armored corps.

The battle over water supplies became even fiercer when we moved to the villa, that is to say, to the detention camp, which had a well whose pump broke down every other day. Sometimes there was not even enough water in the well to operate the pump. Then to draw water we had to let various utensils down into the well on ropes, which we would haul inside. Consider how much water was needed for a two-story building housing sixty women who bathed, used the bathroom, washed clothing, and cooked. All of it had to be drawn either with a primitive pump or with buckets on ropes, and by young women who had suffered difficult conditions, first as underground resistance workers and then for years as prisoners. It was not surprising that we were not strong and fell ill one after another, but we could not live without water, since cleanliness was of paramount importance. Every day there were fewer women strong enough to draw water, and that only made it more difficult for those who were left. We may have received a special building for our detention camp, but that tiny change had been written in our blood, since the administration was still the same and wanted to continue prison rule. The administration consisted of a drunk prison director and his wife, the same White Angel.

The nickname we gave her was a euphemism, since there was little similarity between her and an angel. We called her that because in summer she wore a garment resembling a nun's habit, white from head to toe. She even dressed the dogs in white. She was clever, cunning, and evil-minded. We had a whole series of troubles and back-and-forth battles with her, and finally some improvements were made, although no solution was ever found for the problem of providing a constant supply of water.

Unfortunately we had to fight this battle by ourselves, with no help from the outside world. We appealed to national institutions, the Chief Rabbinate, and influential people for aid and moral support, and all our pleas fell on deaf ears. There was only one organization willing to help us, but it could not give us practical help, since as a thorn in the side of the government it was hunted and ostracized by the official Jewish institutions: the Revisionist movement, voicing its opinions through its publication, the *Observer*. We had another avenue through which to seek help, lawyers, both those sent by the Irgun to maintain contact with the women in prison, and those sent by the inmates' families. It was difficult for them to have an effect on general prison conditions; they could only deal with the files of individuals. Some of them did manage to help us, however, among them Attorneys Kritchman, Zeligman, Heggler, Lebbel, and Levitsky.

In the meantime, the prison directors were replaced. The White Angel used to have the convicted criminals work as her housekeepers, and that was forbidden by law. Her house was on the other side of the road, outside the prison gates. One of the prisoners decided to "release" herself, and she simply picked up her feet and ran. Only then were the authorities made aware of the fact that the Angel had for years been employing prisoners as her personal servants. She had her pride, and unable to endure the shame of losing her post, she tried to poison herself. She was saved at the last minute, but she and her husband were forced to leave.

A new prison director was appointed. "A new broom sweeps clean," runs the saying, but he wasn't much of a new broom for his employers. We exploited his desire to get into our good graces, yet even he didn't solve the problem of the water supply, but merely saw to a few minor improvements and repairs.[22]

The detention camp was located in a building which had once been the villa of a wealthy Christian Arab. In spite of his money he had not needed more than two bathtubs and showers. That would have been enough for an ordinary family, but for a camp of sixty to seventy women inmates such sanitary arrangements were pure hell. Since the building was a kind of cottage, the top story only had one bathroom and shower, which apparently had never been used, and therefore we had to make do with one shower and one toilet. Worse, the condition of the plumbing was shocking; the drains became stopped up every other day, and since the shower was attached to the bathtub, after every shower water had to be bailed out of it.

A few scenes from the ongoing tragicomedy of water in the Bethlehem prison follow.

Scene 1. No one ever visited Bilhah Hermoni because her husband also had the "privilege" of being a guest of His Majesty, and their relatives were afraid that visiting would be too dangerous. She was not the only one, there were other women in the same situation. The day in question was mail day, and Bilhah had a well-developed sense of humor and quite an imagination; since she might receive a letter from her husband, she wanted to take a shower and dress up as though

---

[22]I must state again that the main problem of the camp was geography, and if forces outside the prison had applied pressure the inmates could have been moved somewhere else. This did not happen until the sword was almost resting on the necks of the women in Bethlehem, when in 1947 the United Nations announced the Partition Plan, and women imprisoned in Arab areas were in the gravest danger. I kept badgering both the National Council and Asireinu, an organization working for the good of Jewish prisoners regardless of their political affiliations. Since I was in the outside world I could pressure various institutions, but meanwhile the price of neglect was high.

she were receiving a real visit from him and not just a letter. In fact, letters were the only contact with home for those who could not receive visits.

Bilhah was on duty in the kitchen that day and was first in line for the shower, both because of her work and because of the letter she hoped to receive. When she finished in the kitchen she ran to the shower. "Wonderful!" she called out to us, "There's lots of water!" and she began to wash herself. A few minutes later a cry came from the shower, "Oh no! The drain's stopped up and the water won't go down!" This meant that after she had finished showering she would have to bail the water out of the bathtub and get dirty again. We told her that as soon as the letter came we would bail the water out, the important thing was for her to finish showering because the letter might arrive at any minute. A few moments later she cried out again, "Help, this is awful! There's no more water and I can't rinse the soap off!" The "rescue team" ran to the bathroom and found her standing in a pool of water, her face and body soapy.

We ran to the well, drew up a bucket of water, and poured it over her. In the meantime Thomas, the prison director, arrived with the mail, and the policewoman who accompanied him called out, "Bilhah Hermoni, letter for you!" The guards knew that she wrote only to her husband, himself a prisoner, and for that reason gave her the message out loud.

Soapy Bilhah cried out in desperation from the shower, "This is the end! I can't stand it!" and this from a normally quiet, phlegmatic young woman. She couldn't control herself and began swearing, not only at the heads of state but at Anton, the villa's expert plumber. Somehow or other she finished showering and left the bathroom, still bearing traces of soap here and there. Some of us volunteered to bail the water out of the bathtub, and she went to receive her "visit": the letter.

Scene 2. "Oh no," cried Pnina Effron from the kitchen, "the water in the sink won't go down, the drain's plugged up and the water's pouring out onto the floor. I can't wash the dishes and it's time to set the table!" No sooner had she finished, than the women began to shout, "Anton! Anton!" and for good measure the High Commissioner was cursed, as were all the enemies of Israel. The wretched noodles were thrown out because there was no water to rinse them in, cooking stopped, and the wash could not be done.

Scene 3. Shaulah Ivriah was miserably unhappy and alone. Not only couldn't she have visitors, but she also received no letters, because the CID was anxious to know with whom she was in contact, and her friends were unwilling to give them the pleasure of obtaining that information. Shaulah had all kinds of completely illegal and conspiratorial ways of sending and receiving regards from her relatives, but since there was no specific date for the receipt of an illegal communication, and since these communications were "visits" for her, she too had to look her best at all times. Since she could not receive her own mail or visits, she was happy for anyone who could and did, and participated in the joys and sorrows of her friends.

It was a hot summer day, and Shaulah had just finished working in the kitchen. It had been a difficult day. The camp had grown and now housed sixty-five women. Many of them were ill, and the number of women who could work in the kitchen had grown smaller. Soaked with sweat, she ran to the bathroom to bathe, even though it wasn't her turn.

The day happened to be a holiday, and people were coming to visit Julie and Nelly. Shaulah understood the hints being sent through the window: regards to Shaulah. She picked up her clean clothing and ran to the bathroom. "Girls," she called out, "we're in luck! There's cold water."

Only a few minutes had passed when she cried out, "Girls! Help! Bring water, there isn't any more!" Once again the women ran to the well and brought water. After a while they began to get anxious. Shaulah had been in the bathroom for a long time, too long. One of the women knocked on the door and asked, "Shaulah, did you fall asleep, or don't you feel well?"

Shaulah answered in a voice choked with tears: "Don't ask," she said, "the drain is stopped up and I'm bailing out the water." Haya Ben-Tzvi opened the door and was horrified to see Shaulah soaked with sweat, bailing water out of the tub. "What a wasted shower," she said angrily, as sweaty now as she had been before she had gone into the bathroom.

Scene 4. Winters in Bethlehem were colder than on the coast, but if the window pane happened to break in the bathroom (or anywhere else), the Mandate government was not quick to replace it. If the purpose of the glass had been to prevent someone from escaping, it would have been repaired immediately, but there were bars to foil attempts at escape, and the function of the glass was only to guard against wind and cold, and who cared if it was cold and windy in prison?

It was finally Judith Mozer's turn to take a shower. The door opened, and Deborah Baruch came out complaining and flushed with anger. "Judith," she said, "the drain is plugged, and maybe you'd be better off not going in than to have to bail out water afterwards." But Judith had just finished giving her room a thorough cleaning, and she had to have a shower. She had no choice but to enter the freezing bathroom, trembling with cold.

She began to shower when suddenly she cried out, "Girls! Help! Bring water. There's no more water, I'm freezing and I have to rinse the soap off!" Sonia and Frieda were waiting their turn just outside the bathroom door, and they ran off to bring water. There was just one kettle of hot water in the kitchen, it had been boiled to make tea. Since there was only a small quantity, they decided to add cold water so there would be enough to rinse all the soap off Judith, because it would take time for the guard to open the door for them to get water from the well, and in the meantime she was covered with soap and freezing.

These four scenes can barely give an idea of the plumbing experiences that embittered our lives. Experts had decided that another shower could be added, but only on the condition that the bathtub be pulled out, and we wouldn't agree to that, since we did our washing in the tub. After protests and endless demands, a different place was found for the additional shower. They tried to fix the shower on the second floor but nothing worked: the pipes weren't wide enough to carry the necessary amount of water.

The plumbing, or lack of it, was one of the most serious causes of disease among the prisoners. More than one of us fell ill standing in the shower, soapy and wet, with the cold wind blowing in through the broken window, muttering, like King David in 1 Chronicles 11:17, "Oh that one would give me water to drink of the well of Bethlehem."

Throughout it all we knew how to laugh at our suffering and to mock our troubles. More than once we laughed aloud as the world turned upside down for whoever was in the shower, with the water that was supposed to come out of the shower-head disappearing, and the water that was supposed to go down the drain steadily rising. We were all fated to have the same experience in the shower, and much as we wanted to help each other, it was difficult to keep from laughing when one of the women was helpless and stuck in the bathroom. We told all kinds of jokes and stories about Anton——his alleged expertise, his helper, his tools. Laugh as we did, even today many of us still bear the scars of the lack of water and the awful plumbing; some of us have rheumatism as a souvenir, some of us suffer from other ailments.

The late Rabbi Herzog[23], who was asked to try to help in the matter of water, visited Bethlehem and was struck by the heavy vessels we were forced to use. He tried to comfort us, saying, "Rachel herself carried water, but not in such heavy vessels."

The problems got worse from day to day, and when they became unbearable, the prisoners' patience came to an end and they rebelled. They broke into the prison office and took it over, disconnecting the telephone and destroying everything that came to hand. It was only then that the prison authorities were forced to solve the problem of water once and for all.

---

[23]Chief Rabbi of Palestine

✳ ✳ ✳ ✳ ✳ ✳

Chapter Eight

Medical "Treatment"

One of the most pressing problems in prison was that of the medical treatment received by the prisoners. The healthy spirit of the inmates overcame the agonies of being in prison, and keeping up morale was something the women could do by themselves, but preserving physical health was not dependent on having courage and a strong personality.

We used to have a joke: Why is the prayer of the Eighteen Benedictions arranged in the following order: "heals the sick, loosest the bound, and keepest thy faith to them that sleep in the dust"? Answer: "Because by the time the doctor comes and releases the patient of her torment, the dead will have come to life."

It was a bitter joke, and fortunately for us it remained one, but for those incarcerated in Eritrea it was bitter reality. One of the people sent there, Naphthali Lubinzik, an old-time fighter, died as a result of "successful" medical treatment. He passed away before the horrified eyes of his comrades, suffering from a mild disease, amoebic dysentery, a disease easily and simply treated outside prison.

As previously stated, the conditions in Bethlehem were inhuman. A distinction should be made between the conditions prisoners live under and the treatment they are given by those in charge, since there is no connection between the two. The best treatment could not overcome or eradicate the awful conditions because they were part and parcel of the prison building itself. Every detention camp had additional space, they had sports fields and rooms set aside for activities of various kinds; we, however, had nothing of the sort, and our bodies began to weaken and deteriorate because of lack of sports and physical exercise. The cramped quarters adversely affected our nerves as well.

The cellar we lived in had been variously used as a storeroom and a pigsty. The walls were covered with mildew, and several months passed before we managed to force the prison administration to make repairs. In the meantime the damp caused some of the prisoners to come down with bad cases of rheumatism. There wasn't enough food, and what there was, was of poor quality despite the help we got from people outside. Our daily rations consisted of two teaspoons of sugar, a few olives, a pita and a half (which had not been properly baked and only the crust could be eaten; the inner part had to be thrown away), and ten grams of milk. We had a small amount of lamb twice a week, an occasional egg (usually powdered egg), and a small amount of vegetables, usually rotten. After a long struggle which involved sending the food back to the storeroom, nutrition improved somewhat, but in the beginning, we would have been unable to remain alive without food packages from friends and relatives outside.

However, the worst problem was never solved——the lack of physical exercise and intellectual activity. Under normal circumstances the body is constantly in motion and one is too busy to pay attention to physical complaints, but in prison, even under the best of conditions, the inmate is virtually motionless and has nothing to occupy his or her time, and so he or she becomes aware of these complaints as soon as they appear.

It is written in the *Sayings of the Fathers* that "he whose head aches should occupy it with studying the Torah," but we couldn't study anything because there was no place to study. Simple remedies which relieved the suffering of sick people outside of prison were often not strong enough to help those inside. The inmates were helpless, there was no doctor to turn to who could be trusted, and there was no way of replacing the doctor who could be called. This made it difficult for us to get well, because a basic condition for healing is trust between patient and doctor.

The situation was particularly difficult when one of the prisoners was taken ill at night. The doctor couldn't be called because it was forbidden to open the door at night, any door; the pain had to be borne till morning. There was no way of getting even minimal help. The mere thought that help was far away made the person more sensitive to pain and increased her fears and apprehensions.

I experienced this myself. Before I was arrested I had never been sick and had never imagined that it was only natural for sick people to suffer and be afraid. Today, when I feel pain, I don't run to a doctor, since the knowledge that I can get medical attention any time I so desire is enough to calm me and make me feel better. In prison the feeling of helplessness was enough to drive one mad.

The subjects of medical treatment and of the doctor himself were very painful and troublesome. The doctor who treated us was an Arab named Ma'aluf (he was killed by Arabs during the War of Independence), and he had all the qualities necessary for his job: he was base, mean, vile, and utterly lacking in compassion. The only thing missing from his repertoire was medical knowledge. Going to him for treatment was terrible, not only because he didn't want to help Jewish prisoners, but because he simply didn't know anything about medicine. For every pain he prescribed alkaline powder, which we threw away because whenever we took it, the pains got worse.

When I first came to Bethlehem, Rachel Ohevet-Ami was ill and weak, and as a convicted prisoner was not permitted to receive extra or special food. Only when more women prisoners arrived did the general problem of diet arise. Dr. Ma'aluf had to prescribe white bread instead of the pitas which even a healthy person couldn't have eaten, to say nothing of a person with an intestinal disorder. After a long struggle the doctors began to prescribe special diets for the prisoners, and I was given quite a lot of food after the CID said, "Food, yes, release, no." The ill women were given special food instead of being released. It eased their pain but did not cure the diseases which spread among the prisoners.

Asclepius will have to forgive me, but I don't remember the names of all the doctors who came to the prison. We had one who claimed he was Jewish, although no one could state with certainty what his nationality was. What was true of his predecessors was true of him, except that he had an additional virtue: he aspired to speak only English, although he had no command of the language. The prisoners didn't go to him when they felt sick, and he had nothing to do with his time. His conduct was intolerable, and we quarreled with him endlessly.

He was replaced by a woman doctor. The two things that characterized all the doctors sent by the prison authorities were lack of medical knowledge and boorishness. It seemed to us that they had been chosen on the basis of these two qualities, but the woman doctor was the worst of all. We wouldn't admit her into our room, and even the prison superintendent agreed with us.

Only after people outside the prison had interfered and public opinion was enlisted by the National Movement did a woman doctor come to Bethlehem who would be remembered for her good works. She was Hannah Perlman from Jerusalem, a doctor who worked for the National Sick Fund. She was Jewish, a cultured woman, knowledgeable and professional, full of the milk of human kindness, and she did everything in her power to ease the lot of the prisoners. To her sorrow, and to ours, her resources were limited, since an English doctor was her superior and she was answerable to him, and he was answerable to the Ministry of Health.

In any case, Dr. Perlman helped us more than was humanly possible. Although no longer young or strong, she didn't care how many hours she worked, and was not afraid of hard work. She came to the prison more than once when she was not authorized to come, and sometimes even went to the hospital in Jerusalem to visit prisoners, never forgetting to bring a gift with her. She made her patients forget that they were prisoners.

Thomas, the prison superintendent, said more than once, "I see that you are quite anti-British."

"I am not anti-British," she would answer, "I am a Jew, and as such I am pro-Jewish, and it is my duty to take care of my own people."

She was not concerned only with her Jewish patients. Having a conscience, she cared for the Arabs as well. In addition to obtaining material with which the Jewish prisoners could make pajamas, she got nightgowns for the Arabs, and also improved their food.

She continued to come to the prison even during the dangerous days after the 29th of November, 1947, when the Partition Plan was voted on and passed. Once her life was saved by a miracle when some Arabs decided to murder her but instead killed Mrs. Thompson, a probation officer whom they had mistaken for Dr. Perlman.

When conditions in Jerusalem worsened, the other Jewish doctors became afraid to go to the jail to treat the Jewish prisoners, but she had no such fear. When one of the members of the Lehi had an attack of appendicitis, the prison authorities refused to let him be taken to the hospital lest he escape, and Dr. Perlman offered herself as a hostage in his place.

The CID caused her many problems, making it difficult for her to perform her duties as a doctor, but she overcame the difficulties with the help of the prison superintendent, who understood and valued her devotion to her patients and her dedication to her profession.

A noteworthy incident occurred at the government hospital in the Russian Court in Jerusalem.

It was not until the beginning of 1942 that prisoners were sent to the government hospital. Conditions there were primi-

tive, and the doctors were Arabs and Englishmen who had neither the knowledge nor the desire to be of any use. Their attitude toward their patients, who except for us were all Arab
peasant women (the Arab women who had money went to the
Jewish hospitals, despite the fact that it was forbidden), was
despicable. More than once an Arab nurse in the hospital
would look at a woman lying in bed, decide that she had died,
and without authorization from a doctor, have her sent to the
morgue. The Arab nurses were outstanding for their vulgarity
and arrogance; they were all city-bred and treated the peasants
like animals. Their conduct was dictated by ignorance and apathy about the plight of their patients, and it is difficult to set
these things down on paper.

One morning I saw one of the nurses mixing Lysol and
water in a bowl. She was planning, with the help of a rusty
pipe, to "treat" one of the Arab patients. It seemed very strange
to me, and when I asked, I was horrified to hear that she was
planning to rinse out the woman's uterus. With Lysol. And a
rusty pipe. I began to shout and managed, at the last minute, to
save the woman from a painful death. The nurse wept and
begged me not to tell the hospital director, while the patient
herself couldn't stop singing the praises of the Jewish terrorist
who had saved her from certain death. After that the Arab
patients always consulted with me before they agreed to
receive medical treatment.

In the midst of the Arab women, many of them suffering
from communicable diseases, were the ill prisoners from
Bethlehem. After we insisted and refused to capitulate, we
were given food that was more suited to the European palate
and served in separate dishes. What the Arab women received
could not be called food.

The nurses decided which bed each patient would be
assigned. Therefore we had to teach them (1) to treat us with
respect; and (2) to make our beds first and to wash their hands
before they came to treat us. It was a difficult situation, because
there were many nationalistic nurses who resented our telling

them what to do and how to behave. When we appealed to the English hospital inspector, however, we won our case. I demanded kosher food, and the inspector ordered a Jewish nurse to bring me food from outside the hospital, but in the meantime to go to the kitchen and look in the refrigerator for any food which might be suitable for me; the next day I received kosher food.

Prisoners from Bethlehem who were hospitalized were awarded a special bodyguard, an Arab policewoman who sat next to our beds day and night, not to mention the high-ranking Arab and English police officers stationed in the corridor. As a result, the other patients considered us superwomen and had great respect for us.

Mr. Charlton, the chief prison superintendent, used to visit us every now and then and ask if we had any special requests; these were usually granted. I demanded and received a newspaper, and thus learned something about the general level of British intelligence. I had a subscription to the *Observer*, and it used to be sent to the prison, so the head of the hospital sent someone to Bethlehem to bring it to me, although it had been sent there from the central prison in Jerusalem. I benefited from this arrangement, because the women in Bethlehem exploited the opportunity to send me coded messages inside the newspaper.[23] Complaining that they were being left without a paper, I would send it back to Bethlehem the next day, and thus get news to them from the hospital.

We also used to exchange information via the laundry. I would sent my dirty clothes to Bethlehem, and they would send me back clean clothing. Director Thomas wanted to change the arrangement and refused to allow them to send me

---

[23]In Hebrew the vowels are written below the consonants, but only in children's books; normally they are left out. We would add the vocalization beneath the letters of the words of the message, and thus whoever knew the code could spell out the words simply by looking for the pencil marks.

clean clothes. During Mr. Charlton's first visit at the hospital, I complained and he settled the matter. When I returned to Bethlehem, the prison director complained that when his wife had been a patient at Wallach Hospital, she had worn hospital gowns. I told him that there was a difference between a Jewish hospital and a government hospital.

No real medical treatment was given at the hospital, and almost no tests were performed. There was an Arab doctor from Syria whose mother was Jewish. Something about two Jewish prisoners who were fighting the British Empire must have moved him (Adinah Laor and I were in the hospital at the time), and he wanted to treat us by using a stomach pump, but the equipment was rusty, and what he tried to do caused me indescribable suffering.

The X-ray room was so primitive that it was difficult to perform the simplest test, and we usually went and came back without the X-ray being taken. But we profited from looking through the window of the car we were in and seeing the streets of Jerusalem and the people walking around freely on them. Once my fellow Irgun fighter Carmela and I even witnessed an attack by the underground, and heard the echoes of the shots and explosions.

On one of my first visits to the hospital, I was taken in a military van which was high and cumbersome to get into and even more cumbersome to get out of. When we arrived at the hospital, an English policeman came over and extended his hand to help me out. Needless to say I chose to jump out by myself, the results of which were severe pain and a report sent to the CID claiming that "Tzila Heller is not sick, she laughs and can run and jump like a young girl." The new director told me about it when I returned to the prison.

While in the hospital I had tests done which showed that I was suffering from hepatitis. When I asked the prison superintendent whose diagnosis it was, the CID's on the basis of external evidence or the doctors' on the basis of examinations, he had no answer for me. That was the beginning of a long con-

troversy between us, and the result was that all during my stay
in prison he would remind me that people made mistakes. I
would answer that the CID's mistakes were the source of great
suffering for many people, not only with regard to a fictitious
report, but also with regard to unnecessary incarceration. His
answer was always that with regard to my arrest no mistake
had been made.

I was hospitalized a few times, once for a tonsillectomy, once
or twice for tests, and no doubt I would have been hospitalized
many times more if I hadn't decided once and for all that I was
never going back there.

One day I couldn't breathe and suffered intense pain. Dr.
Perlman rushed to the prison and immediately ordered an
ambulance. It was not the kind of incident to put the camp in a
good mood, and my cellmates began to cry. I felt awful, and
guilty that I had caused my friends such sorrow.

Four English policemen carried me on a stretcher, and all the
women accompanied me to the door. Suddenly I heard an
angry laugh, and Pninah Bejaio cursing in Hebrew. I couldn't
understand the laugh until I was put into the ambulance.
Through the window I could see a cavalcade of vehicles full of
English policemen armed with Tommy guns, guarding the terrorist on the stretcher.

The second time they wanted to put me on a stretcher I
decided against it because of what it did to the morale of the
other women. Leaning on the shoulders of two policewomen
(it was forbidden for inmates to pass the gates by themselves),
I bit my lips and barely got to the ambulance. I paid for the
effort by lying in bed for hours without being able to open my
eyes or say a word.

My tonsillectomy was performed in the hospital by a Jewish
doctor, Dr. Frankel, in the presence of Mr. Charlton, Director of
Prisons for the Jerusalem area. It was a difficult operation,
according to the doctor, because of the amount of infection present. Having Mr. Charlton in the room made me more ambi-
tious to pass the test, and although I fainted from the pain

(anesthetics were not used for tonsillectomies in those days), I didn't move or make a sound. Before the operation I asked Charlton what he was doing there: was he perhaps a doctor? did he want to be sure that I really needed the operation? He didn't answer, so I continued and said, "So why *are* you here? To make sure I don't escape?" And he answered, "It's always a good idea to keep an eye on you."

✳ ✳ ✳ ✳ ✳ ✳

Chapter Nine

A Night to Remember

The late afternoon of Saturday, January 19, 1946, was gloomy and unpleasant. The Sabbath, the day of rest, was slowly yielding to the approaching specter of six gray days of activity. The week was stealthily invading, stealing into our hearts, bringing silent, inexplicable melancholy. It was a hard enough time for those in the outside world, but ten times harder for those in prison, and a hundred times harder for those in the prison hospital in Jerusalem. The wonderful scenery added its own touch to the general picture. We were two young Jewish women in an Arab government hospital, the only Jewish patients among the fourteen there.

The shadows penetrated the room and climbed the gloomy walls. It was an hour when people didn't notice how their thoughts wandered. My thoughts were unfettered (the ropes to bind thoughts have still to be invented; perhaps before long technology will find the solution), and traveled the space separating me from everything that was precious to me. I could hug my child and tell him a story that would make his innocent eyes sparkle with curiosity and interest. "Mommy, tell me just one more story," he would beg, "but a nice one, not one that scares me."

Such a sweet child, he couldn't bear frightening stories, but what could be more frightening than the story of his mother?

Bad men came to take her away from her Benjamin, from the house, they took her far away and closed her up behind bars.

"No, Mommy," he used to say, "not scary stories, maybe we could sing a song?" "Yes," I would say, stroking his head and beginning to sing.

And without knowing exactly when or why, I would begin singing those same songs, like the one about "The Two Banks of the Jordan River," both banks ours, but how strange it was to sing the song in prison; both banks of the Jordan belong to the Jewish people, but in the meantime even our own lives di not belong to us.

I suddenly came back to reality, and the dark walls of the room seemed to be laughing at me. A wisp of my previous train of thought remained with me like an echo: the voice of my son asking, "Mommy, are you going to the cinema tonight?" He was afraid to be without his mother for an hour or two, poor thing! How many years had he spent without his mother, without his father?

The cinema? It was enough to make me laugh. It was now the hour when the first showing usually began. The young women of Israel would be getting ready to go out, trying on their best dresses, powdering their noses and putting on lipstick, getting ready to enjoy the evening. After the film they would go to the Cassit, the most fashionable cafe in Tel Aviv, or perhaps try one of the newer ones, gossiping all the time about what their friends were doing and who had a new boyfriend or girlfriend. They would make nasty remarks about those criminal terrorists who were endangering the Yishuv in Palestine with their acts of terrorism, occasionally leading the British to impose a curfew, during which they could not go to the cinemas or the cafes but would be forced to sit at home. To sit at *home*? What a joke! It must have been real torture for them to sit at home.

And inevitably, of its own accord, the troublesome thought would be there, at the front of the prisoner's mind: Who knew when he or she would be able to go to a cinema or a cafe? A war of independence was not like a crop, to be harvested in a certain season. It was a seed sown in fields of ice and snow, and until it could be harvested . . . Well, as a certain CID officer said, "Hair will grow on my palm before a Jewish state is established, even if all the Jews want it, and they don't. All your leaders and most of the Yishuv are completely opposed to the stupid idea. You are Don Quixotes, tilting at windmills, and if there are some madmen who think otherwise, we know how to take care of them. But *women* having such idiotic ideas and taking part in such stupidity, married women, mothers? That's worse than a crime, it's madness."

And who knows, I thought, who knows, maybe they are right. How many years had Ireland been fighting for its independence? The units they counted in were not years, but tens of years, hundreds.

I belonged to the fighting National Military Organization, the Irgun, but what effect did a small organization have, forced as it was to fight on so many fronts at once? The fiercest front of all was the stupidity and pettiness of its own people. How much effort we had to put into each military operation. Would the Irgun have enough strength to continue its operations and to increase them until the foreign invader was forced to leave the country?

The sounds of shots and explosions broke my reverie as the fighting underground organizations answered my questions. The Irgun and the Lehi had attacked the prison to release the freedom fighters.

They attacked and we put on a "performance" in the hospital. Because of our special situation we had to pretend not to care about what was going on outside, not only not to care, but to be innocent of all knowledge of it while our hearts were pounding and we said a prayer for the fighters—— that they would hammer at the invaders, strike them in the name of the homeland enslaved by an enemy, smite them for the millions of our brothers and sisters who had gone to the gas chambers and the crematoria while the gates of salvation had been locked: the gates of the homeland! Smite them for freedom and for the rebirth of the Kingdom of Israel, and smite them for us, the women locked behind bars, sacrificing our youth on the altar of the war of liberation!

And without even noticing what I was doing, I began to say the prayer of the ancient Hebrew warrior, he who smote the Philistine, the prayer of David son of Jesse of Bethlehem, which we used to recite at all our modest Irgun functions, the 144th Psalm:

Blessed be the Lord my Rock,
Who traineth my hands for war,
And my fingers for battle;
My lovingkindness, and my fortress,
My high tower, and my deliverer;
My shield, and He in whom I take refuge;
Who subdueth my people under me.

Lord, what is man, that Thou takest knowledge of him?
Or the son of man, that Thou makest account of him?
Man is like unto a breath;
His days are as a shadow that passeth away.
O Lord, bow Thy heavens, and come down;
Touch the mountains, that they may smoke.
Cast forth lightning, and scatter them;
Send out Thine arrows, and discomfit them.
Stretch forth Thy hands from on high;
Rescue me, and deliver me out of many waters,
Out of the hand of strangers;
Whose mouth speaketh falsehood,
And their right hand is a right hand of lying.

O God, I will sing a new song unto Thee,
Upon a psaltery of ten strings will I sing praises unto Thee;
Who givest salvation unto kings,
Who rescues David Thy servant from the hurtful sword. . . .

We whose sons are as plants grown up in their youth;

Whose daughters are as corner-pillars carved after the fashion

of a palace; . . .

Happy is the people that is in such a case.

Yea, happy is that people whose God is the Lord.

What a combination! The hands of warriors and poets were extended to us from the far reaches of history two thousand years old. And my prayer went heavenward: Preserve them, O Lord, in the fire of battle!

The storm raging outside the hospital walls brought terror to the hearts of the Arab patients. They understood its meaning and feared for their lives, afraid that the fighters might break into the hospital and comforting themselves with the hope that Jewish fighters wouldn't harm sick people. To be on the safe side, they tried to get some kind of assurance from their "representatives": us! We calmed them and assured them that not only did Irgun fighters not attack hospitals, but that they were also careful not to harm Arabs.

A few minutes after the attack begun, the Englishwoman in charge of the hospital came into our room in an effort to preserve the honor of Albion in the eyes of the "natives." Erect and proud she passed between the beds of the Arab women and tried to calm them. Then she came over to our beds, paused for a moment, and with a smile that could have signified anything and everything asked us how we were, then continued on her way without waiting for an answer, proud and erect.

The reaction of the Arab policemen, however, was quite different. They ran helplessly through the hospital corridors, consoling themselves with the fact that they were in a hospital and not under siege in the prison. The cool British policemen with their stiff upper lips panicked. The hospital was put on stand-by alert and stretchers were made ready, as were all sorts of medications and equipment for the operating room, and the doctors went on duty.

When the attack was over, everything stopped and became silent, especially our hearts. We were anxious over the fate of the fighters and wanted to know the outcome of the action; we couldn't fall asleep, and the night dragged on endlessly. All our efforts to get information from the Arab policemen were fruitless because none of them knew anything, and when they did hear something from the doctors, their Eastern imaginations took over and they improvised wildly.

A typical example will serve to illustrate the respect and fear they had for the Jewish fighters. One of the Arab policemen who came to work that morning told us that during the attack the police had arrested a Jewish girl who had been wounded in the leg. He used gestures to show her weapons, and they included two pistols, one in each hand, a belt full of hand grenades, and a submachine gun. When he began his story I saw no reason to disbelieve him, but as he described the girl and her weapons I realized that it was all a figment of the fertile Arab imagination. I was pleased to learn how frightened they were of us and how much they respected our fighters' fortitude and bravery.

We only learned what had really happened when the newspaper arrived. Irgun and Lehi fighters had attacked the prison. Several British officers had fallen, and one of our men had been sacrificed, but at the time we didn't know who he was.

Our windows looked out over a yard in whose right-hand corner was the morgue. From the moment we read the newspaper we kept a watch over it, knowing that the body of the brave soldier lay there.

He had fallen as an unknown soldier, and as an unknown soldier he would be buried, a fighter who had sacrificed himself on the altar of his nation's liberation.

Suddenly Carmela and I felt the weight of the sacred duty which lay upon our shoulders. We two had to take leave of him in the name of all our friends, in the name of the high command of the Irgun which had ordered the mission, and in the name of the tens of thousands of people yearning for redemption. Above all, we had to part from him in the name of his mourning family, his father and mother who couldn't even come to his funeral, lest his identity be known to the British and the CID wreak their vengeance on the family. If any of his relatives were in the ranks of the Irgun, they would continue the work of their heroic brother, and they would not be alone in their tragedy, for there were many other families whose men had been sacrificed on the altars of the enemy.

It was a terrible feeling. We felt that we were inadequate for the task. We did everything in our power to fulfill the mission, reciting the prayers we knew by heart, among them the prayer for the dead: *El Malei Rachamim* ("God the Merciful").

The dead fighter's body was kept in the morgue for a few days. Sometimes the CID would bring it outside to take photographs. Once I managed to catch a glimpse of his face, which was strong and beautiful, and it seemed to me as though he would soon wake from the sleep of death and, like Samson, rise up against the enemy.

When they finally took him to be buried, alone and lonely, the floodgates burst in our hearts and the tears flowed. All the suppressed anger, all the feelings gathering momentum for so many years, all the distress, the hope and disappointment, all welled up demanding release. His eulogy came from the depths of my heart, from my subconscious, but I could not express it in words, because no words could convey the meaning of what I wanted to say. It was expressed in my burning tears, in the blood flowing in my veins.

"Dear friend, brother in war and suffering, partner in pride, sorrow, and victory! You gave what was most dear to you and sacrificed your young vibrant life on the altar of a war for liberation and freedom. No one knew your name when you fell, and no one will put a name on your grave. But with God as my witness you are not alone. All your comrades in arms walk behind your coffin, and tens of thousands of eyes accompany you to your final resting place, the eyes of the heroes and fighters of all the generations. A huge family is with you, the family of the fighters of Israel. They were always few in the face of many enemies both at home and abroad, and their deaths brought honor and glory to the Jewish nation. The State of Israel also walks behind your coffin——at a distance, perhaps, but it is approaching and will soon arrive, for you have paved its way.

"Forgive us, dear brother, for we are but two fighters who belong to a great nation, and we stand here bent and broken, and cannot find the words. We know that no matter what is said, it will be insignificant in the face of your heroism. In the name of all mothers everywhere, in the name of your mother, we bring you this last blessing, and say goodbye."

Two years later, after I had been released from prison and the State of Israel had been established, I described, at a women's conference, what happened that night, and I mentioned, among other things, the heroism and emotional fortitude of the mothers who could not, because of the circumstances, say a final goodbye to their sons, victims of the War of Independence. Tears stood in the eyes of the audience as I described that awful night. A few minutes later a note was passed to me from the audience stating that one of my listeners was crying, and that she was the mother of Abraham Bachar from Petach Tikvah, the man who had been killed during the attack on the prison. I tried to change the subject, but it was hard for me to continue, and I had to end the lecture. I immediately went to look for her and begged her forgiveness for having wounded her feelings. "No, no," she said, "quite the opposite, this is the first and only time I have ever heard the story of what happened to my son, because once he left home I never saw him again. I couldn't go to his funeral, and he was buried as Abraham ben Abraham."

I stood in awe of that mother's bravery. Most blessed among women is the Hebrew mother who gave birth to such a generation of fighters!

Chapter Ten

Holy Work

Daily life creates new words and terms, renews old terms and gives them modern meanings. Thus the traditional Yiddish expression *yeshiva bocher*, the boy who sits and studies the Torah all day, was transformed. Dr. Abba Achimeir, Dr. Yehoshua Yevin, and their comrades-in-arms from Brit Biryonim took the old-world, Diaspora expression (exalted as it was) and turned it into a national revolutionary expression. The same thing happened with "Holy Work." "Holy Work" referred to the women who worked in the Temple, weaving and embroidering, and bringing their handicrafts to the Tent of Meeting. Here, behind prison walls, we gave new meaning to the ancient Hebrew expression. We too were engaged in holy work; the very fact of our imprisonment was holy work to promote the new Temple that would come into being. We too did delicate handicrafts, and the prosaic raw materials were threaded with our love for those outside, and absorbed into the fiber of their being the best of our songs and heart-felt prayers. Many women excelled in handicrafts, and they were imbued with the spirit of holiness and purity of our being behind bars in Bethlehem, the cradle of the Kingdom of Israel.

The only thing we had to entertain us and occupy our time (beside reading and studying) was handicrafts, and they served several purposes. They were a way of smuggling mail in and out and keeping us in contact with the outside world. In addition, they enabled us to make presents for our children or our husbands (most of whom were also imprisoned). Finally, they were a way of thanking friends and family who worried about us all the time; this was the only way we could repay them for everything they did for us.

Every time one of us had a birthday we turned it into a real celebration, and giving presents we had made ourselves was a major part of it. The gifts were made under the watchful eye of a prison guard whose job it was to prevent us from putting anything contraband into them. They were usually made of absorbent cotton or cardboard cartons covered with embroidered silk. We made boxes for cosmetics and jewelry, notebooks, and pin cushions. These had to be examined by the authorities, but the napkins and knitted goods we made were not.

We used to sit in the corridor which served as the work area for everything we did. It was where we ate, prepared food, picked through rice (which was infested with insects because it was wartime, and supplies of good food, even staples like rice, could not be relied on), and did handicrafts. Most of the time the guard was so bored she fell asleep, and we used these opportunities to insert special material into our work, that is to say, illegal mail. It had to be inserted in such a fashion as not to arouse the suspicion of the guard or of those women against whom we had been warned. Sometimes, when it was hard to insert a note, we would make two things which looked similar, one while the guard was watching and the other "underground," and then switch them at the last minute.

All this soon became a matter of routine, and the "mail" was delivered without incident. We had the feeling that the guards had no idea that unauthorized things could be done, or how. They knew nothing about our "mail," and except for a bomb we could have inserted anything we wanted—or maybe I should say except for rice and coffee, two items which were in very short supply in the outside world at that time. If the guard on duty had sharp eyes, it was necessary to hide things and find ways to circumvent her.

When it came to handicrafts, Bethlehem was an excellent school. Strictly speaking, one should have to go to prison to learn how to do them, but we were already in prison, and I at least benefited from the lessons. I remember that a few days before I was arrested I went into Judith Gorenstein's kitchen and saw wool and knitting needles on the table. I picked them up and asked her how it was done, and while I was speaking I managed to drop several stitches, causing her to cry out in alarm. I only understood the significance of what I had done after I had learned how to knit in prison. As a matter of fact, when she came to visit me after I had been in Bethlehem for about a month and a half, the first thing I told her was that I had learned how to knit, and that from now on she could trust me to pick up her knitting, because I had learned enough not to drop stitches.

A lot of the raw materials for our work, such as embroidery floss, were sent to us by the National Women's Union. They also sent us clothing, most of which had been received from South Africa, where they were always very devoted to us. We wore the clothing that was in good condition but put the silk dresses to other uses; the black ones were usually ball gowns, and since we had no immediate need for them, they furnished important material for our handicrafts. Much of the clothing we passed on to new immigrants who had managed to reach the country and were helped by the institutions which sent packages to the camps.

Making purchases was another problem for us. The other detention camps had canteens, and some of them even had coffee shops, but we were at the mercy of the guards, as they were the only ones who could buy us the materials we needed. The result was that we had to content ourselves with whatever they were willing to bring us. Often we did not get what we really wanted, and we had to reimburse them for whatever sum they said they had paid. The worst thing was that they always made sure we knew they had done us a favor for which we had to be grateful.

At the end of 1945, when the Arab boycott became stricter, we found ourselves in a ridiculous situation. We had to ask an Arab woman to buy Arab merchandise for us at a time when the Arabs were boycotting the Jews. As was our custom, we brought the problem to a general meeting, and after much deliberation we decided to stop ordering from the guards and to obtain what we needed from Jewish sources and to buy Jewish merchandise. We often had to wait a long time before we received what we wanted, but we felt much better about it.

The prison authorities provided absorbent cotton, although not, of course, for handicrafts but rather for hygienic purposes. We fooled them to the point where they themselves, without knowing it, became our accomplices in the transmitting of the very information whose transmission they were so eager to prevent.

With regard to work as well, we were worse off than the men in the detention camps. They had special work rooms, or at least special corners reserved for work, and they had tools. We had to do our work in our own rooms, or in the corridor which served as our dining room under the watchful eye of the guard. At mealtimes we had to gather everything together, and more than once we ruined everything by stopping in the middle and had to start over later on. When one works in special places the mood is different, too. We sat in a corridor through which people passed all the time, and it was both unpleasant and inconvenient, because we were doing exact work which required all our concentration.

Our visitors and the people we corresponded with always wanted to know what we did all day long. The answer was simple: sometimes the days were too short because the electricity was turned off at ten o'clock. We fought for an additional hour and half of light in our rooms, and eventually were put in charge of turning off the lights ourselves, although at a specified time.

There were days when we worked particularly hard. When visiting days approached we were anxious to finish presents that weren't ready. Sometimes we didn't have the right materials; the sack from which one wanted to make a pillow had yet to be dyed. Then we would sit for long hours, in winter ruining our eyes in the light of the kerosene stove which had been lit for warmth.

What a paradox. We were in prison but didn't have enough time for what we wanted to do! I think that was a mark in our favor. Anyone who has not been in prison doesn't know the real meaning of the expression "killing time." We were very successful when it came to killing time, and the days passed quickly and the year ended. Sometimes, when I think back on those days, I am amazed; we used the time well in spite of the fact that we couldn't study anything, and we felt the lack of studies very keenly. I can testify to the fact that almost none of the women in Bethlehem played cards; to this day people laugh at me when I try to hold a hand. Some of the women knew how to play bridge or gin rummy, but they could almost never get enough people together for a game.

In addition to doing handwork, we read a great deal. We avidly read books in various languages, and if we came across a good book we would read it more than once. We read about science not only to have something to read but also to learn as much as we could. Some of us studied English, and others the Bible. It is true that our studies were not intense. Some detainees and prisoners learned Russian from a woman who knew the language, and others tried to learn Arabic. We knitted a great deal, and some of us could read and knit at the same time, Ada Stecklis being the local champion.

What didn't we do? This may seem surprising and even incredible to many people, but we didn't gossip. We had neither the time nor the inclination for it. More than once I said that if people came to the prison they would see that there was no truth in the theory that women gossip all the time.

Our physical appearance was very important to us. Whenever we left the confines of the prison, whether to be interrogated by the CID or to go to the hospital or to the doctor, the guards who accompanied us were always annoyed because we were better dressed than they were and looked better, too, and the CID officers were very jealous. They wanted to see us looking miserable, depressed, and pitiful, and before them was a camp full of proud women who even in their hour of sickness needed no pity, whose morale was high, and who were in good spirits regardless of imprisonment and suffering. In such situations one's external appearance speaks volumes.

Conditions of misery and distress are the proving-ground for generosity and friendship, as shown by the examples that follow.

It was winter. One of the prisoners fell ill and had to be taken to the hospital. What she wore was very important, and a "war" almost broke out among her fellow inmates. "My woolen dress is warmest," said one, "take it!" Woolen clothing was vital in Bethlehem during the winter, even if one wasn't in the hospital, but the woman with the woolen dress was willing and even eager to give it up for the sake of her friend.

If a good book arrived everyone wanted to read it, and everyone had to wait her turn. As soon as someone finished reading the book, it would be virtually snatched out of her hands. If on visiting day someone brought one of the prisoners a good book from home, everyone would want to read it, and the prisoner would make up a list according to who had asked first. But if one of us had to go to the hospital, she didn't have to wait in line, and could have any book she wanted, even if she wasn't due to read it for weeks. She would receive it immediately, even if the woman reading it hadn't finished, because the hospital was even more boring than the prison, and there was no way to get books there.

If only someone had photographed the contents of the suitcase of a prisoner or detainee on the way to the hospital. I doubt that her own family would have packed the same things for her as did her fellow prisoners who had only known her for a short time. And it wasn't just the women in the same room who packed her suitcase; everyone participated in the operation. One contributed warm slippers, another a robe, a third perfume, a fourth special soap. No suitcase left the prison without a Bible. Any prisoner or detainee who had to go to the hospital was greatly encouraged and supported by all the others.

When I was taken to the hospital on a stretcher, there was no way I could pack my belongings, but I never mentioned to anyone what I wanted put into my suitcase. When I opened it in the hospital to look for a towel, I was surprised to find a large bottle of cologne, a bar of good-quality soap, a comb and a mirror, a pillow and handkerchiefs, and four or five books that I had wanted to read but would have had to wait at least a month for. I am ashamed to report that I became quite emotional and my eyes filled with tears, despite the fact that I knew that this was standard procedure, and that I would have done, and had done, as much for the other women.

My cellmates (Hasiah, Pninah, and Yaffah) had been in charge, and it was immediately obvious that great care had gone into packing the suitcase. More than once the Arab policewomen who sat next to my bed pointed out to the nurses and the other patients what friendship there was between the Jewish prisoners, and sometimes it was the main topic of conversation for the day. They also said that it was hard to break down that kind of person, and they even quoted the Arabic proverb which said that one twig was easily broken, but a bundle of twigs would always remain whole.

And so it was; as David Niv,[24] exiled to the detention camp in Kenya, wrote, "They will never break our spirit! We will never bow, we will never surrender!"

---

[24]David Niv (1915—1988) was an Irgun activist and served in the Jewish Brigade during World War II. His three-volume history of the Irgun was published in 1967.

✳ ✳ ✳ ✳ ✳ ✳

Chapter Eleven

"What a Nice-Looking Villa!"

There was a rich Arab who owned a villa which stood next to the prison. Only a very rich Arab could permit himself a villa, but it was small and never housed more than four or five people. He died in 1942, and the authorities decided, as a result of pressure exerted on them, to confiscate it and turn it into a detention camp; two years passed before the decision was put into effect.

We called the camp our villa, but the name was deceptive. After the hell of the prison it was practically paradise, but we lived in special circumstances and they caused special problems which made our lives more difficult. At times we were more than sixty women, young and old, from different backgrounds and even from different underground organizations. Sixty in a space meant for four or five! Unpleasant things happened; it was only natural that they would, and they will be mentioned, but I want to paint an overall picture of what life was like in the camp.

It should be remembered that we were fighting against the Arabs who had attacked us and to change the official policy of restraint of the institutions of the Yishuv. We were not only interested in bettering conditions in the prison, but in gaining recognition for ourselves as underground fighters.

Within the enclosure was a path leading from the prison directly to the villa. There was no way of knowing if there had always been bars on its windows, since Arabs often built their houses that way. A large iron gate, less rusty and difficult to open than the prison gate, closed off the entrance to the court-yard.

The building itself had two stories, or rather it had a base-ment and a first floor. The first floor included a long, wide cor-ridor with two to four rooms on each side, an office, a kitchen, and toilets, and from it a staircase led down to rooms which had once been, according to what the guards told us, a pig sty and storeroom. These rooms were relatively large and had high ceilings.

The guards claimed that when the government comman-deered the house, the owner's wife, as an act of revenge, uprooted all the flowers in the garden, including the rosebush-es, but try as she might she couldn't uproot the fruit trees. As a result we had the double pleasure of eating green almonds, plums, apricots, and olives, and of seeing the trees in bloom. We worked in the garden and laid out beds of flowers and veg-etables.

Inside the building we tried to make our rooms look "nor-mal." The windows were high and had wide mosaic window seats facing the garden. Niches in the wall became clothes clos-ets after we had hung up curtains to cover them. We turned our beds into sofas by rolling up the blankets lengthwise and using them as bolsters. We had vases on the tables full of flowers either cut in our garden or brought by visitors. We hung pic-tures of our families on the walls or stood them on the book-shelves.

Living conditions were very bad. There were no special rooms for study or work, and we had to do everything in our bedrooms. One woman would read, another would embroider, a third would hum to herself. There were only the bedrooms, and depending on their size, they housed between five and ten women. None of our attempts to set aside a special time for study was successful because everything depended on our moods, and we weren't all in the same frame of mind at the same time. This was also true for our attempts to set aside an hour for reading. It was hard to get a detainee interested in studying if she had just gotten a letter from home that made her cry or want to cry.

The corridor served as our dining room, and it was far from ideal, because when all of us sat together at a holiday meal and one of the women was sick in her room, writhing in pain, we all had to be quiet lest we disturb her. Since there were so many of us and we were often sick and in pain, the whole building turned into a hell. Or sometimes it was the other way around; the ill woman would ask the others not to keep quiet but to enjoy themselves as much as possible, and her suffering would be that much greater.

What happened in prison never would have happened outside: a situation in which sixty women took it upon themselves to be silent so that one woman might not be hurt or disturbed, and it only goes to show how civilized and humane were our relations with one another, and how unified we were in spirit.

Either out of malice or out of a desire to limit our freedom as much as possible, the prison administration had divided the villa's yard into two parts. The area across from the prison was separated from our side by a high fence, and we were forbidden to enter it. Our part of the yard had trees and plants growing in it and was too small for so many women; it goes without saying that we couldn't use it for games or sports. All we could do was walk back and forth, back and forth, an activity characteristic of all prisons and which causes loss of muscle tone and physical deterioration. When we first moved from the prison to the villa, we weren't allowed in the yard during most of the day, and only after a long hard struggle were we permitted to stay there until sunset, when we were locked in our rooms.

As previously mentioned, the prison administration was also responsible for the detention camp, and it was difficult for them to accept the fact that the camp's rules and regulations were different. As a result, whenever we wanted to make the conditions in our camp more like those in other camps, we had to fight hard and threaten to go on strike.

In the villa we managed to obtain better eating utensils. There were knives and forks in the kitchen, and spoons, and glasses we had brought ourselves instead of the prison cups. While we detainees were moved to the camp, the convicted women remained in the prison with its terrible conditions, and their lot was not improved at all, although we tried to help them as much as we could.

The villa had ordinary doors, and the keys were in the hands of a guard who locked the doors from the outside in the evening and opened them in the morning. Each door had been fitted with a fairly large peephole, and the guards used to check throughout the night to make sure that we were in our beds. They carried large flashlights which they shone on the faces of the sleeping women. At first it was hard to get used to the idea that you were being watched all the time, even in bed, and it was symbolic of our situation. The beam of the flashlight woke us up more than once, but in time we got used to that also.

Our situation was completely at odds with logic, and even with minimal justice. We belonged to the so-called fair sex, the weaker sex, yet our punishment was double; not only were we imprisoned in the coldest place in the country, but the conditions we lived in were inhuman. Even when they decided to set up the camp, they put it in the worst possible place from the standpoint of topography and climate. As a part of the prison we were subject to prison conditions and discipline.

Some of us claimed that the English could understand men being rebels, but couldn't understand and therefore hated women rebels, and avenged themselves on us ten times over. But there was another factor: the Jewish national institutions, by completely ignoring the camp's existence, were no less responsible than the British for our situation. They should have at least demanded that the camp be moved to a more suitable place, a demand I presented before the National Council (which eventually became the government of the State of

Israel)[25] in 1947, when relations with the Arabs worsened (I was
out of prison then, and with the help of Rabbi Goldman we
began to demand that all the imprisoned and detained women
be moved to territory held by Jews, something that should
have been done as soon as they were arrested.).

If the demand had been made earlier, we could have done
something to preserve the detainees' health: most of us developed rheumatism as a result of the dampness in the basement,
and others developed internal ailments resulting from forced
inactivity and improper medical treatment. We suffered by
being subordinate to the prison, and one of the most salient
examples of our victimization was the way our freedom of
movement was limited within the confines of the camp.

The rooms were open during the day, but access to the yard,
which was small in any case, was arbitrarily limited. A door led
from the basement to the yard, and it was opened at ten o'clock
in the morning, and all the women who decided to go out into
the yard had to stay there until noon. Then the door was
opened by the guard again, and everyone had to go inside. In
the afternoon we were only allowed into the yard for one hour.
If for any reason someone was late in getting out, she had to
spend the whole morning inside.

Sometimes a detainee who had gone out would have to go
back in again, often for the most prosaic of reasons (there was
no bathroom in the yard), and then one of two things happened. If the guard was a decent sort of person (a rare occurrence indeed), she would open the gate and the woman could
go inside, although she couldn't go out again. Either that, or
the guard opened the gate and we all had to go back inside and
stay there all morning. This was particularly unfortunate on
sunny winter mornings, when the air was warm outside and
cold and gloomy within, and we were denied our perfectly natural right to enjoy the sun in the camp yard.

---

[25]The Va'ad L'umi, or National Council, was officially recognized by
the British as representing the Yishuv and the Jews of Palestine.

This state of affairs caused more than a few arguments and problems for the guards and prison authorities. When the guards made our lives difficult, we knew how to pay them back in kind. We appealed to the highest authorities, and they came to inspect the situation for themselves, in the end rescinding the arbitrary rules, although of course not all at once. First the gate was kept open all morning, and then for two hours in the afternoon. Finally it was kept open all during the daylight hours, but we paid for our success with our blood, suffering, and health!

Most of the guards were analphabetic Christian Arabs, and we had nothing in common with them, no way of speaking to them. The secretary and two or three of the guards knew English or French, so that we could communicate with them a bit, but the overwhelming majority of them knew only Arabic. A large percentage of the prisoners didn't know Arabic, and when they were released from Bethlehem, even after years of imprisonment, they still hadn't learned the language. We were at a loss when it came to communicating with the guards. There were some words and short sentences we learned within a few weeks or even a few days, like the Arabic for "forbidden," "impossible," "no," "warden," "release," "prisoner," "political prisoner," "guard," "lawyer," and one or two other things.

Every other word the guards said was "forbidden" or "impossible," for fear of the "warden." Naturally we didn't pay too much attention to all the things we were forbidden to do, and most of the time the guards' shouts fell on deaf ears. What were we permitted to do, according to them? If we sat and cried and were pitiful the guard would do us a favor, she would clasp her hands and weep for us, "poor miserable wretches." We didn't allow them the pleasure, and when they yelled and cursed we would simply shrug our shoulders, meaning, "Leave me alone, don't bother me." When that happened the guards would come running to one of us who knew some Arabic and weep and wail and beg for mercy, and this out of their fear of the warden. Needless to say we showed good-will and pitied them, and that was usually the end of the argument, and in that way we would exchange roles: we would take pity on them instead of the other way around.

It was very important for us to keep the camp clean. We decided, in spite of the difficulties involved, to scrub the floors, something none of us was used to doing and something we didn't have the strength for. However, there were no shirkers, and we all worked and helped one another.

All the packages received were put into a storeroom and became common property, equally distributed. Even clothing was held fully in common, that is to say, if one of the detainees had to go to a doctor or to an interrogation, she chose the dress she wanted. When it came to clothing there was no mine or yours. We knew how to accept one another, overlooking one another's whims and the moods each of us suffered from at one time or another.

This does not mean that we never argued or disagreed, but the arguments were never serious and always ended well. We took everything that was good to the villa, but some of the evil came with us too; evil seems to be an integral part of human nature. Despite the fact that in the villa we were no longer twelve or thirteen women, but fifty or sixty, our social life was not much changed, and more than once I thought that people living outside prison walls might do worse than to take our example of how people could live together. As I have already mentioned, there were unpleasant incidents as well, we were only flesh and blood, not angels, but the good far outweighed the bad.

Problems arose in the villa for the following reasons: (1) the change in conditions, (2) the large number of women, (3) the length of our imprisonment, and (4) the state of the women's health.

In the prison the cleaning was done by convicted prisoners, but in the villa the whole building was our responsibility and we had to do everything alone. The floors were made of

Jerusalem stone (a kind of marble), with cracks between the slabs, and there were a lot of stairs as well, all of which made them harder to clean.

Our decision to scrub all the floors once every two weeks was exaggerated, especially since a number of the women were sick and all the work fell onto the shoulders of those who were relatively healthy, many of whom, and I among them, became ill as time passed. There was never enough water, it was hot outside, all of us wanted to wash in the only shower, and each of us felt she had the right to be first: "I did the laundry," "I did the cleaning," "I cleaned the rooms," "I worked in the kitchen." This was a cause of strife more than once, and sometimes the arguments became heated and passionate. Kibbutzniks also shared facilities, but there were always many communal showers, and so the problem was never as serious.

The psychological aspect was also distressing, in that not only were we incarcerated, but we restricted ourselves voluntarily in other ways and devised our own rules to keep our social life civilized and to preserve tranquillity insofar as was possible. Not everyone can adapt to the laws of society, and when you are free you can abandon one society and its laws in exchange for another, but in Bethlehem we had no choice, and whether a prisoner or detainee wanted to or not, she had to stay and she had to obey the rules. But there was a limit to that too, and often we bore grudges, and eventually they would come to the surface and make themselves felt. Not all of the detainees belonged to the underground freedom movement; some had simply been unlucky and were in a foul mood, but nevertheless they too had to obey the rules.

The rooms were cleaned in the morning, and when there were not enough cleaning materials and water, it was only natural that there would be arguments over the mop and pail: "I asked first," "No, *I* asked first." In a prison that sort of thing becomes terribly important, because each woman feared that if she didn't stand up for herself she would have neither the time nor the water to clean her room, and in an hour she would have to perform some other duty.

All of these restrictions and obstacles increased the general feeling of bitterness and led to emotional outbreaks. It was usually something trivial that caused the blowup, for each of us was a walking powder keg: one woman didn't receive the visit she had been expecting, another didn't receive any mail or got a letter that did nothing for her morale, or someone was just in a bad mood.

Outside of prison you would deal with a situation of this kind by going to a film, to the beach, to a coffee house, almost anything, but here? No wonder there were arguments and misunderstandings about things that would be meaningless to someone who had never been in prison.

I could have avoided writing about this, but it is impossible to give a true and objective picture of prison life without mentioning the little things that are so important behind bars. For example, rice. Because we had to cook for sixty women, we were given large amounts of rice. It was dirty and infested with worms, and had to be picked over grain by grain. How were we to go about it? Should the work be assigned to sick women? It was unthinkable to ask a few sick women to spend hours doing such a boring task.

The problem was sent to our highest forum, our "general assembly," for a solution, and among all the other things that had to be decided was how to clean the rice. After the problem and its ramifications had been thoroughly discussed, it was suggested that on certain days of the week, at set hours, all the women except those working in the kitchen would sit and pick through the rice. This was done in the corridor which served as our dining room at an hour when there was a special radio program. (Before we obtained a radio we used to put on our own "show"; we would sing and tell stories and jokes.)

In time, for those women who were superstitious and believed in signs and omens, "Rice Day" became a favorable day, a day that brought good news, such as a release order or letters or any other good thing. It chanced once that quite the opposite occurred on Rice Day, and that was the infamous speech of the chairman of the Jewish Agency, David Ben-Gurion,[26] in which he told the nation to hand over, inform on, and throw out of the schools and places of work any person suspected of being a terrorist.

Whenever something was disputed there was only one solution: the general assembly, the times for which would be announced at meals. If a bed became free in a better room, an assembly would be called to decide who would move in (and of course health was more of a consideration than seniority), an assembly would be called to decide whether or not to write letters and whether or not to accept a new prison decree. Everything touching on our lives was debated at those meetings: drawing water, choosing representatives for dealing with the prison authorities both in Jerusalem and Bethlehem, who would be in charge of the storeroom, who would do the laundry on which day (so that there would be enough soap for everyone). Everything was brought before the general assembly: the release of women (which would improve conditions), the admission of new prisoners, how many sick inmates there were. Of course we had many differences of opinion, but we were completely democratic, and the majority always ruled.

Interpersonal issues were also brought up, and certain sensitive matters were debated in a smaller forum, with two or three women from the Irgun or the Lehi meeting to solve the problem. There were things that could not be discussed in front of everyone, such as the problem of mail and questions of principle, and we would only refer such matters to the general assembly after we had debated them ourselves and decided that the topic could be made public.

---

[26]David Ben-Gurion (1886—1973), Israel's first Prime Minister and leader of the Mapai Party, was chairman of the Jewish Agency Executive from 1935 to 1948.

There were also intraorganizational matters which were dealt with by the members of the concerned organization, but there were few issues of this kind, and as a rule we didn't interfere one with the other in such things.

The bigger the camp grew the more problems there were, and the greater and more pressing the need for changes. As a result the meetings became more frequent. Occasionally a prisoner did not join our "commune," that is to say, she would not fit into our social framework. In two or three instances we felt that certain women could not be trusted, one of them being a woman who decided, on the grounds of her own egoism and personal convenience, that instead of eating with the other prisoners she would dine alone, feasting on the packages sent her by her family, who could afford to indulge her. That sort of woman wasn't invited to meetings.

During the ten years in which women were imprisoned in Bethlehem, between 150 and 180 passed through its portals, and there was only one woman who decided to remain on her own of her own free will, but it is doubtful that she was content. Her family sent her everything she needed, but as the saying goes, "Not by bread alone . . . ," and that was doubly true in prison.

Some meetings concluded with everyone in a good mood, singing songs, and some ended in a quarrel; it depended on the subject being debated and the tone of voice of the debaters. If the meeting ended badly, its influence would be felt and the atmosphere lingered in the camp for a long time; and for all the light there were patches of shadow here and there, but they were few and far between and faded quickly.

Many readers will be quick to say, What about cultural life? Can it be that for ten years so many women from different cultures and of different ages and different viewpoints were imprisoned together in a detention camp and studied nothing, wrote nothing, created nothing? In the Diaspora women in the same situation created their own cultural revolution, they studied and passed matriculation examinations and even university examinations.

The ordinary person sees years spent in prison as a single unit, and if they were, it would be possible to accomplish great and wonderful things. If a detainee had known how long she would be imprisoned, she would have been able to formulate a program for work and study. However, we were like people walking on quicksand; things kept changing, and our situation was always uncertain.

Between 1937 and 1941 the detainees generally remained in Bethlehem for only a few months. Only Rachel Ohevet-Ami had been sentenced to a long term, but she couldn't study under prison conditions, although she did teach herself secretly.

The absence of a room set aside for the purpose of study was another factor which made it hard to concentrate. Whether she wanted to or not, the inmate would be swept along into the general mood of the other detainees, for better or for worse. The bewitching possibility of release beckoned from time to time, based on all kinds of promises given in letters or at meetings, and made it difficult for many inmates to enter into the ordinary routine of prison life. The same thing happened when new inmates arrived with news from the outside world or when prisoners were released; both interrupted the routine of learning.

Nevertheless, determined efforts were made to study. Esther Raziel taught Bible, Peninah Effron gave English lessons, two detainees began to learn shorthand; I gave a course in theoretical military training. There were those who started to learn Arabic, French, and even Russian, but because of the lack of minimal studying conditions, they didn't continue.

On the other hand, we had many successful discussions and debates on various issues. We used to read Dr. von Weisl's articles about the international situation,[27] Dr Bader's articles

---

[27]Zev von Weisl (1896—1974), a physician, was a leader of the Revisionist movement and then of the New Zionist Organization. He was a prolific writer on economics, world politics, and literary subjects.

about domestic affairs,[28] and the clever and funny columns of
Y. Winitzky, who aimed his missiles straight at the authorities
and managed to outwit the most rigorous censors. And we
knew to our sorrow that one day we would be forced to stop
reading them, because they, like us, would be "invited" to
spend their time behind bars.

Every morning we read from the Bible, and those who were
"lucky" enough to remain in Bethlehem for many years read
through the whole Bible more than once.

Early in 1945 the wonder of the twentieth century, the mov-
ing picture, made its way into the prison. A film was shown
once every two weeks, but the truth was that we were not particularly eager to see them. They were of poor quality, cheap,
and irritating, and we didn't want to waste our time on them,
although heaven knows we had enough time at our disposal.
We felt that our intelligence was being underrated and our dignity insulted by the mere fact of such films being brought for
our "enjoyment," and when we saw that our repeated requests
for good films went unanswered, we relinquished the dubious
pleasure of going to the cinema. That was the end of our experience with films, which could have brought us a bit of entertainment, had it not been for the arbitrary decisions of the
authorities.

Only in 1946 were a radio and a refrigerator brought to the
camp, during the time of Lord Gort.[29] An interesting incident
occurred when the radio technician asked one of the guards
where the water was, because he wanted to use a water pipe to
ground the electricity. She was so ignorant that she brought
him a bowl of water.

---

[28]Yohanan Bader (1901—1994), Irgun activist and journalist, later
became a Herut member of the Israeli Knesset and often spoke on
economic issues.
[29]Lord Gort (1886—1946) was British High Commissioner for
Palestine from October 1944 to November 1945. During World War II
he commanded the British forces in France (1939—40), and subsequently was governor of Gibraltar and then of Malta.

zsipporah Flomin and Shulamit Shmueli arrived at the villa after they were arrested with Michael Eshbal and Joseph Simhon while "acquiring" weapons at the British camp at Sarafand, a few miles southeast of Tel Aviv, today an Israel army camp called Tzrifin. Eshbal was wounded in the stomach, and Simhon in the knee, and after they were given first aid they should have been rushed to the hospital for treatment. Tsipporah was a nurse. She and Shulamit pretended to be the girlfriends of the two men, and when they were stopped by the British police they claimed that they were going out for a good time. The British didn't believe the story and arrested them.

Tsipporah told the men to call a doctor immediately if they felt ill, because otherwise their lives might be in danger. The men saw things differently, and in spite of the pain they didn't reveal that they were wounded. For some reason they were not examined when they arrived, and only in the morning, during a routine examination, were their wounds discovered. Syringes and other first aid equipment were confiscated from Tzipporah and Shulamit; the men were tried and sentenced to death, but thanks to the courageous war waged by the Irgun, which kidnapped British officers and held them as hostages, the two were pardoned. Tzipporah and Shulamit were brought to the camp and never stood trial; apparently the British were not interested in trying women. Tsipporah was very important to the camp, especially after Adah was released, because she was the only trained nurse and the number of detainees kept growing.

Michael Eshbal fell during the raid on the Acco jail, and Joseph Simhon was killed in a work accident while drilling for oil in the independent State of Israel.

The political detainees who arrived in Bethlehem had usually been given a password for whoever was in charge from the Irgun or the Lehi. But sometimes someone was arrested without having been able to get in touch with the organization while still outside, and she didn't have a password. When that happened a representative of each organization, either Julie for the Lehi or I for the Irgun, would speak to the woman to discover whether she belonged to one of the underground movements.

Vicky Kimchi and Deborah Barazanti, two young Bulgarian girls, were brought to the camp. The general opinion was "Bulgarian equals Lehi," but during our first walk around the villa's yard with Vicky it became obvious to me that they both belonged to the Irgun; she knew the password and gave it to me. When a new inmate came who didn't belong to any organization but who obviously wasn't dangerous to us, she was never discriminated against, and we didn't try to recruit her into an underground movement until she had decided for herself which one she wanted to belong to. Sometimes a woman chose not to belong to any organization, but such cases were rare, and in any case her life was no different from ours, she had the same rights and duties as everyone else, and belonged to the commune like the rest of us.

Once a young girl from Petach Tikvah was arrested——I think her name was Shulamit——and she arrived wearing the blue shirt of Hashomer Hatzair, a leftist organization. It was the custom in the camp that whenever someone new came to the villa, the guards would take three or four women to the storeroom to bring her a bed and a mattress and all the rest of the equipment detainees were issued.

When we saw the girl we had mixed feelings; we had pity for her but were amazed that anyone wearing a blue shirt would be arrested. I was reminded of the saying, "Better to fight for the Russians so as to be taken prisoner by the Americans." And I thought, my God, if an Irgun woman, wearing a Betar shirt,[30] found herself in prison with a load of Hashomer Hatzair women, what would happen to her? What irony; something similar happened in the prison at Latrun, and

---

[30]Betar shirts were brown. Jabotinsky chose the color in 1925 to symbolize the earth of the country; Hitler chose the same color more than ten years later.

we saw there what happened to the mothers and their children who found themselves among kibbutzniks (the story will be told in the chapter on Latrun).

We took the new girl into our room. We were thirsty for knowledge of the outside world, and new prisoners were questioned endlessly for every scrap of information they might have. But if we saw that a woman really knew something, we would stop questioning her so that she would not reveal too much. But no danger of that sort was expected from this child. We sat there and let her talk, drinking in every bit of news.

The situation outside the prison was very tense in those days, and many people were being arrested, but we knew a lot about what was happening because of the illegal mail we received. Nonetheless, it was interesting to hear the opinions of someone who had been outside until quite recently, even if she was only a child, especially one wearing a blue shirt. We followed her stories with great interest until a guard came in to ask some women to come and take her equipment.

We treated Shulamit as though she were wearing a Betar shirt, and she couldn't believe it, because she had heard all sorts of stories about "criminals" and "terrorists" and the "dissidents" who ought to be destroyed, and here she was, being treated by them like royalty. Her whole arrest was an act of stupidity, and in fact she was released a few months later, but it seemed to me that when she left, both the shirt and her sentiments for it remained behind.

There was another incident in which a member of the Haganah was arrested; I can't recall her name. She wasn't very intelligent, but what she lacked in intelligence she made up for in conceit and arrogance. Around that time an Irgun member from Jerusalem named Daniel Yanovsky was kidnapped, and this happened only a few days after he had visited us in Bethlehem to bring us gifts for the holidays. There had been a newspaper in his pocket, folded with the headlines outward, and we read that Wilkins had been killed. Yanovsky had been sent by the Irgun in Jerusalem and was forbidden to carry anything that might identify him, as were we, but we saw the newspaper and understood other hints, and as the proverb says, "A word to the wise is sufficient," and that was especially true for inmates in a detention camp.

In any case, Yanovsky had been kidnapped by the Haganah, and the new woman herself told us, no more and no less, that she was one of the kidnappers and it was only by chance that she had been arrested. I would like to point out that it was a heroic feat for us, and took a great deal of strength of character, not to break every bone in her body. For as David lamented in 2 Samuel 1:20, we wanted to "Tell it not in Gath, publish it not in the streets of Ashkelon; lest the daughters of the Philistines rejoice," the daughters of the Philistines being the Arab guards and the British prison administration. In addition, we knew that an order had been given for restraint when dealing with renegades. She was with us in the commune for a few weeks, and not everyone was willing to talk to her; indeed, we really had nothing at all to do with her, one way or another, and only heaven knows how hard it was for us to practice self-control!

Once a woman named Yocheved from Kibbutz Givat Brenner was brought to Bethlehem. She had been arrested at Kibbutz Hulata, and told us that it had been as a result of a *kumsitz*. We laughed and said *"Kum sitz,"* which means "Come and sit down" in Yiddish, and in fact she did "sit" in prison for several months.

Yocheved lived with us and ate food prepared in our common kitchen, and she must have told people on the outside that most of our food came to us in packages from beyond the prison walls. In spite of the fact that she was with us for months, she got nothing but sandwiches from Kibbutz Ramat Rachel (which was close to the prison in Bethlehem), since if an ample quantity of food had been sent to her, the "terrorists," heaven forfend, might have eaten some of it.

She shared our food, that was fine, but were we to share hers? Never! What was important to us was not the food; giving her food didn't impoverish us, and we wouldn't have become rich even if the kibbutz had sent her crates of food, the way the Tel Hai Fund[31] and our families did. But through the behavior of its members we became acquainted with the people who ran the Haganah, so famous for their "pure morality" in those days.

Two members of the Haganah arrived, arrested purely by chance, a piece of bad luck, as they would say, and they spent their time in the prison with Rachel and the convicted members of the Irgun and the Lehi. While they were there, friends of these two "important" women sent them a refrigerator. The camp didn't receive a refrigerator until 1945, and the prison only had one for as long as the two Haganah members were there. During very hot weather it was hard to be without a refrigerator, but what could we do? There was no one to send us one; the government didn't want to, and the Tel-Hai Fund was too poor.

Still, it was more important for the convicted women to have one than it was for us, and the whole time the "high society" prisoners were in Bethlehem, they had their refrigerator. When they were released they took it with them, but I believe they didn't want to and were only following Haganah orders.

I could cite many more examples of intransigence and anti-social behavior on the part of people whose slogan was "comradeship between nations," and who forgave Arab rioters but were cruel to their own people.

The woman from the Haganah received illegal mail a few times, and I knew that when it came to that sort of thing the Haganah was still in the Stone Age, whereas the Irgun had all kinds of new techniques for sending hidden messages. Once I saved a cake that she had been sent, claiming that we were going to have a birthday party and we needed the cake whole. I knew that the Haganah was capable of putting a note into a cake, which was a prehistoric method of sending illegal mes-

---

[31]A fund set up to help members of the Betar and Revisionist youth movements.

sages, and when I brought her the cake I said, "Please take out your mail first!" and she did.

Once she received pajamas, and the belt aroused my suspicions (I used to go out to get packages when they arrived). I didn't want to tell her that there might be mail in her pajamas, and I didn't want her to get caught because of her ignorance, so I picked up the pajamas before they could be inspected, brought them to her, and said, "Please take your mail out of the belt." I never asked her what was written in the notes she received.

The treatment she received was particularly significant in view of the fact that Peninah Bejaio was in the camp, and she had been kidnapped by Yocheved's friends from the Haganah and held prisoner at Kibbutz Yagur under terrible conditions. She herself was not tortured, but friends of hers were.

When Peninah came to the camp she was sad and depressed. Irgun members from Jerusalem who knew her were amazed because they were used to her being a happy, mischievous girl full of energy, always in a good mood, whatever the conditions or situation might have been. It was obvious that simply being arrested had not caused her depression, and after a few minutes some of her friends decided to ask her why she was so unhappy. She could barely keep from crying. When she calmed down a bit, she told us that it was the circumstances under which she had been arrested and not the arrest itself that had shocked her so.

The incident occurred on May 12, 1945; it was one of the ugliest ever and will be remembered to the eternal shame of the informers who collaborated with the foreign regime. In the streets of Haifa one could still hear the echoes of the people cheering the parade celebrating the victory over the Nazis. The Second World War had ended, while the war of the Jewish people for its own country had just begun. The Irgun decided to direct its efforts at the oil sold by the Arabs, thicker in the eyes of the Western world than the blood of six million slaughtered Jews, and the Achilles' heel of the democratic countries.

With this goal in mind, a group of Irgun fighters, one of whom was Peninah, set out in a truck loaded with landmines. The target was the Anglo-Iraqi oil pipe which brought crude oil from Iraq to the refineries in Haifa. They were to sabotage the pipe by placing mines under it every five hundred yards on each side. Unfortunately, the pipe ran through Arab villages, and when the truck reached Kfar Hassidim (a Jewish settlement) it was stopped as suspicious by the Jewish sentries[32] whose job it was to defend Jewish settlements from the Arabs.

The truck was ordered to park near the police station and surrounded by sentries. The station commander was amazed to see the haul of landmines which had fallen into his hands. He alerted the regional head of security, which in those days meant the regional head of informers and kidnappers. It immediately became obvious to the Irgun fighters that they would have to abort the mission, but they were more worried about the truck, which was the only one the Irgun had in those days. (The historian who someday writes the chronicles of the underground war of liberation will be amazed when he discovers how poor the resources of the underground fighters were, and what small quantities of weapons we had with which to fight against the forces of the British Empire!)

The driver of the truck managed to fool the sentries and, before they knew what was happening, to drive off with the truck. The sentries wanted to open fire but were afraid that the mines in the truck would explode. A small pick-up truck full of milk cans was parked near the station, and it was pressed into service to overtake the Irgun truck, but to no avail.

The sentries were afraid that their prey would escape, and brought Peninah and the men to Kibbutz Yagur, whose "holy ground" had been chosen as the place where freedom fighters

---

[32]The sentries were policemen, but since they were Jewish they didn't wear the same uniforms as the Mandate policemen. The sentries' uniforms were khaki, those of the police, blue.

would be held and tortured. The building they used as their makeshift prison had previously been a children's house.

A squad of sentries armed with "pure" weapons guarded outside of the building, while members of the notorious Information Services waited inside.

These men, who claimed to be in favor of Jewish morality and the unity of nations, first tied the male prisoners' hands behind their backs and then put them in separate rooms. At dawn two thugs entered each room, blindfolded the resistance fighters, and said, "You're going to be interrogated, and if you don't tell us what we want to know, you'll be sorry."

The interrogations were accompanied by threats and beatings. They usually began in the early morning hours and lasted throughout most of the day. During the three days of their arrest and interrogations, the men's hands were bound behind their backs, and the bonds were only loosened at mealtimes.

This torture lasted for three full days and took place on the property of a kibbutz founded and built with public funds and symbolizing the new, ideal society.

Before dawn on the third day the thugs again entered the rooms, bound the hands of the underground fighters with *police* handcuffs, blindfolded them, and put them into a vehicle. After having gone about a mile the vehicle stopped, the blindfolds were removed, and the men found themselves in an official van full of Jewish policemen. The policemen claimed to have found them in a ditch, this despite the fact that they were sitting in the same van into which they had gone directly from the kibbutz. The story was ridiculous, and had been fabricated to camouflage their kidnapping and torture.

From there they were turned over to the CID in Haifa, one of the stations on their journey to Eritrea, while Peninah was sent to Bethlehem.

As far as she was concerned, Yagur hadn't been much of a honeymoon for her either. Her interrogators woke her up several times a night and shone a bright light in her eyes, trying to get her to reveal the names of Irgun commanders, arms caches, and so forth. "Your friends have already given everything away," they said over and over, "why are you being so stubborn?"

Peninah was kept strictly isolated during her whole time in captivity, until she was turned over to the police. That was the reason for her depression. Over and over again she asked herself how people could treat their own brothers in such a fashion when their only crime had been to fight to free their homeland, how they could inform on and betray them to a foreign, hostile ruler.

The British government "thanked" the members of Kibbutz Yagur a short time later by searching the kibbutz thoroughly for hidden weapons. Did it never occur to any of the informers that there is justice in the world, and that history often arbitrates it?

And in Bethlehem the kidnappers had been delivered into our hands, but all we did was grind our teeth and clench our fists in silence, nothing more; our consciences would not permit us to take action, nor would the directives from the Irgun, which stated that there was to be no fratricidal war. The enemy would have liked nothing better, it would have distracted us from the real war we had to fight. I am not ashamed or embarrassed; the directive was just and so were those who carried it out.

At about the same time we heard another directive, this one calling for traitors. We heard it one Rice Day while we sat in the corridor, separating the rice from the worms and insects. We were listening to the radio, and after the news at noon we heard a speech by the man who later served as Israel's Prime Minister for so many years, David Ben-Gurion. In his unforgettable voice with its unmistakable cadences he called for collaboration between the "national institutions" and the CID in the following words:

1. Drive them from the workplace! "Anyone who belongs to these gangs, anyone who supports them, not necessarily by using a gun or throwing a bomb, but all who distribute their lit-

erature and put up their announcements should be expelled from the office, factory, or orange grove and not given any other job. The same is true of a high school student if he distributes their literature; not only should their vile, polluted material be taken away, but they themselves should be thrown out of school."

2. Don't give them shelter! ". . . and the second thing we must do: we must not shelter them. . . . I know that here we come into conflict with one of our highest instincts, the human, but especially the *Jewish*, instinct, but if we don't want to be cruel to the Jewish people, now being utterly destroyed, we cannot now be overcome by a false sense of pity. We cannot shelter these criminals who are endangering our future."

3. Do not give in to threats! ". . . and the third thing, do not give in to their threats, which are so extreme that even people far removed from these gangs and utterly objecting to their actions claim that we cannot oppose them because it would lead to a civil war."

4. Collaborate with the British! ". . . and to the extent the British government and police are interested in stamping out terror, we are interested in cooperating with them. It would be stupid and suicidal if, because of the just complaints we have against the British rule of this country in other areas, we avoided helping them and being helped by them in areas in which, insofar as is possible, we have common interests. . . . If we don't help them and they don't help us, we will not get rid of the terrorists. I reject the piety, benevolence, and charity which would be justified under other circumstances and at other times."

We sat there, young Jewish girls who had sacrificed the best years of our lives on the altar of Israel's liberation, sitting behind bars, and listened, stunned and hurt, to the abominable words of the chief informer. The "living legend" had sunk as low as was possible, and had called for schoolchildren to be betrayed to the CID for the "sin" of loyalty to their country!

Since we were not under his control and refused to follow his instructions, Ben-Gurion decided to fight a physical fight against us, not just an ideological fight, and to deprive us of everything possible: food and shelter, education and medical services.

Only a few days passed and his speech bore fruit. We began to receive entire "shipments" of students from schools. Girls from the teachers' seminary, from high schools—some of them members of the underground, some of them victims of vendettas who had been turned in by people who used the leader's call for informers to settle their own personal scores. We were reminded of the words of the poet Uri Tzvi Greenberg,[33] who said, "The pain is great, so is the disgrace," and asked, "Which is greater, say, O man!"

The spirit of that speech has always remained with me. Whenever I heard Ben-Gurion's unmistakable tones, I remembered it and was shaken anew.

---

[33]Uri Tzvi Greenberg (1895—1982), recipient of both the Bialik Prize and the Israel Prize, supported the underground struggle and was noted for his intensely nationalistic poetry.

※ ※ ※ ※ ※ ※

Chapter Twelve

Mail and "Illegal" Mail

More than once in Bethlehem I asked myself who had invented the form of human communication called the letter. It seemed to me that it must have been someone in prison who had no other way of communicating with the people he loved.

Alone as we were, and cut off from everyone who was dear to us, letters were the only thing binding us to our families, a kind of paper bridge over which we could cross to visit each other. The day a letter came was a holiday, no less and perhaps even more of a holiday than visiting day, because visits were limited to a few minutes. The tension before and during a visit was great, and it was over almost before it began, but a letter was different. A letter could be read again and again, quietly and without pressure, and new things could always be found in it. In addition, letters could be saved, and one could sit and read all the letters from a specific period and learn what was going in each family member's life during that time.

The Yiddish song, "A Letter from Mother," had a special meaning in prison. That must have been why the CID tried so hard to deny us the pleasure. Among the restrictions in Bethlehem and the prohibitions against having something dangerous in one's possession, such as a watch, which might be used to bribe a guard, one of the most conspicuous was the ban on writing materials.

The rule was arbitrary, and we had to fight a long, bitter battle to change it. They were afraid that giving writing materials to prisoners might lead to illegal correspondence with the outside world. At first we could only have pencils and paper once a month when we were allowed to write letters, and it made no difference if on that day a detainee was ill or not in a letter-writing mood. At the end of the day we had to give back the pencil and any unused paper; actually, there wasn't much paper left, since each of us only received one sheet.

We decided to fight back and went on strike, but not the sort of strike found in the chronicles of the labor movement; this was a correspondence strike. "If you won't let us write home the way we want to," we said, "have it your own way: we won't write home at all."

For someone not in prison, this may seem like a strange threat, and not particularly threatening to the people in power, but such strikes in the prisons and detention camps were very effective. We had no official support, but we ripped away the mask of the British regime's "humanity," with which it had been trying to hide the real conditions in the prisons and detention camps. The British knew that every strike was widely publicized outside the prison. Then the families, which had to patiently suffer the imprisonment of their loved ones, went into action and revealed to the public, both in Israel and abroad, the true face of the oppressive regime which allowed innocent people to be imprisoned for unlimited periods.

News of the strikes caused a storm in a wider circle, and people who were not involved politically could not help but be involved on a personal level, and this was most unpleasant for the British. For such "petty" interests it wasn't worth their while to complicate matters and alienate an entire population which accepted the imprisonment of women, some of them mothers of small children, for years on end.

Even behind the prison walls it was convenient for them if life went on as usual, so they wanted the prisoners and detainees to write home. They never learned the addresses of any Irgun and Lehi commanders from the letters, but sometimes they might benefit from something written thoughtlessly or in haste.

Therefore, the British had to give in, although not all at once, but as slowly as possible. At first, His Majesty allowed us pencils and paper twenty-four hours before "Writing Day," and then later, when we moved to the detention camp in the villa, we could have writing materials all the time, although the pages were numbered. I kept a notebook with numbered pages as a souvenir. We didn't need the favors of the prison clerk, Jemila, nor did we need Mr. Graham's paper; actually, we didn't need the prison mail either, because we had our own methods of getting mail in and out whenever we pleased.

Somewhat later we learned that we were not the only ones with a pencil problem. The same difficulty affected those who were incarcerated in Eritrea, although they were in a detention camp and not a prison. A copy of a letter found its way into our hands, written by one of the men there and sent via the camp commander to the commander of the British military forces in the Middle East. It said,

> I, a prisoner in a camp whose name cannot be mentioned for reasons of national security, ask you, with all due respect, to let me have *a pencil*. I am a high school graduate and am diligently trying to continue my education insofar as I can.
> As a result of my unexpected move to this corner of the world, I can no longer continue my accustomed activity because I lack a pencil to write with.
> In accordance with the Atlantic Charter and the goals of the current war, as stated by the United Nations, relating to the entire world, including this charming corner, it is the right of every man born of woman to enjoy education so that he may enlighten his mind and let truth, developments in science and research, and technical progress overcome the pagan gods of barbarity and of medieval Nazism.

I believe, therefore, in the light of the principles of justice and democracy, as understood by the United Nations (with Britain first among them), that your kind and honorable self will use your undisputed influence to allot me a pencil.

I deeply request your pardon for troubling you with a matter so seemingly insignificant, but it seems to be far easier to build buildings and detention camps overnight than to provide writing materials for the prisoners. The problem must be much more complicated than it seems, and I therefore have decided to bring it to the attention of the institution most capable of dealing with it.

The day after this letter was received, the prisoner in question was allotted a pencil as a personal gift from the commander of the British Middle East forces, along with the request that he take back the letter.

Many people read our mail, both incoming and outgoing, and that was in addition to the strict censorship it underwent, which more often than not left the letters looking like spaghetti, because parts deemed objectionable were cut out and not merely effaced.

There was also internal censorship. A prisoner would sit down to write a letter, her heart bursting with things she wanted to tell her family, when suddenly in her mind's eye she would see not the faces of her loved ones, but the faceless form of the CID censor. At that moment the pencil would fall from her hand, the flow of words would dry up, and the paper would remain blank, with only the censor's cynical Cheshire cat grin floating in the air.

There was another kind of letter which deserves to be documented, but my powers of description are not sufficient for the task. These were the letters from the women of Bethlehem to the men in the detention camps both in Israel and abroad, in Eritrea, Sudan, and Kenya. The Histadrut had an expression, "working couples," by which they meant families in which both husband and wife worked for the national Jewish institutions and received a double salary. In our world there were also working couples in secure jobs: one in the prison in Bethlehem, the other in a prison camp someplace in Africa or in Latrun, Acco, or Jerusalem, and their salary was also impressive. Some families were really "fortunate" in this respect, having a son or two in Eritrea and a daughter or two in Bethlehem.

It is no wonder that under such conditions many strange things happened to the mail. For instance, Adinah Lichtmacher sent a letter to her husband, who was imprisoned in Acco, which surprised him no end. She belonged to the Lehi, and her husband, Michah, belonged to the Irgun. They both came from the same city as Nathan Friedmann or Yellin Mor,[34] and were arrested after visiting his wife in Bethlehem. They had just been married, and spent an extended "honeymoon" as guests of His Majesty. She wrote the letter to him two years after their arrest, and said "In a little while we will have a child." She was referring to Esther Raziel, but he didn't understand. Esther's husband, Yehuda, was with him in Acco and explained it to him.

When it came to working couples, the cruelty of the mail situation became more intense. Prisoners could only write and receive letters once a month, and if a wife wrote from Bethlehem to her husband in Eritrea, she couldn't write to her parents, and vice versa. The women found a way to get around the rule by sending collective regards to everyone from everyone by name in all their letters. There was nothing the authorities could do, because the law only limited the number of letters, but not the number of people who signed each letter. They tried to limit the number of sheets each letter could cover, but in the end that regulation too was revoked.

All these tricks were designed to make it easier to send regular mail, but there was another kind of mail, and it was out of

---

[34]Nathan Friedmann or Yellin Mor (1913—1980) was one of the commanders of the Lehi. Arrested and convicted in connection with the assassination of Count Folke Bernadotte, he later was a member of the Knesset.

*Tzila giving a lecture at the Zionist
Congress in Jerusalem, 1965.*

The gate at the Bethlehem prison.

Tzila's family, Passover, 1924.

*Tzila, far right, second row, at the reunion of women
prisoners at her home, 1953.*

"Villa Salim," a private villa originally owned by Arabs but taken over by the British and used as a way-station for transfer of prisoners after arrest.

Binyamin before Tzila's first arrest.

Tzila and her son at Etzel's training ground, before her first arrest in 1941.

Tzila's husband and son, after her husband's repatriation from a German prisoner-of-war camp in 1946, while Tzila was still in prison.

Binyamin at age 8, in a photograph intended to be sent to Tzila in prison at Bethlehem.

Tzila and her son, after her release in 1943.

The women's prison in Bethlehem.

Dr. Pearlman, the doctor for the prison and detention camp.

The detention camp (Villa Salim)

*Rabbi Aryeh Levin, the rabbi of the
underground prisoners.*

Prisoners and detainees, transferred from Bethlehem to Itlit in 1948.

The "Bethlemhem women," in a gathering in Tel Aviv. Standing, right to left: Amalia Shiff, Devora Shapira, Frieda Wagshal, Esther Beckman; seated: Berachah Birnbaum, Chisya Shapira, Rachel Habshush, Devora Kalfus, Judith Yehezkel.

The arestees of 1940-1944 in a gathering in Tel Aviv. Standing, right to left: Frieda Friedman-Yelin, Malkah Weingarten, Hayah Srulowitz, Hasidah Lifshitz, Naomi Orenstein, Bela Shechter (Putzi). Seated: Gertl Mordechai, Rachel Habshush, July Elazar, Ruth Schechter, Gali Fisher. Front row: Adina Lichtmacher, Miriam Rubowitz (Goldman), Tzila.

The "Bethlehem women" in a gathering in Tel Aviv in 1953.

The Arrestees and Detainees of Bethlehem, participating in Kenes Dor Hamered in Tel Aviv, 1958.

One of the letters sent to Tzila Heller thanking her for her participation in sending books and clothing to the fighters' camps.

A request to lighten the rigor of Tzila's house arrest in 1943.

Binyamin Amidror, a captain in the armor division, in Kham Yunis after the Sinai Campaign.

Meeting with Prime Minister Manachem Begin, July, 1982.

the question for the censors even to know about it, and for this reason it was sent in other ways; this was the illegal mail.

As is well known, inmates smuggle all kinds of forbidden things into prison. Common criminals have a list of more or less standard items, but for political prisoners the smuggling is political as well, and it includes letters, contraband materials, and tools for breaking out of prison. I will only deal with letters and illegal literature. By letters I don't mean the kind sent in envelopes, I mean coded correspondence, sometimes even sent as regular letters, everything done according to what was necessary and what was possible.

Notes and letters were usually smuggled into prison in cakes of soap or in tin boxes, but especially in food packages, via someone in the prison or camp who had been bribed. None of these was a viable system in Bethlehem. There were very few Jewish guards, and they usually couldn't be trusted. Contacting Arab guards was dangerous, so we had to find original methods of getting messages in and out. Cakes and bread were cut into when they arrived, and the same was true for soap. Packs of cigarettes were opened and emptied. The procedures were stricter than in other places because women were in charge of the prison, and in such matters it is much harder to fool a woman. The prison authorities and the CID were as quick as we were when it came to learning about ways of smuggling things into and out of the prison, and they were always on the alert.

Between 1940 and 1941 there were very few underground fighters in the Bethlehem prison, and the illegal mail was not well organized. The Jewish guard, Rayah,[35] would smuggle a

---

[35]A number of Jewish policemen and policewomen cooperated with the underground even though they were not members of any resistance movement. Several of them were guards in the prisons and detention camps, but there were very few Jewish guards in Bethlehem, and even fewer who were willing to help the prisoners.

letter in to Ruth from her boyfriend outside, or if the family of one of the women contacted her privately, Ruth would take in a letter for them. This would be done strictly as a personal favor. Of course, since the boyfriend was also an officer in the Irgun, sometimes he might use this method to pass on information, but that was only done incidentally.

After I was released, I recall, I had to relay something to the prisoners about getting special treatment for Rachel, and about what she had to demand or do to help those of us who were outside, and we were afraid to endanger the guard. We couldn't tell Rachel about any of this on a visit, so our difficulties were great.

Once I had to get a note out when a rebellion began among the Lehi women, and I had no way of doing it. By chance I learned that one of the Jewish convicted criminals was about to be released. The convicted women knew to the day when they would complete their sentences, unlike those of us who were simply detained, and never knew the day or the month or even the year we would be set free. I met the woman in the kitchen and persuaded her that as a Jew she had to help the imprisoned

---

One of them was Rayah Mazcoriah. She had three small children and was her family's sole support. When she was the listener on visiting day, we could say what we wanted without fear that it would be reported; she simply didn't hear anything. In some cases Rayah was the only person who could contact prisoners' families, and she walked endless miles to deliver letters or pass along messages. More than once she had to sleep on a bench because she had missed the last bus back to Jerusalem and didn't have the money for a hotel.

Rayah did what she did because of her immense humanity, and endangered herself by smuggling things like cigarettes, pencils, and knitting needles. Sometimes she bought things for the prisoners with her own money.

Her contribution was as important as the work done by those of us who fought actively in the underground. She took many risks over the years, deriving strength from her feelings of compassion and patriotic duty.

freedom fighters. I even found a way to get the message out, a way popular with women prisoners worldwide, but unless the need to pass the information along was really very urgent, I would never choose to use it. The message was delivered the next day. I gave her an address with which she was familiar, and she was never in any danger.

When I was arrested in 1944 and the detention camp was in the villa, there were fifty or sixty of us, and our needs and demands grew in proportion to our numbers. We had a great desire to know what was happening outside the prison walls, and the possibility of contacting people outside became greater. We engaged in handicrafts, making things which were sent out of the prison, especially embroidery or knitting, but in a knitted sweater or an embroidered napkin there is no place for even the smallest note, and everything we received from the outside world was subjected to the most careful scrutiny by the prison administration.

In the camp, however, we made things filled with absorbent cotton, and they were wonderful containers for letters. The inspection of packages which came into the compound at Bethlehem was also less stringent in the camp than in the prison. I emphasize Bethlehem because in other prisons it was easier to smuggle mail, even easier than in our camp, as a result of the prevailing conditions.

Contact was maintained in two ways.

1. The mail was put into the packages we got once a week from the Tel Hai Fund. The families of the prisoners would bring packages to Fund offices in various parts of the country, and they would be sent to the head office in Jerusalem, together with packages sent by the Revisionist movement in cooperation with the Irgun. The packages, each with the name of the recipient printed on it, would be sent in a special car with a messenger to Bethlehem, whereas parcels meant for all the detainees would be sent with the name of only one woman on them. Since I had nothing to lose after my third arrest, and since I didn't hide the fact that I belonged to the movement

which had sent the packages, they all had my name on them during the time I was in prison. The guards knew that the packages belonged to the Gema'ah, or "tribe," that is to say, the national institutions. Our poor "institutions," so guilty in the eyes of the guards. They also thought that the Gema'ah sent the packages we received from the Chief Rabbinate and from the Community Committee in Jerusalem, and we didn't bother to teach them to distinguish between the two senders, both because we were ashamed that the institutions didn't take care of us and because of general tactics of secrecy and intrigue.

2. The other method of maintaining contact was during the visits our parents paid us. In prison only a few packages were received, and all of them were examined and the boxes were removed. We got everything after it had been carefully examined, and almost everything arrived in small pieces. The packages our visitors brought were no bigger than those sent from Jerusalem. Things were different in the camp, however, because the number of packages received was great, and because they were delivered to the prison, they had to be brought to the camp by one of the convicted prisoners. We demanded that the packages be opened and examined in the camp in the presence of the people to whom they had been addressed. Like our other demands, this was not complied with immediately, and we had to use pressure and threats. Only then was a room allocated for the mail where all the packages were put and from which the prisoners could take them. Here too we only got crumbs and pieces of things, but the situation was better than it had been in the prison. We fought long and hard to teach the prison administration and the guards to give us our cakes whole, not to cut our food into pieces and not to open our packs of cigarettes. In that way we prepared the ground for smuggling in contraband material, not just notes and letters, but newspapers, magazines, and illegal manifestos. Usually we read the manifestos before they had been posted in the streets of the cities.

The sending and receiving of letters never stopped; quite the opposite, it kept increasing.

In the middle of 1944, along with many other young women, Miriam Birenbaum was arrested. She and I had known each other before I was sent to prison; I had been her commanding officer, and her family belonged to the National Revisionist Movement. They owned a bakery and used to bring Miriam boxes of rusks and other food. Sometimes the number of boxes was very large because there was a great demand for rusks in prison, as a result of both the huge number of sick women and the desire to vary the diet and substitute something for the bread, whose quality was poor. I had a feeling that Miriam would not be in prison for very long, she was too young and her family too rich, and I decided to work out a plan with her to ensure that after her release the boxes would continue to arrive, not necessarily containing rusks, but rather food for the soul, and contact with the outside world.

Miriam "lived" in the basement of the prison. All the girls in her room were young, all Irgun fighters whose commander I had been, so that I could do in their room whatever I could do in my own. I asked the others to leave and remained alone with her. We experimented with opening the boxes and closing them again, gluing them shut with flour-and-water paste after I had stuffed the boxes with newspapers. I let the more experienced Irgun fighters try to find the boxes which had been doctored, and although they knew that some of the boxes hid something, they didn't know which. We conducted many experiments and they were all successful.

After a while Miriam was released, earlier than had been expected because she suddenly fell ill. As soon as she could she contacted the Gurion family and Esther Raziel, and the work of the "factory" improved, because they used better glue and because outside there were more and better possibilities. The boxes kept coming as usual, and among ourselves we always remembered the Birenbaum family, which never forgot us and continued to provide us with rusks and food as if Miriam were still with us. Only a very small number of trusted women knew what was in the boxes besides food. In that way a lot of illegal mail entered and left the camp, much of it thanks to the efforts of Isaac Gurion and his wife, Tzipporah.

Appetite, say the French, comes with eating. When Esther Raziel Naor was released, she put her brain to work. Now, instead of just one kind of box, they started using long ones, wide ones, all different shapes, but the principle was the same.

The boxes were only one of the ways we smuggled mail in and out, and people outside the prison who received mail from us, that is to say family members who were also Irgun fighters, started looking for additional ways to establish contact with us. Sometimes they would put notes into boxes of candy and the heels of shoes, but that was dangerous, because the prison authorities once tried to inspect the soles of some shoes.

But no joy comes unmixed with sorrow, and one fine day (although it wasn't a fine day at all, it was a dark, brooding, dangerous Friday) the ax fell. As previously mentioned, the convicted Arab prisoners used to bring us our packages from the prison building, and on this occasion we could see from afar that the boxes were open! They were large boxes, and the women were carrying them on their heads. Could anything be done? Our anxiety was unbearable. I had nothing to lose, I had already been arrested and my chances of being released were negligible, but the CID knew that the packages had been sent by the Tel Hai Fund, and if they found anything illegal inside they would both shut down the Fund's offices and declare the whole Revisionist movement illegal, and all because of our desire to have contact with the world outside the prison.

We were filled with remorse but there was no time to feel sorry for ourselves; we had to act. An immediate emergency meeting was called which included Julie from the Lehi, Esther Auerbach, Peninah Bejaio, Peninah Effron, and Hayah Ben-Tzvi, all Irgun commanders, and we had to decide whether or not I should refuse the packages, since they had not been opened in my presence. If I refused, I could claim that I was not responsible for what was inside them and that anything suspicious had been planted by the CID. But we could always hope for a miracle; perhaps the illegal mail had not been found even though the boxes had been opened. In that case, if I refused to accept the packages I might make the situation even worse, because the CID would become involved and the chances of the mail being discovered would become greater.

We decided to accept the packages and let the dice fall as they might. I vowed that if the mail was there and everything turned out all right I would ask my mother to make a contribution to charity.

We were terribly excited and anxious. I would have to wait for Maria, the guard, to open the storeroom, which might be in an hour or two, and during the time I would feel as if I were being raked over hot coals.

That same day I had been given some fish to prepare. There was nothing wrong with the fish, but I went into the kitchen angry and upset and determined to make trouble, saying that the fish were no good and I had nothing to cook. The poor fish quickly found their way into the garbage pail, and I demanded that the storeroom be unlocked immediately because I had to find something to cook for Saturday (I was on a strict diet because of my illness). My anger about the fish was sufficient to justify my foul mood and the uproar I was causing.

I entered the storeroom and deliberately overturned a container full of food, all of which had to be picked up. I asked for someone to come in and help me and threatened the guard, saying that otherwise she would have to do it because I didn't have the time, it was Friday and I had to finish cooking before the Sabbath. Loudly I cursed the government for not providing me with enough food and forcing me to need packages from the outside, and how lucky I was that people had sent me food; otherwise, what would I do?

The poor guard worked hard to collect all the spilled food, since quite a number of paper bags had been torn. I searched through all the boxes, all of whose sides had been opened, or rather, three of whose sides had been opened because they were all open on top. Suddenly I came upon a box which according to all the signs should have contained mail. My heart began to pound. Again I started cursing the government and the prison administration, and happily called out that I had finally found the food. I shoved a lot of food into the box and called to the guard to open the door because it was getting late. The other women in the camp understood what I was doing. I had no food and the Sabbath was very near. I was so upset and anxious that if someone had laid out a feast I couldn't have eaten so much as an olive.

I took the box and ran into the kitchen, where we put on another little performance. One of the women pretended to be angry and grabbed the box from me, asking me by what right I had taken the box she needed for her clothing. It was all a show, of course, but we managed to get the box into our room. Now we had to make sure that the other women didn't come into the room, just the four of us, and we hid behind the curtain and started to take the box apart. By that time we were nearly desperate, but finally, there in a corner of the box, in a place where the knives of the prison director couldn't or didn't reach, was what we were looking for, and it was more precious to us than caviar.

There was no end to our rejoicing, and we felt that a miracle had occurred. Silently we thanked God. All of a sudden I felt exhausted from the show we had put on for the guard, and from having to pretend to the women that the fish, which would have made a wonderful meal, were spoiled, and finally from the happiness I felt when I realized that the Tel Hai Fund was not in danger. A rumor quickly went through the camp that I didn't feel well, that I'd had an attack and no one could come into my room. It was an attack, not of any illness, but of pleasure. The four of us began to read the material we had been sent, and it was doubly enjoyable because we had gone through such a terrible time to obtain it. I cannot reveal here what was in the material, but even today I can feel the thrill that ran through me as I read it.

When the rabbi came to visit the following Thursday, I asked him to help me fulfill my vow by telling my family to make a contribution to charity, and he did. He was smart enough not to ask any questions. I told Mr. Thomas that in the future I would not accept any packages which had been opened in the prison. If he wanted to open them, I said, he could, but only in the camp in the presence of the detainees to whom they had been sent. No more packages were ever opened, and the matter passed without further incident. To be on the safe side, we told people outside not to send us any more messages until further notice, and contact was only renewed two or three weeks later.

On one occasion the guard named Blossom decided for some reason to open a small package which had aroused her suspicions. Usually there were ways we could tell if something had been hidden in a package, and when I saw her pick up the box I dropped three bags of noodles. The contents fell all over the floor of the storeroom. Cursing in Arabic, I took the package out of her hands and demanded that she help me pick up the noodles because I had to cook them. It was bad enough that the government didn't give us enough food, I said, but that she had pushed me and made me drop the noodles was intolerable. It worked, and in the end Blossom never opened the box and we threw the noodles into the garbage.

Another time I saw a message sticking out of a candy box. I took the box out of the guard's hands and with a flourish offered her a piece of chocolate, I even put it into her mouth, at the same time telling her all kinds of stories about the candy, why we had gotten it, and that in fact it was supposed to have been a surprise present for Hasiah's birthday, and thus I saved the box and the note.

The note had been put into the candy box by a family which was new at sending illegal mail and didn't know exactly how to do it. If they had been caught, their daughter would have spent much more time in prison than she did.

There were all kinds of strange incidents, but I have only recounted what happened to me. Surely there were other women who went to get their packages and at the last minute saved the mail from being discovered by the prison authorities. We sent illegal mail from 1944 until the camp was disbanded. All during this time not one piece of illegal mail was ever found. Mr. Thomas used to say that he knew that illegal mail was going in and out of the camp, but he didn't know how.

Once a note came for one of the women we had been warned against. We didn't want her to know about the illegal mail, but I had been given instructions to deliver it to her. For various reasons I couldn't inform the people outside that I could not permit myself to endanger the whole mail system because of one note. I did something I never would have done under normal circumstances, but in this case the end justified the means. Since it was a private message and not part of a conspiracy, I asked one of the women to read the note and tell her what was in it as if she had heard the news from someone who had come to visit. But before I had a chance to inform the people outside that I didn't want illegal mail sent to that particular woman, another note arrived for her. This time one of the women put it in her room while she wasn't there, so that she would find it without knowing how it had gotten there. Finally I got word through to the Irgun, and no more mail was sent to her.

We were very anxious about the mail, and for good reason. Besides the packages, we received coded messages in books. Esther Raziel used this method more than anyone else because she had the greatest amount of patience and willpower to sit and put pencil marks under one letter after another. It was really interesting to lie in the yard or on a sofa during the winter, pencil and paper in hand, deciphering the code.

In the camp we usually used the code to transmit messages to the prison, as if we were exchanging books with them. We also contacted the women in the hospital, using the code with books and newspapers. Those were the methods I used, in any case; the women who belonged to the Lehi probably had other methods. Our mail was separate from theirs, needless to say. Sometimes letters for them would come in our mail, and we would pass them on as soon as they came.

Another way of getting mail from the outside world was via the Arab prisoners from the prison in Jerusalem who were sent to Bethlehem to do repairs. From them we received messages from the men and sometimes cigarettes; the guards were their accomplices. We mostly had to fear the women guards. It was a difficult situation, because the minute a man set foot in the prison all the women would be locked in their rooms. Those in charge of morals and modesty were worried about every minute a woman prisoner and a man might be together, especially after one of the Arab women suddenly became pregnant, and if there was ever an instance of a child fathered by the Holy Ghost in Bethlehem (in accordance with the beliefs of the prison director), it certainly wasn't this particular child.

Eventually we persuaded the guards that there was no need to keep watch over our morals, and they stopped locking us in our rooms. As a result we could talk to the policemen and the male prisoners and find out exactly where the smuggled mail had been put and how to get it.

Yehoshua Zeitler sent regards to his wife Bella, a prisoner in Bethlehem, by writing his message on the underside of a plank brought by the prisoners to fix the wooden floor of the bathroom.

The Lehi women sometimes used to put messages in the soles of shoes. Nelly Fisher was an expert at inserting them, and the shoes would be sent out of Bethlehem to be repaired. They also smuggled messages out in book bindings, usually to their comrades in the prison in Jerusalem.

We often sabotaged utensils or the bars on the windows so that prisoners from Jerusalem would be sent to fix them, and thus we could continue to contact our friends. When we moved to the villa, the repairs were done by ordinary hired workmen. This must have been because we had been found out, and the prison authorities wanted to put an end to the contacts we had developed with Jerusalem.

Once when my mother came to visit she hinted that "the walls had ears." I laughed and tried to make a joke of it so that she would not worry, but I seriously considered what she had said.

When Shoshanah Raziel returned from a visit to Dr. Ticho in Jerusalem, friends and family hinted to her on their next visit that there were microphones hidden in the walls of the "Villa Salem."

We took the rumor with a grain of salt. It might have been true, because the building had been specially fitted out as a detention camp. The bars on the windows had been strengthened (Arab buildings in Bethlehem had barred windows as a matter of course), the garden had been divided by a high fence, the outer fences had been topped with barbed wire, and the inner doors had been replaced. Who could say that listening device hadn't been planted in the walls?

We weren't afraid of divulging Irgun secrets because we never discussed them, but we used to read the orders of the day and secret circulars aloud in our rooms, so while the rumor made us more careful, we saw it as a source of entertainment. As usual, we didn't like to let an opportunity for fun go to waste.

We decided to scrape the walls around the light switches and wall sockets to see if the rumors were true. Sonia Rekuzin was our local electrical expert, and she told us what to do. Our next problem was how to get to the ceiling; that was the most logical place to put a listening device. The ceiling was high and we had no ladder, so we put one table on top of another and a chair on top of that, which was the only way we could get up so high. But how could we do it without arousing the suspicions of the guards?

We decided that the time had come for gymnastics, and we practiced making pyramids. For that we needed the tables, and we accustomed the guards to seeing us making pyramids with them. After a while we began engaging the guards in conversations in their room to make sure they stayed there, while at the same time some of the women scraped the ceilings and looked for hidden microphones. After a while Sonia said that there were no signs of microphones in the ceilings. For the sake of intrigue we called the microphones we couldn't find "those damned whatsits," and whenever one of the women started to say something and we didn't want her to continue, we would say "don't forget the damned whatsit."

We became more careful of what we said, just to be on the safe side, and when we read material aloud, we did it almost in a whisper.

There were other ways of getting illegal mail in and out, and since lack of space prevents me from discussing them all, I have only mentioned the principal ones. The only people who can understand how important it is for someone behind bars to receive the commander's order of the day, a circular, or an illegal newspaper are those who have had experience with it.

My mother, then already almost sixty years old, played an important role in sending and receiving illegal mail. Sometimes, when we couldn't wait until Friday, the day for sending packages, we gave a package containing concealed mail to family members who had come to visit one of the women. The visitors never knew what they were taking out of the prison with them. But not my mother. She always knew what was in the little suitcase or box she took, and not only that, more than once (Esther told me this once I was free) she had suggestions of her own about how and where to hide the mail. During visits she always found a way to tell me on which page of which book the code was found, and where the mail itself was. She brought me not only my son, but other spiritual comfort, and she should be honored for her composure in the face of danger, her devotion to her people, and her willingness to help the freedom fighters of Zion.

I expressed my feelings for her when on her sixtieth birthday I asked the Jerusalem radio to play the song "A Yiddishe Mama" and dedicate it to her. As we sat and listened to the song, our eyes filled with tears and overflowed.

Someday a monument will be erected to honor the Jewish mothers who sacrificed so much for the establishment of the State of Israel, and I can see it in my imagination: an old woman walking along a road, one arm laden with bundles, the other leading a child, and she is walking forward, her head held high with pride.

Chapter Thirteen

Visits

We marked time from one event to the next: the days and weeks till mail day, a holiday, visiting day. Anything and everything not part of the usual gray prison routine made life more interesting, and waiting for something more pleasant to happen made the time seem to pass faster.

Visiting days were the happiest days for the convicted prisoners and the detainees, but saddest for those who had no family, or whose friends were afraid that visiting the prison might endanger their own safety. Sometimes the authorities forbade any visitors at all, and that was the worst thing that could happen. I was lucky in this respect because during the time visits were prohibited I was not in prison.

There were different rules for convicted prisoners and detainees. Prisoners could have a limited number of visitors every two months, and an unlimited number on holidays and feast days. Sometimes the Jerusalem branch of Betar organized "pilgrimages" to Rachel Havshush Ohevet-Ami on holidays. Needless to say, a hundred or a hundred and fifty people could not get in to see her, but some of the instructors and commanders, as well as her family members, were allowed in. They usually exchanged only a few words with her, and of course not all of them at the same time, because they didn't want to take time away from her parents, for whom every second spent with their daughter was precious.

The detainees could receive visits every week and every holiday, with an unlimited number of visitors on the holidays. Visitors only had to give their names and addresses to the guards at the gate, and it goes without saying that since there was no need to present identification, none of them ever gave their real names and addresses. These conditions were in force until 1942, when things changed.

As for the convicted Arab prisoners, all their relatives used to visit them, and the status of the families was reflected in their behavior. If the woman came from a poor family, a crowd of people dressed in rags would come to visit, shrieking and wailing. If, however, the woman came from a rich family, the rich and important people from her village would come with expensive gifts, although in these instances as well, most of the their time was spent in waiting.

The Jewish convicted criminals had the saddest visiting days because they usually led the saddest lives, cursed by fate and with no families to care for them. The official Jewish national institutions were totally indifferent to these women, while the Christian and Moslem institutions occupied themselves with the prisoners of their own faiths. The Jewish prisoners were simply ignored by their own people. It was an inhuman situation, and it was painful for us to see. Insofar as we could, we gave them food from our own packages.

The spot which the authorities designated as the meeting place for the detainees was next to the room of the mentally ill inmates. There might have been a certain justification for this choice, because in the eyes of both the prison authorities and the Jewish institutions, we were a bunch of madwomen.

At the north end of the corridor on the second floor, where the mentally ill women were kept, there was a barred door next to which a small table had been placed. We had to stand in back of the table while our visitors stood on the other side of the door. The atmosphere, both physical and emotional, was awful. The hair-raising screams of the ill women and the stench issuing from their room lent the scene a nightmarish air. The impression it made on our families was terrible, and they assumed that we lived under these conditions all the time.

The physical distance between the prisoners and their visitors was too great to hold quiet conversations, and intimate discussions of family matters were out of the question. In addition, someone from the CID who knew Hebrew, English, and Arabic was always present, so every word which passed between us had to be carefully considered. Sometimes there was no one from the CID, and then the guards tried to force us to speak English or Arabic, languages which they understood. When this happened we had to forgo the visit, causing our relatives—and ourselves—much pain, especially since many of them had come from far away.

On holidays, when the prison director knew that many visitors would come, a large table would be brought for the packages. The director herself would put in an appearance to supervise the proceedings, wearing one of her white outfits (starched and ironed by Rachel), and looking like a nun.

A few days after I was arrested and brought to Bethlehem, I was told that someone had come to see me. I was surprised to have a visitor so soon, especially since it had been raining heavily all day. There before me stood Hadassah Brande, wearing a torn raincoat and drenched to the bone. The poor woman had made a mistake and asked the Arab bus driver to let her off at the prison (*beit-sohar* in Hebrew), and since she didn't speak Arabic he hadn't understood and had let her off at an Arab village called Beit Tsor. She was unable to do anything but gesture, and the villagers called the local "expert," who knew that there was a prison for Jewish women at Bethlehem; he brought her there by bus. In the meantime she was well received by the villagers, who were kind to her even though they knew that she was going to the prison to visit terrorists.

It was strange that I, who was imprisoned, had to feel sorry for her, who was free. Hadassah hadn't come solely for the pleasure of seeing me, she was following Irgun orders, and as a result she caught a cold. Even today, when we occasionally meet, she still hasn't forgiven me for the way I laughed when she told me her story, but what else could I have done but laugh, with her standing on one side of the gate and me on the other?

The worst problem of all was that of the young children who came to visit their mothers behind bars. It was almost too awful to write about.

For several months after I was first arrested in 1941, I was the only mother in Bethlehem. Then Tovah Savorai was arrested; she had a daughter. My son was then only four and a half years old, and I thought long and hard before I decided to let my mother bring him with her on her visits. I was afraid of how seeing me in prison might affect his young mind, and that he might suffer emotional and psychological damage as a result of the treatment he received at the hands of irresponsible people who knew why his mother had been arrested. On the other hand, I could not overcome my great (and only natural) desire to see him, if only for a few minutes. If only I could caress him, kiss him . . .

I was given permission to see him in the yard near the prison office, so that I could hold his hand.

I will never forget the look in those small, pure eyes as they took in everything. His eyes were deep wells of longing, of love and sorrow mixed with innocence and awful questions he didn't know how to ask: what was I doing there, why wasn't I at home with him, when would I come home? Why did all the other children have mothers and fathers?

It was only with the greatest difficulty that I kept the tears welling up in my eyes from pouring out, and the sorrow in my throat from choking me. I prayed to God for the strength not to frighten my child with my tears.

He was too young to ask questions. I told him that I would only stay there for a short time and then I would be home and would stay with him forever.

Later my mother told me that he used to listen to conversations and later ask her difficult questions, more than once putting her in an unpleasant position.

It was terrible for him to be searched by the guards, and I asked them not to do it. I volunteered to search him myself while they watched.

On one visit he brought a box of chocolates and gave it to me, and he was astounded when a guard took it from my hands. He didn't understand that she had taken the chocolate to examine it, he thought that the present he had brought was being stolen from me. In the boarding school where he lived, they almost never had chocolate, and giving it up was a sacrifice made on the altar of his love for me, and then a strange woman came along and took the gift away. He couldn't understand or accept the situation and began to cry, and it was only with great difficulty that I managed to calm him.

When I asked where he had gotten the chocolate, he told me the following story: He and grandma were riding in the car and grandma started talking to someone. When they stopped in Jerusalem, the man bought the chocolate and told him to give it to his mother. My mother filled in the missing details. While they were on the bus to Jerusalem she struck up a conversation with one of the other passengers, and when she told him where she was going, he bought the box of chocolates and told her to give it to me. I never found out who he was, the man who expressed his friendship for me and the other prisoners, but somehow I would like to thank him for being one of the lights in those dark days.

Since I had been arrested during the winter and it was very cold in Bethlehem, I decided it would be best if my son not come to see me till it got warmer, and several months passed before I saw him again.

A short time after his first visit, the prison director asked me how I dared to be politically active and in the underground when I had such a small child at home. I answered that being arrested did not prove that I was an underground fighter, only that I was suspected of being a member, and that suspicion could fall on anyone.

A short time after my son's second visit I was released, and I "visited" him for two years as a free person, until I was again arrested in 1944.

The first year I was imprisoned I did not have visitors every week because my mother couldn't come to Bethlehem from Tel Aviv so often, and as previously mentioned, friends didn't rush to endanger themselves, and justifiably so. The only people who visited me were my mother, my son twice, my bother Naphtali, my friend Judith Gorenstein and her husband Isaac, the late Mrs. Herzog, Hadassah Brande, and Mrs. Ebolitz.

Once, when I went to receive a visitor, I was surprised and pleased to see Mrs. Herzog. She was no longer young, and activities like prison visits were very difficult for her. She became very emotional when she saw me behind the iron gate, and asked if I could come out, because she wanted to hug me. I stretched out my hand and she kissed it. I calmed her and tried to pretend that I felt better than I did. I said that I didn't need anything, that I could rest a lot and do handiwork.

Mrs. Herzog was very anxious to see Rachel, whose conditions she had worked so hard to improve. She always did whatever she could when a case of human suffering was made known to her, but she was particularly worried about Rachel. When I was not in prison she and I worked together to help Rachel, but she was not permitted to see her, because as a convicted criminal Rachel could only have visitors on holidays or once every two months when her parents came, and Mrs. Herzog was religious and did not ride on holidays.

I told Mrs. Herzog how we prisoners usually spent our time, and then the visit ended. Again I extended my hand and again she kissed it, once for Rachel, once for all the incarcerated women, once for me. She brought baskets full of things for us, and all the prisoners thanked her.

Sometime later Mrs. Ebolitz visited me, a woman also not in the first bloom of life but willing to help any underground resistance fighter. She was worried that we had to eat dry bread, because at that time life was very hard in the country and many people lacked food, especially fats. She brought us a special preparation of coconut oil so that we would have something to spread on our bread. There was nothing she wouldn't do, this Hebrew mother, for Hebrew daughters so much younger than she but who shared a common ideology. She became terribly emotional, far more than I, and in her presence too I pretended that I was content and did not lack anything.

Both Mrs. Ebolitz and Mrs. Herzog were members of the National Women's Union, and I was very grateful to the organization, which not only remembered us but was sufficiently concerned to send people to visit such a wretched place. Among the women who concerned themselves about us were Mrs. Rappaport, Mrs. Plotkin (who never missed an opportunity to send us packages), and Dr. Danziger.

Mrs. Rappaport was the Union's chairwoman, and one of her special contributions was the establishing of kindergartens for the children of those who had been arrested. They provided these unfortunate children, one or both of whose parents were behind barbed wire, not only with food and care, but with the comfort and encouragement that came from knowing that their parents were heroes fighting for their people.

A short time before I was released a ban was decreed on all visits, and it was in force for two years. The detainees tried to find substitutes for official visits, some of them funny and some of them simply painful.

Nelly Fisher knew that on a certain day at a certain time her brother would come to the gate. She asked the doctor for a laxative, and of course she didn't take it, but it was a wonderful excuse for her to have them open her door when the time came. The gate was on the western side of the compound, whereas the window in her room faced east. The women in the room on the west side watched the path to see who was coming, and when they saw her brother they signaled her. She called the guards to unlock her door, but instead of running right, to the toilets, she ran left, to a door in the corridor which faced the path, and was thus able to exchange a few words with him.

Their parents were in Mauritius, where they had been exiled as illegal immigrants by the British Mandate.

The other women used similar tricks to meet their visitors.

As a result of the tremendous pressure brought to bear by the families of the detainees and by the National Movement, this arbitrary rule was eventually revoked. In 1944, a short time after I was arrested, visits were reinstated, but by that time we were in the detention camp.

Everything was done in stages. At first we were allowed a visit once a month, on Wednesdays, and every detainee could have a visit. Permission for the visit was wrapped in red tape and in addition it was dangerous for a potential visitor to go to the CID in Jerusalem, and very few people were willing to risk it. Thus only older family members came to visit, because young brothers and sisters would probably be arrested or at least noted by the CID. Parents and relatives, most of them old, who had received permission from the CID had to take an Arab bus to Bethlehem and wait at the prison gate, sometimes for hours, for a visit of ten minutes.

At first these visits took place at a small barred window through which it was barely possible to discern the face of the person the prisoner had waited a month to see, usually her father or mother. Only one person was allowed in, and if both of them came together one of them waited outside, looking at the building in which their daughter was imprisoned. There were some "lucky" families that had two sisters in prison together, and then both parents could come in to see how the young lives of their daughters were being spent behind bars.

Meanwhile, the number of Bethlehem mothers with small children grew, and the problem of children's visits became much more serious. In the prison, as previously mentioned, Tovah Savorai and I were the only mothers. Her daughter, Harutah, was less than two years old at the time of Tovah's arrest, and for the two years during which there were no visits she never once saw her child. In the detention camp, however, the number of mothers was doubled. Esther Raziel Naor left two children at home, one three years old and the other only eighteen months, and Emma Germant left her two-year-old child with neighbors because her husband had to go underground (he was later betrayed to the CID).

We couldn't decide whether or not it was a good idea to have the children visit. Esther was afraid of the impression the prison would make on them because they would have two parents to visit: her husband was in the detention camp at Latrun. Tovah and I decided to do everything in our power to make it possible for our children to visit.

After a long struggle we won the right for two names to be put on the CID authorization, one adult and one child. For me the visits turned into nightmares, because I couldn't speak to both my mother and my son at the same time. Eventually one visit was authorized for the child and one for the mother, but it was still very difficult, because one cannot be with a four- or five-year-old child and not give him all of one's attention. In this respect I was lucky, because Johnny Graham, the prison director, came to the camp drunk as a lord. When he was in that condition it was easy to extract promises from him. In the presence of the Arab guard, I asked him to allow my son to enter the yard via the garden and be alone together with me for a few minutes. Apparently there are people who get so drunk that their personalities change, and good replaces evil. He agreed and told the policemen to show my son into the yard. If I recall correctly, Nelly exploited the opportunity to ask him for some letters from her parents which were being kept in the prison office, and he agreed to that too.

From that time on, the children were let into the yard. We would take blankets and spread them on the ground for the children to sit on. Yael, Emma's two-year-old daughter, was interrogated by the CID. They asked her if there were weapons at home and the names of the "uncles" who came to visit. I'm sure she belongs in the *Guinness Book of Records* as the youngest person ever interrogated by the police.

My son was the oldest child, and therefore less restrained in his movements. He used to climb the trees in the yard, almond and olive, plum and apricot, and sing the songs he had learned in kindergarten and later at school. First I played with him alone, and then all the other detainees joined us. All the children received presents and a great deal of love.

In time the children's visits became very important for the detainees, and they could hardly wait for them. The visits lasted more than half an hour, and when the prison administration was changed the tradition of the children's visits remained. The length of the visit depended on the policewoman on duty, and we usually managed to exploit the good relations we had with them to prolong the visits.

My mother willingly and lovingly suffered through these visits, waiting outside in the cold of a Bethlehem winter or under the burning rays of a summer sun. She had suffered worse things, and she knew that at least I had some small measure of pleasure at seeing my son, and what won't a mother do for her daughter?

I remember one time when we were sitting on the ground under a tree and Mr. Charlton, the prison administrator of Jerusalem and Bethlehem, came for a visit. He walked over to us, and I didn't want him to stand there looking down at me, so I stood up. He asked me a few questions, including whether my son understood English. My son understood the question, apparently because Mr. Charlton had pointed his billy-club at him. He said, "Tell him I will begin learning English in the fifth grade."[36] I translated what he had said, and Mr. Charlton was amazed that the child had understood and wanted to know how. I was uncomfortable, because I was afraid that he might suspect that the children were being used as intermediaries, but it passed without incident.

---

[36]According to the British Mandate law, all children began to study English in the fifth grade.

The visits got longer and longer, although it was hard for us to lengthen them indefinitely because we knew our mothers were waiting outside without shelter from the elements. However, when my ex-husband returned from the POW camp he brought the child, and I allowed myself longer visits.

As previously mentioned, the visits took place in the yard in a room used as a storeroom, but we could only go there when the camp gate opened for the visitor. There was a short distance in which the detainee and her visitor could run to meet each other and hug and pass information about where the secret messages were hidden, so that in the end our visits were more pleasant than those in other detention camps. We could kiss our mothers on almost every visit, and there is no way to describe the pleasure we had from the children when they came.

Both Auerbach sisters from Haifa were in the camp. Every time their aging parents came we used to teasingly ask them if they had left anything in Haifa, because they used to bring suitcases packed with everything they thought we might need. They knew that we lived in a "commune" and felt that they had to bring enough for everyone. When it came to our diet, we had lean weeks and fat weeks, depending upon our visitors. Some of them could barely pay the bus fare to Bethlehem, but they brought us things anyway, and then we were sorry and wanted them to take something home with them. However, we couldn't return the packages, and we protested in vain that there was no need to bring anything because we had everything we needed.

After the visit was over the detainee would return to the building, shaken by everything she had heard and by the very fact of the visit itself and by the hurried exchange of kisses. The women on duty would go out to collect the packages, although most of the time no one knew who had received what and no one really cared, except for personal items like books or cologne. If someone received chocolate, the box was brought to the kitchen. Often visitors would bring gifts sent by others, since the families visited each other, passing regards to and from all the women in prison who were from their city.

The detainees would get up on the window sills when they knew that someone was coming with regards from the outside. From there they would call out to the visitors, who would call messages back. All this would happen in the short distance between the gate and the visiting room. And if the woman didn't manage to run to her visitor, those on the window sill would use the time to talk to the visitor; and if she did manage, they would talk to the visitor on his or her way back, because by then the woman would be back inside. If the visitor was experienced, he would stoop to tie his shoelace or something similar, and then the visit with the women on the window sills would last even longer. Usually all of the women who wanted to pass along verbal messages would be able to, and thus personal visits became general visits, to everyone's satisfaction.

I saw my mother and son separately from one another; when she came in he would stay outside with the other visitors. Most of the time I would be able to run to her and hug and kiss her, and these were my most cherished moments. My mother was truly brave. She always knew how to overcome her feelings and use the occasion of our meeting alone to tell me where the "material" was to be found and what the code was, and that was uppermost in her mind despite the fact that she hadn't seen me for a month, had brought the child with her, and had such a long journey from Tel Aviv to Bethlehem. As a member of the Irgun she performed the duties assigned her, and this instead of simply giving her daughter a kiss. If by chance she didn't manage to give me the illegal material on the way to the visiting room, she would drop hints about what it was and where. She used to make the trip carrying important "baggage," the child at her side, going first to the CID and then to Bethlehem. It was hard even for young people to climb up to the villa, and my mother was not young.

When I appealed to the prison administrator to provide a roofed area where the visitors could wait protected from the rain and snow, he answered, "Don't you know that all the women of Bethlehem do their washing on Wednesdays because they know that it never rains or snows on visiting day at the prison?" That was nothing less than the truth, because I don't remember one single rainy or snowy Wednesday during all the years I was imprisoned there. I can only assume it was divine intervention.

Every visiting day was a holiday for all of us, and we went from one Wednesday to the next the way people outside went from Saturday to Saturday. We would count from the holiday of Wednesday to the day of rest of Saturday, and from Saturday to the following Wednesday, breaking the week into two parts, and thus the time passed.

We prepared feverishly for each visiting day. We didn't have access to a hair dresser, but there were women who knew how to cut and set hair, although in the most primitive way, and we used to wear our best clothing and even put on perfume. It was all to put on a show for our visitors, to keep them from feeling sorry for us, and make them think we had every material thing we needed—what we really needed was our freedom, of course.

What we did made life much easier for our visitors, because they could go home having seen us in good spirits, and that would keep them till the next visit, and it turned the event into something pleasant instead of the torture and suffering it normally would have been. It was another mark in the fighting Jewish women's favor, and the CID and foreigners took notice of it as well.

Visits to the hospital, on the other hand, were more difficult and gloomier. We never knew when visitors would arrive, and we could only have a limited number of them. I would receive my mother and son wearing a robe, and even if I got out of bed we were still in a hospital and the atmosphere was depressing. Perfume couldn't hide the smell of disinfectant, lipstick couldn't hide our paleness, and laughter couldn't hide the sadness in our eyes.

In the hospital we could discuss whatever we wanted to with our visitors because there was usually no one listening to our conversations, and if there was, she tried to make herself scarce. Bella Schechter once came to visit me in the hospital after her release. She told me things that she could never have told me if anyone else had been there. As a result of her visit I gave Frieda regards from her husband for the first time, and she learned things about him that she never would have known otherwise. My sister Rebecca also came to visit me, and when her husband returned from the internment camp we had long conversations.

After my release I heard a story about one particular visit to the villa. When my mother and son arrived at the camp, the policewoman stationed at the gate told them that I was no longer there. My mother spoke to her in Arabic, but every time she asked were I was, no answer was forthcoming. The guard took advantage of her position, arbitrarily refusing to tell her anything, but finally another policewoman told my mother that I had been taken to the hospital. By that time she was in tears. My son was eight years old at the time, and he began to cry as well, but then he stopped and said, "No, I won't cry, I'm a man." Ruth Schechter was waiting outside to visit Putzi and her sister, and she heard everything and later told me about it.

The first time my ex-husband came to see me was very difficult for both of us. It wasn't a Wednesday, but they told me that I had a visitor. I had no idea who it could be and was very surprised. When that kind of thing happened, all the women went into action, one to comb hair, another to choose clothing. It was noon and I didn't feel at all well, but of course I couldn't let my visitor see me in anything less than the best possible spirits. But who could it be? No one visited except on Wednesdays. Sometimes a lawyer came, but we usually knew about those visits well in advance. According to the radio the prisoners from overseas had returned, but I had no way of knowing whether Aryeh, my ex-husband, was among them.

Just then the prison director came into the room and said

that my husband was there but for bureaucratic reasons he couldn't let us meet. My emotions at that moment can be well imagined; we hadn't seen each other for years, and we hadn't been able to write to one another. I had heard vague reports about him and assumed that he knew where I was, but I never imagined that he would come to visit me in prison. I was still trying to make sense out of what I had just been told when the director returned and told me that the bureaucratic objections had been dealt with and I could go to the visiting room.

Even now it is difficult for me to describe our meeting. I was overcome with emotion. Aryeh told me that he had learned about my imprisonment while in England after his release from the POW camp, and the first thing he had done when he returned to Israel was to find out about getting me released, but before that he wanted to see me. The CID put every obstacle they could in his path, but he had not allowed them to stand in his way.

We met, husband and wife, both fighting for the liberation of our people, on either side of a barbed-wire fence. One fought the Nazis, who sought to destroy the Jews, and the other fought the British "friend" who closed the gates of the homeland and prevented the salvation of the Jewish people.

✳ ✳ ✳ ✳ ✳ ✳

Chapter Fourteen

Holidays

Most of the holidays of the Jewish people are national holidays celebrating the passage from slavery to freedom. Sukkot commemorates the Exodus from Egypt, for as it is written in Leviticus 23:43, "I made the children of Israel to dwell in booths, when I brought them out of the land of Egypt." Passover (Pesach in Hebrew) is the most important holiday of liberation. Shavuot commemorates the giving of the Law on Mount Sinai, when the Jews, former slaves, became a nation. Hanukkah commemorates the Maccabean revolt, the victory of a few over many, at home and abroad.

The leaders of the Jewish people were also their lawgivers, and knew well how to unite public and private rejoicing. Jewish mothers have always known how to instill the holidays in the hearts of their children, so that even those who are not observant during the rest of the year always return to the fold at holiday time. The traditional holidays attract them like a warming fire, and they come to thaw their souls; the ice melts, and once again they belong to the Jewish nation. No matter how rich or poor, the holidays bring an extra measure of light and happiness to every Jewish home.

But not in prison. The holidays slip apologetically between the bars, unannounced, as if to say, "We know that there are no holidays here, no joy, we know that we bring not an extra measure of light and happiness, but of sadness and suffering. However hard you try to overcome your homesickness and

168

your longing for parents and children on ordinary days, it is ten times harder for you now. You sit here while your hearts yearn to be at home, sitting at the family table with the people dear to you, your souls full of joy. We can do nothing about it, nothing beyond simply wishing you a happy holiday."

That was how holidays passed in the prisons and detention camps. But if we knew how to chase the gloom away and keep up our spirits on ordinary days, we knew even better how to turn holidays into events which would never be forgotten by those participating in them. The private, individual family was replaced by the "fighting family," and the light shed by the war of independence shone brightly and lit the dark. It would not be an exaggeration to say that few people have ever celebrated the holidays of Israel the way we did behind bars. Perhaps it was because only we could truly understand the special significance of the liberation on which the holidays were based, and only here that the holidays of the individual returns to their sources as national holidays in every sense of the word.

Bethlehem and the "weaker sex" contributed fully to the celebrations. Detention camps sprang up all over, both within the country and abroad, but the conditions in Bethlehem were completely different from those in the men's camps. What was most readily apparent was our lack of basic necessities, as has already been mentioned in the earlier chapters, and it was particularly noticeable at holiday time. Cantors and rabbis were sent to the men's prisons and camps to lead the prayers and to encourage the men, but we had to fend for ourselves.

The third time I was arrested I arrived in the camp after Passover, so I became acquainted with the problem during the days between Rosh Hashanah and Yom Kippur. We were given prayer books for Rosh Hashanah, and while the Passover Haggadah may say that "we are all smart, we are all clever, and we all know the Law," none of us had ever conducted a congregational prayer service. But some divine spirit must have been watching over us, because we were sent some women who knew how to pray.

While the prison may have been a kind of "ingathering of the exiles," we did not segregate ourselves along ethnic lines. Our cantors were Esther Raziel, Hayah Ben-Tzvi, and Esther Auerbach. Deborah Ashkenazi, whose father was a rabbi, helped her.

On Yom Kippur more women were pressed into service to lead the prayers. Hayah Ben-Tzvi conducted them all, aided by Esther Raziel, Esther Auerbach, and Leah Ashkenazi. We also had problems with setting the tables in the traditional manner and with cooking the foods properly, but we managed everything by working together. We decided to do things in accordance with the customs of those whose families had been in the country longest, and this satisfied all the ethnic groups. Many of the traditional dishes were missing because we couldn't get the required ingredients, but we did everything we could and the holiday was properly celebrated.

We even conducted *Tashlich*, the casting off of sins. There was a pool in the part of the garden closed to us, and we had to work long and hard to explain to the prison director that Jews had a custom of casting their sins into water, so that he would allow us access to the pool, which was the only suitable place for the ceremony. Perhaps he authorized it because he saw our war against the authorities as a sin. It was a unique Tashlich, held only by women in the presence of policewomen.

It was hard to know how to say the traditional grace after meals on holidays, especially when we came to the part about blessing the "heads of the house," in this case the prison authorities, whom we graced with a special blessing all our own.

During Sukkot we put up a booth in the yard, and it was decorated by Adah Stecklis, Shaula, and Sonia. Since we didn't have the services of a cantor, we performed the duties ourselves. We used to say the prayer "Releaser of the Imprisoned" with special emphasis, and also "Healer of the Sick," because so many of us were ill. To this day when I pray I remember how we prayed then.

Preparations for the holidays were begun early in the day, but we couldn't go shopping for what we needed and had to make do with what was brought in to us. The holiday atmosphere cut through the barbed wire, leaped over the wall, and took over the prison, but it was a sad time for us nevertheless. In our imaginations we could see our homes and remember preparing for holidays when we were still free. It would make us forget the bitterness of our surroundings for a while, and on the wings of imagination we would fly home and sit at the family table until someone brought us down to earth by exclaiming, "What are you dreaming about? The pancakes are burning and the milk is boiling over!"

We usually managed to overcome our emotions and keep in good spirits. We wore our best dresses and made sure that our less fortunate comrades also had something nice to wear. Everything was spotless, and while there was no crystal on the table, our souls were as bright and pure as crystal, etched with pain and trouble. We would conclude the prayer of the "Eighteen Benedictions" paying special attention to the verses "May there be no hope for informers" and "Build Jerusalem the holy city in our day," and we would finish the meal with "Next year as free people." We believed that with all our hearts, and we knew that no matter how hard the road was, and no matter how many obstacles it was strewn with, sooner or later the day would come.

On Hanukkah we lit candles in a menorah and sang the traditional songs. On Purim we put on fancy dress. Wine was smuggled in vinegar bottles, and people sent us packages of hamantashen and cakes. We chose someone to play the part of Queen Esther, and the atmosphere became quite festive. We even celebrated Tu B'shevat (Arbor Day), when the fruit trees in the garden bloomed white, pink, and red. We dressed up and went out into the garden, and no matter how cold it was, our hearts were warm.

In 1946 the rabbinate began sending rabbis to lead us in prayer. Passover, 1946, was the first time someone from the outside visited us on a holiday, and his presence lifted our spirits to the festive atmosphere. We felt that people cared about us and that we hadn't been completely cut off and forgotten. After my release I learned that a woman had been sent instead, and that her services would have been willingly dispensed with, because she added nothing and caused only unhappiness, making the detainees and prisoners miserable.

There were other holidays in Bethlehem, but by that time I was no longer there. The great Rabbi Aryeh Levine, the rabbi of the men in the Jerusalem prison, who became a legend in his own time, came to Bethlehem. He only came on weekdays, but he turned those days into holidays for the prisoners and detainees.

Rabbi Levin knew how to restore faith, warmth, and love to their hearts. His pious good heart could be read in his eyes; they expressed his goodness, gentleness, warmth, and mercy, and his very presence was comforting. The women welcomed every word he said, and he was genuinely happy to be able to do the smallest thing for the prisoners and detainees, begging them to tell him what they wanted. He was old and venerable, and no one wanted to bother him, but he would ask again and again what he could do to help, and no one dared refuse him.

To bring family members peace of mind, Rabbi Levine passed regards on to them the same day without giving a thought to his own personal inconvenience. If he could help one of the imprisoned women, he took no notice of time or place. This began only in 1946, and unfortunately his visits were infrequent because all sorts of obstacles were placed in his path, and they could not always be overcome. His visage shed light in the darkness in Bethlehem and strengthened the detainees' belief in the triumph of good over evil.

After I was released, Rabbi Levin *shlita* told me that his wife had accompanied him every time he came to visit. She would stop at Rachel's Tomb to pray for the prisoners and detainees, remaining there until he came to fetch her, and he used to find her red-eyed from weeping.

I had my own private holiday, but it turned into a victory celebration for the Jewish people and for the underground. It was my son's birthday, the sixth day of the Jewish month of Iyar. I used to celebrate it quietly behind bars in Bethlehem, but it was fated to become a national holiday when in 1948 the State of Israel was declared on the same day. For me it became a double holiday, because when my son Benjamin was eleven years old, his brother Jacob was born on the same day, the day the British left the country.

Lag B'Omer (an agricultural holiday between Passover and Shavuot), which is celebrated with bonfires, was not neglected in Bethlehem. We had our best celebration in 1945, when our "bonfire" consisted of a can of kerosene with rags for a wick. We were in a wonderful mood and put the "bonfire" in the corridor which served as our dining room, turned out all the lights, and made the guards turn off their light too, although they didn't want to, and danced around the fire. The shadows we cast on the wall frightened one of the guards, and she ran away in terror, claiming that she had seen ghosts and devils.

We laughed and danced even faster and more happily, enjoying ourselves no end until finally we went to our rooms for the night. The guards had to plead with us to do so, saying that they would be severely punished by the prison administration if we didn't. We began to line up for the bathroom, and that kept us in the corridor even longer. Only the women who were really tired waited in line, and that left more time for the dancing to continue.

The celebration continued even after we were locked in our rooms. Ollie, a Bulgarian girl, sang to us in her sweet voice, and the detainees sat on the window sills and sang into the night, answered by the songs of the prisoners across the yard, which frightened the guards no end. Usually we were locked in our rooms when the shifts changed. When we remained in the corridor until late at night, they would lock the doors leading to the stairs lest we see the policemen. It was a matter of "morality," of course.

Birthdays were special for us too, those of the children of the Bethlehem detainees and prisoners as well, and we used to send them presents.

We would celebrate the birthday of a detainee in the camp in whatever manner her roommates thought best. One way or another the women would let the dates of their birthdays slip out without thinking, and someone would make a note of it; if not, detainees would simply be asked when their birthdays were. Sometimes they were quite surprised that the rest of us knew their birthdays, not remembering that they had casually mentioned the date.

Birthdays were celebrated in different ways. Sometimes a detainee woke up in the morning to find that everyone else had gotten up early, and when she opened her eyes she found the room full of her friends laughing and wishing her a happy birthday. Only then did she notice the presents, flowers, and cake on the stool next to her bed. It didn't matter that she herself had participated in similar celebrations many times before, she was always surprised when it happened to her. The most strong-minded and least sentimental woman always became emotional when her birthday was celebrated, and sometimes the emotion was so strong that while we could see her lips forming the words "thank you," we never heard anything because she couldn't voice them.

Sometimes the surprise was prepared when the detainee wasn't in her room; she might be on kitchen duty, or maybe she was deliberately lured from her room on some pretext or other. When she returned she found a table covered with gifts and a room full of women singing and dancing in her honor.

Usually the presents were homemade, but if there was any doubt as to what she might like, a book or picture was ordered from the outside. It wasn't the monetary value of the gift that caused the joy and emotion, but rather that someone had remembered and cared enough to do something, and when the detainees in the other rooms heard the singing, they all came running to wish her a happy birthday.

Women who were released always noted down the birthdays of their best friends and sent them cards and presents when the time came. It often worked in the opposite direction as well, and those outside received cards and presents from the detainees.

The celebration wasn't confined to the inmate's room. The kitchen also made a contribution, depending on what was on hand at the time. If someone's birthday fell on a holiday it was postponed, since two holidays are never celebrated at the same time.

We also sent presents to friends and family members on the outside when their birthdays came around and on holidays. We were very enthusiastic about making gifts for these occasions. We sent—anonymously, of course—a Bible with an embroidered cover to Menachem Begin, commander of the Irgun, on the day the revolt was proclaimed in 1944. The decision for the final form of the gift rested in the hands of Hayah Ben-Tzvi, Hannah and Ester Auerbach, and Peninah Bejaio. For the sake of secrecy and intrigue we had embroidered the words, "To our father from his daughters behind bars," and we used illegal mail to congratulate him on the outbreak of the revolt, wishing him the best of luck and promising to do everything we could to help.

The Lehi fighters sent hand-made presents to Yair, the son of Abraham Stern, who was born after his father died.

Rebecca Perl, Chaim Landau's sister-in-law, was with us when her sister, Chaim's wife, gave birth to their son, Uzi, today chairman of the Knesset's Committee on Defense and Foreign Affairs. She and the Auerbach sisters worked hard knitting things for the child even before he was born, and so did Peninah Effron, Judith Moser, Hayah Ben-Tzvi, and the detainees in Rebecca's room. Before he was born they knitted everything in white, just to be on the safe side, and then in light blue when we knew it was a boy. Everything knitted for him carried our faith, energy, and love. When Efrat, Esther's daughter, was born, there was real competition among the women to see who could knit the most beautiful gift.

Those of us who were imprisoned in Bethlehem will always cherish the memories of the holidays and recall them when we celebrate today in freedom, telling our children what it was like back then, when the darkness and despair of prison and barbed wire were dispelled by our loyalty to our people and homeland.

✳ ✳ ✳ ✳ ✳ ✳

Chapter Fifteen

Days of Mourning and Remembrance; Hunger Strikes

We were very strict about keeping national memorial days. The most important of them was Tisha B'Av, the ninth day of the month of Av (July—August), the day on which the Temple was destroyed. People on the outside may not have fasted on the ninth of Av, but in the camp it was a day on which we both fasted and did not work; the kitchen was closed. We read the Book of Lamentations aloud. The day was recognized by the prison authorities, and they left the doors unlocked later than usual, both the evening before the fast day and the evening after, even though there was no official British recognition of the occasion.

We held memorial services on the anniversaries of the deaths of Herzl,[37] Jabotinsky, Trumpeldor,[38] Sarah Aaronsohn,[39]

---

[37]Theodor Herzl (1860—1904) convened the First Zionist Congress, authored The Jewish State, and is generally regarded as the father of the Zionist movement.

[38]Joseph Trumpeldor (1880—1920) was one of the great heroes of the Revisionist movement. An ardent advocate of self-defense and the military virtues, he played a key role in persuading the British to organize all-Jewish fighting units during World War I. He was killed on Feb. 29, 1920 while leading the defense of Tel Hai against an Arab attack.

[39]Sarah Aaronsohn (1890—1917) was a leader of Nili (the Hebrew acronym for the words "The glory of Israel will not fail" in 1 Samuel

Shlomo Ben-Yosef (the first person hanged by the British),[40] and David Raziel. The women from the Lehi held a special service for Abraham Stern, whose *nom de guerre* was Yair. In 1947, the year of the hangings, to our sorrow there were many more memorial services held. Those for David Raziel and the twelve hanged men had to be camouflaged as "private," because none of us had ever confessed to belonging to any underground resistance group. (When we used to read illegal mail in secret and in a whisper, the Arab guards would say, "Now they are praying.")

The service we held for Sarah Aaronsohn, the Nili heroine, was particularly thrilling. For us she symbolized the fighting underground pioneer spirit, renewing the Land of Israel. We felt that we and the Nili fighters were linked by history, although the way we were fighting for our independence was different. Sarah and her comrades fought so that the British might invade the country to oust the Turks, and we were doing our best to get the British out. The road to liberty is long and hard and takes many turnings; it changes with circumstances and the weapons in the hands of the fighters. The British had promised us a national home and then betrayed us, despite Nili and despite the Jewish battalions of Jabotinsky.[41] From allies they became enemies, and we were following in the footsteps of Sarah Aaronsohn in our fight to throw the traitors out of the country.

15:29), a spy organization that helped the British against the Turks during World War I. Arrested and tortured by the Turkish police, she held out as long as she could, then killed herself to avoid revealing anything about the group.

[40]Shlomo Ben-Yosef (1913—1938), a member of Betar, was executed for attacking an Arab bus in retaliation for Arab attacks on Jews, even though none of the passengers was hurt.

[41]Largely as a result of political agitation by Jabotinsky and Joseph Trumpeldor, the British agreed to recruit all-Jewish fighting units to help liberate Palestine during World War I. The first such unit was the Zion Mule Corps, organized in 1915; it, was succeeded by the Jewish Legion in 1917.

When we compared ourselves to Sarah and the Nili fighters, we felt we were discussing the immediate present and not the past. In those days the Yishuv had ostracized Aaron Aaronsohn[42] and his Nili comrades the same way that we of the underground resistance were now ostracized. They had accepted the gold he brought the hungry settlement and then slandered and outlawed him. The Nili fighters were hanged, tortured, and persecuted for the sin of loving the Jewish people, while the leaders of the Yishuv continued to collaborate with the rotten and hostile rule of the Ottoman Empire.

Sarah, a child of the Carmel, had breathed the clear mountain air from her childhood. Could she not have lived her life quietly, instead of choosing the path that led through torture by the Turks and ended in a heroine's death?

Absalom Feinberg had the soul of a poet and was lost in the deserts of Egypt, and Abraham Lishansky was persecuted by enemies from without and "brothers" from within; both fought in the ranks of Nili.[43] We were links in the same chain, and Sarah was part of the soul of every detainee in the Bethlehem camp.

The lack of a proper flag was one of the problems of the memorial services. The prison director refused to provide us with one, and while several attempts were made to send one from the outside, he wouldn't let them through. Left with no other choice, we had to fashion a flag by ourselves. The robes we got from the prison authorities were blue. We took a white tablecloth, folded two pieces of blue material into stripes, cut a Magen David (six-pointed star) out of paper, and made our-

---

[42]Aaron Aaronsohn (1876—1919), Sarah's brother, was the overall leaders of Nili.

[43]Absalom Feinberg (1889—1917) was the co-founder of the Nili group with Aaron Aaronsohn. Joseph Lishansky was a Nili activist. The two were ambushed by Arabs in the Sinai desert while on a mission to Egypt. Feinberg was killed; Lishansky, wounded and left for dead, was rescued by a British patrol.

selves a flag. It may have been primitive, but despite that, and maybe because of that, it was the most wonderful flag ever made.

We had pictures of Jabotinsky, Herzl, and Ben-Yosef, and David Raziel's sister Esther and his widow, Shoshanah, had pictures of him as well. On the anniversaries of their deaths we would cover the table with the flag and place the picture on it, and instead of candles, which we were forbidden to light on weekdays, we would use oil lamps which stayed lit for more than twenty-four hours. We would gather around the table, stand at attention while the mourning order was read, and then sing Betar songs. Then each of us would say something personal about the person being mourned, an anecdote or a memory.

In 1944 we held a thrilling and impressive ceremony in the villa in honor of David Raziel, in which both Esther and Shoshanah took part. Esther read the mourning order as we stood there united, each one of us aware of the direct connection between our war and the fact that we were behind bars, and thinking about the mighty family of fighters we belonged to, which was contributing the best of its sons to the war of liberation; if one fell, another took his place.

These ceremonies were unlike any held on the outside, just as the singing of the national anthem and of revolutionary songs was different behind bars. It seemed as though they were here with us, as if the walls had toppled and the bars had been cast down. Our souls and imaginations took wing, and in our mind's eye we saw ourselves far distant in time and space, as part of the future, striding on the altars of victory. However, it was enough for a guard to open the door and glance into the room for everything to disappear, as if it had all been a dream.

Only Irgun fighters took part in these ceremonies. It had been explained to the guards that these were the private services of one of the detainees and only her friends were attending. There really were private services at which psalms would be read and the prayer beginning "God the merciful . . ." would be said. Every year, on the anniversary of my father's death, I used to visit his grave in the cemetery on Trumpeldor Street in Tel Aviv. I was very sorry that I couldn't go here during the years I was in Bethlehem, and that I had to be alone on that day.

We usually observed all the fast days decreed by the national institutions, although for them many, those days were a substitute for the real war they should have been fighting. We didn't observe these fasts because we felt that they furthered the war effort, but because we wanted to demonstrate solidarity with the rest of the nation, although the rest of the nation, or rather, the institutions, never demonstrated solidarity with us—not with our war, not with our suffering, and not with our sacrifices.

We decided on our own fast when we heard that 251 underground fighters imprisoned in the detention camp at Latrun had been exiled to Eritrea. The news was unexpected, and we were severely shaken, both ideologically and personally. We felt that a historic step had been taken which would not only decide the fate of our war, but would undermine the very foundations of our national rebirth. With one blow the alien rulers had challenged our right to a national homeland. All the work of generations of prisoners of Zion who for eighty years had labored to return the Jewish people to its homeland and to stop the eternal wanderings and exile, the entire struggle of Zionism to ensure a "secure shelter," everything was being undone by the exile to Eritrea, and it meant that the Jews of Palestine had no more rights than Jews anywhere else in the world. Just as the governments of other countries could uproot the Jews and banish them, the same thing could happen here, and it made no difference whether the person was a new immigrant or had been born in Palestine.

We were also shaken on a personal level. Some of us in the underground resistance movement belonged, as previously mentioned, to "working couples," that is, both the husband and wife were in prison, he in the detention camp in Latrun, she in the camp in Bethlehem. Others would have married but for the fact that the woman was in Bethlehem and the fiance in

Latrun. But more important, these were our comrades in arms
and suffering. We felt only rage and pain, but there was nothing we could do.

We held a general assembly to decide how to react. The most
extreme measure of protest any inmate can take is to go on a
hunger strike. We all agreed that this would be the most effective measure we could take, and the only question was how
long the strike would last. Some suggested that we strike till
the bitter end, that is to say, until the Yishuv institutions were
forced to take action to assure the return of the exiles. After
deliberating for a while, we decided that this would be too
dangerous, because we had no direct contact with the outside
world, and if we went on strike the authorities would try to
prevent the news from leaking out of the prison. In addition,
who knew how many of us would be able to hold out?

We looked for another way to protest, one which would not
only make an impression on the apathetic populace outside,
but would make itself known to our exiled comrades, informing them that we were with them in spirit.

We finally decided on a hunger strike that would last for
sixty hours. We waited until Sunday in order not to desecrate
the Sabbath. The only thing we allowed ourselves to ease the
strike was cigarettes.

It was torture. Even under normal circumstances most of
the detainees felt ill. Some of us began to feel the effects the first
night. By Monday morning the situation was worse, and the
number of detainees suffering from weakness had grown, but
no one wanted to end the strike. The Chief Rabbinate sent us
word via the prison authorities asking us to stop, and when we
refused they sent special messengers at noon, but we had made
our decision and were not about to back down. In the afternoon a delegation came from Rabbi Herzog ordering us "in the
name of the Torah" to stop the strike, and Professor Klausner[44]
also begged us to stop.

---

[44]The noted historian Joseph Klausner (1874—1958), a member of the
Hebrew University faculty from its founding in 1925, was close to the
Revisionist movement and in 1949 was Herut's nominee for
President of Israel.

To our great sorrow, our hunger strike did not have the intended effect and did not fire anyone's indignation. It did, however, fire the indignation of both the CID and the prison authorities, and they did everything in their power to break the strike. They were very worried about "troubles."

When the appeals of Rabbi Herzog and Professor Klausner were made known to us, we called a general assembly, where we decided to comply with their wishes. According to our original decision, we should have continued until the next morning. Despite the late hour the guards opened the gates and pressed the Arab prisoners into service to bring us food. We decided to have oatmeal and coffee, but now, with the strike ended, many of the detainees collapsed. Sick detainees who had bravely borne the pain of not eating for so long fell prey to terrible stomach cramps after barely tasting food and doubled over.

The "healthy" women had a great deal of work to do to soothe them. We used vast quantities of perfume to revive those who had fainted, and Adah's hands turned red from rubbing the temples of those who were unconscious. If at all possible, we wanted to avoid calling for a doctor, but we had no choice. It was obvious that three detainees would need injections for the pain, and whereas Adah was a nurse and could have given the injections herself, she had no drugs. The doctor came and treated those in need, leaving ampoules for Adah to use later, if necessary.

We only ate after four hours of hard work. Despite our great suffering and the complications arising from the strike—many of the detainees, and I among them, had felt the effect of the fast almost from the beginning—no one regretted our action, because it had demonstrated our solidarity and identification with the exiled freedom fighters, our comrades in arms, in their imprisonment and in the dream of a liberated Zion.

However, when we received the issue of *Davar*[45] whose lead story was devoted to the "deportation of the terrorists," we

---

[45]A morning newspaper, now defunct.

understood the degree of stupidity reached by the leftist camp
and how great their hatred of us was. As we read and reread
the poisonous story, our hearts filled with anger and we
ground our teeth in fury. This is what a Jewish hand wrote
about the exile of Jews from their homeland for the sole trans-
gression of wanting a free Jewish state:

> Public opinion is divided on the issue of the deportation of the terror-
> ists and those suspected of helping them. Is the reason for this difference
> of opinion the act of deportation itself? Isn't there a general consensus of
> opinion that Jews are not to be deported from the country, either as pun-
> ishment or as a precaution? We cannot ignore the fact that many people
> find it hard to protest in the matter under consideration, but in this
> instance what we have to say is not directed against the authorities and
> the means they used. We want to discuss one particular side of the mat-
> ter. The lesson learned from the reaction of the Yishuv should be taken
> into consideration by those who until now have not been convinced by
> everything written in the Zionist press both at home and abroad, nor by
> everything that has been explained and reiterated so often by the lead-
> ers of the Yishuv, the Zionist movement, and by proven friends among
> world politicians.
>
> The remaining terrorists, whether they are few or very few, should
> make note of the following: among members of the Yishuv there is no
> support for their actions, no one stands behind them, people do not see
> them as representing the public interest in any way, no one will defend
> them. In the small sums of money they manage to obtain, whether by
> blackmail, terrorism, or violence—and even when they are dealt a blow
> such as has now been dealt, which in principle the Yishuv must protest—
> -there is no hint of identification with them and no sign whatsoever that
> anyone is joining them.
>
> The Yishuv in Palestine is firm in its opinion that terrorism is not the
> way, and is not willing to come to terms with the deceptions of gangs of
> megalomaniac madmen who think that only they know the right path,
> and that they are the ones who will save Zionism in the face of the total
> opposition of the entire Zionist nation.
>
> It is doubtful whether in the life of the Yishuv there was ever any other
> issue around which public opinion was so completely united. Everyone,

each in his or her own way, totally rejects these terrorist acts. The damage they do is obvious to all, and from all sides come censure and the demand that they be stopped. And that stubborn little band, if it does not want to listen and understand, and is not daunted by the great dangers its actions have caused to the very undertaking it seems to think it is serving so faithfully, let it not be surprised at the reactions it brings upon itself. In addition, we all suffer as a direct result of what they have done, in that they have given the authorities the opportunity and the excuse to search Jewish settlements and to institute deportations without meeting strong opposition, certainly not the same opposition they would meet if the these things were done to people the Yishuv identified with and saw as its emissaries, fulfilling its wishes and lawful, agreed-upon orders.

I have included the article in its entirety so that readers today, in the independent State of Israel, can judge for themselves and decide whose path was justified.

What could we do in the face of such blind hatred? We took consolation from the fact that at least we had done what we could to express our identity with the exiles, that company of fighters who had been separated from the front.

Our hunger strike was more than just a show of ideological identity, however, for it had practical results. We demanded and received a list of the names of everyone who had been exiled, and the authorities did not hold up the letters they sent us. When we received them we became less apprehensive, because we saw that the exiles had learned Jabotinsky's three Rules of Samson: They fought with *iron*, both the everyday metal and the iron in their souls; they dreamed of the *king*; and they knew how to *laugh* at their captors, and ridicule them.

The letters were filled with contempt and mockery of the authorities, and showed the writers' bravery and iron will to hold out till victory despite the blows they had suffered in being exiled from their homes and separated from their wives and children, their parents, their homeland, and the family of underground resistance fighters.

More than once their letters were full of "windows" made
by the censor's scissors, and often there were so many that it
was hard to tell what the "building" had looked like, but the
wives of the exiles knew their husbands, and by using their
imaginations could usually piece things together. Sometimes
three of four detainees would sit together with one letter to
solve "the riddle of the censor."

In time it wasn't only the "happy couples" of Bethlehem and
Eritrea who were corresponding with each other. They were
joined by new couples who came together as a result of the
communal reading of letters. From letters they moved on to
exchanging gifts. Dried flowers began making their way back
and forth; a special art of drying and ironing flowers was
developed, and these often accompanied the letters. From
Eritrea enormous colorful butterflies were sent to Bethlehem,
and they made quite an impression.

With the liberation, when the detention camps in Israel
opened their gates and the exiles returned as victors to a free
country, many of the young people who had become acquainted with one another by means of flowers and butterflies decided to stay together permanently.

❄ ❄ ❄ ❄ ❄ ❄

Chapter Sixteen

Superstitions

Superstitions are funny things, and sometimes people who are completely different will fall prey to the same fears: don't let a black cat cross your path, thirteen is an unlucky number, seven is a lucky number, and so on. Free people believe in all kinds of strange things, but behind bars, where the only thing the inmates think about is when they will get out, believing in superstitions is only too natural. The prisoner wants an encouraging letter, an unexpected visit, a present to prove he or she has not been forgotten, some kind of change in the monotony of prison life, even a trip to the doctor, a visit from a lawyer, an answer from the CID to a letter sent. Many of us wanted to hear about a successful military operation which inflicted losses on the enemy and brought us one step closer to our goal: we raided an army camp, seized the weapons, and suffered no casualties. If the inmate was a mother, she wanted news of her child, or of her husband, most likely in a detention camp somewhere in the country or overseas. And the most important thing, who could guess what might happen in a few months, weeks, days, or even hours?

We had our own private fortune teller, a woman who could explain everything, and her name was Hadassah Olitzky. She knew how to predict the future from signs and omens—which only she understood—and if things didn't work out the way she said they would, no one ever really blamed her. She was a good-natured soul and never predicted anything bad, all the signs notwithstanding. When the unfortunate thing happened she would say, "I knew it would happen, but I didn't want to tell you." If a butterfly came to rest on someone's shoulder, it meant she was going home. In Bethlehem there were so many butterflies they had to light on something, and so eventually there was a chance of going home someday.

But sometimes Hadassah would say that she could tell by the way the butterfly held its wings that the detainee would soon go home, and she told us never to kill crickets, because they brought luck. In the meantime, however, we couldn't sleep because there was a cricket in the room, and it was making so much noise. "For heaven's sake," she used to say, "it's better not to sleep all night, the cricket will bring you luck and then you'll be able to sleep at home in your own bed!" If the tea leaves floated in the cup, it was an omen, but who can make a cup of tea without at least a few leaves floating on the surface? "Now you're really being stupid," she would say, "because that's a sign that you're going to get a letter. If there are many leaves it means that the letter is long and is on its way, and the more leaves there are, the longer the letter and the sooner it will get here." Once I simply filled her cup without straining the tea and said, "What do you have to say about that? That the letter is already waiting in the office?" "Yes," she said, and it was!

Hadassah never got angry. She interpreted everything the most positive way possible. Birds in the room, she said, brought peace. We didn't believe her. "You'll see," she would say, "soon there will be peace, we'll all go home, the state will be established, and there will be peace and tranquility."

In time many of the detainees learned her system and began to read the signs themselves, but with nothing like her success. If a military operation did not go well and we were depressed, Hadassah found signs and omens to show that we should be in a good mood. "Look," she would say, "it will all work out for the best." Yefim, her boyfriend (that was his *nom de guerre*, given him by Esther Raziel), had written to her and hinted certain things, she was not at liberty to say what. "See what happens in a few days," and if the days lasted weeks and months, well, it wasn't her fault. She was behind bars and could not influence the course of events. She knew for certain that every butterfly hid something in its wings, but she had such a good heart that she could not bear to say anything upsetting. That's what all the detainees did, it was their good deed, and who is unwilling to do a good deed?

Hadassah, Adah, and I lived together in a room in the basement. We had been arrested within a month of one other, and there was no other room available. It was a time of "prosperity" for the CID, and detainees were brought in wholesale. There were five other young detainees in our room: Raphaela Olitsky, Tzipporah Mulin, Zehavah Pograbinsky, Miriam Birenbaum, and Deborah Mashat.

Suddenly, one evening, one of them saw a mouse, jumped up onto her bed still wearing shoes, and shouted, "A mouse, a mouse!" Hadassah came into the room and I decided to try my hand at fortune telling. I called out, "OK, we'll catch the mouse and all the young girls will go home because they saw it first." "Let's hope so," said everyone.

Anyone who had never seen three mature women and five young girls trying to catch a mouse had a treat in store. Adah armed herself with a broom and rolled up her pajama pants and sleeves; she had been in bed reading and therefore was even more angry. The nerve of that mouse, bothering her in the middle of an interesting English novel! "I'll show it," she said, "I'll teach it a lesson it'll never forget!"

Everything on the floor was swept up onto the tables and beds. The young women thought that perhaps the mouse was hiding in our things and would later get into our beds. Adah said that couldn't happen, mice didn't hide in personal belongings, and if we moved them around the mouse would try to escape.

We asked Hadassah what would happen if in our pursuit of the mouse we chanced upon a cricket and hurt it. "That would be a catastrophe," she said, so we had to be careful. In the end we caught the mouse. Our screams cut the air every time we saw it, and it escaped. All of Bethlehem must have heard us. The other detainees came to see what was going on, and some of them couldn't stand by watching without taking part. Orders flew back and forth: bring salt, water, another broom, and if there was no other broom, then a broom handle would do, or any stick. "Maybe we should try to get Johnny's billy-club," said one of the girls (Johnny was the prison director).

Finally we were successful and caught the mouse, not hurting any crickets to ensure that no catastrophe occurred. Perhaps the young girls would go home soon. Adah picked up the mouse by its tail and paraded around the building, displaying it for everyone to see, saying that was the fate of anyone or anything that dared to disturb her when she was reading. The mouse was put in the garbage and later incinerated.

And as a matter of fact, a little while later the young girls did go home, but not all of them. We must have inadvertently stepped on a cricket after all.

When Hadassah was released there was no one to replace her. Everyone tried her hand at fortune telling, but with almost no success. She was the only released prisoner who did not turn around for a last look when she left us, and we knew that it was because she believed that if she didn't turn around she would never be imprisoned again. Then I understood why I kept returning to Bethlehem; it was because every time I was released, I used to turn around to have a last look at the detainees who stayed behind. But Hadassah was consistent to the end, and although we waved goodbye to her she never saw us, because it was forbidden to turn her head. The secret must have had something to do with the story of Lot's wife.

After this we used to ask every detainee who was about to be released if she would turn around or not, because we didn't want to run to the window and wave for no reason. They all turned their heads, waved, and never came back. Sometimes what we think are omens aren't omens after all. Sometimes

Hadassah used to interpret dreams, but in that field she had a lot of competition from other detainees who had become experts before they ever saw Bethlehem. I have no facility for interpreting either omens or dreams, but as I write these words I have no doubt that if Hadassah were here she would find some sign in the multitude of moths and other flying creatures that have been attracted to the light of my lamp, here in Tel Aviv.

✳ ✳ ✳ ✳ ✳ ✳

Chapter Seventeen

Arguments with Thomas

Even when I was arrested I never denied that I belonged to the Revisionist Movement and to Betar, both of which were legal organizations. While it was true that most of the Irgun fighters were also members and supporters of the Movement, there was no official connection between them. More than once when I was in the camp, I argued with Mr. Thomas, the director, a clever Englishman who understood the problems of the Yishuv and its people, unlike his predecessors, who knew nothing at all.

"You Revisionists," he would say, "are no good, you don't obey the Jewish Agency or the National Council." I didn't want to endanger the legal status of the Movement, and so I had no choice but to answer, "It is not the Movement that doesn't obey, but the underground, and no legal political party has any influence over it or can tell it what to do."

And he would continue, "Why was there such a breach between Weizmann[46] and Jabotinsky?" and I would answer, "The situation is approximately the same as that between Churchill and Chamberlain." He would flush in anger at my audacity in comparing my country with his, but I did it every

---

[46]Chaim Weizmann (1874—1952), the first President of the State of Israel, was head of the World Zionist Organization from 1920 to 1931 and from 1935 to 1946.

192

time we argued. Suddenly he said, "Aaronsohn was good," and I answered, "Yes, he was, that was why you threw him into the ocean from an airplane."[47]

Again and again he complained about our lack of political understanding, and when I mentioned some comparisons with the perverted political maneuvering of Chamberlain and others when it came to their dealings with Palestine and the Jews, he answered, "You don't understand British politics." To that I replied, "Exactly as you don't understand our politics." When I saw that things were getting out of hand and that my English was insufficient to explain our position, I suggested that he read Jabotinsky's *The Jewish War Front*, saying that it would help him understand the problems.[48] I ordered the book in English, and when it arrived I gave it to him.

A few days later I asked Thomas if he had read it and what he thought about it, but he didn't answer. To this day I don't know whether he read the book or even part of it. I only know that from that moment on we had fewer arguments, at least fewer political arguments. I mention political arguments because he usually tried to behave well with us, and more than once he would ask me if I had any complaints against him.

I have to admit that I got a certain sense of satisfaction from sitting across from the prison director, a high-ranking officer, and having him beg me to agree that he was a good fellow. I never let him feel that this was my opinion of him. He used to shrug his shoulders as if to ask what else he could do to make us happy. "I comply with all your demands," he would say, "and if by chance something goes wrong, it's because I'm not in charge of everything here. I can't release you, no matter what."

---

[47]Aaron Aaronsohn, the founder of Nili, survived World War I but was killed in an airplane crash in England on May 15, 1919.
[48]Published in London in 1940, this work elaborated Jabotinsky's views in an appropriate Jewish political response to the war.

Thomas used to say that he was at odds with the CID because of us. Even the former director, the White Angel, used to complain about how difficult and inconvenient it was to deal with the CID. When one of us had to go to the hospital and there was a bed ready: no vehicle. A vehicle was found: no guard. They could never coordinate things. However, she never asked us to certify that she had behaved well. Perhaps this was because in her time the English weren't being harassed by the underground to such an extent that they were afraid for their lives the way they were when Thomas was in charge: officers were being attacked in the streets, and kidnapped, and fear goaded him into being a good fellow, or at least trying to seem like one. The psychological aspect should not be disparaged, because it always worked in favor of the prisoners and detainees.

Somewhat later I found out that one of the lower-ranking officers in the Kenya detention camp who was about to return to Palestine had also asked the leaders of the detainees for a certificate stating that he had treated them well. He was afraid that when he came back he would be killed, or at least beaten.

Mr. Thomas and I used to argue about all sorts of things. Once we received nonkosher soap and I returned it, demanding that it be replaced. He was amazed. He said that when he went to the cinema in Jerusalem and was late getting out, there were no more pork sandwiches in the nearby restaurant because Jews had bought them all, and here I was, demanding kosher soap. I said, "Mister Thomas, you aren't responsible for all the non-Jews in the world, and I am not responsible for all the Jews. All I can do is show you that the soap brought to us by our families is always kosher."

In 1944, during the great curfew in Jerusalem, no meat was brought to the prison. I asked Thomas to call the CID and demand meat. The CID answered that the slaughterhouses were closed because of the curfew and there was no meat anywhere in Jerusalem. I told Thomas that the explanation was totally irrelevant and he had to bring us meat from somewhere else. He brought us chickens, but they had not been ritually slaughtered and we would not accept them. Whenever a prisoner or detainee was released we would sing a special song, and when we released these chickens from their potential captivity in our pot, we sang the song for them as well.

Once a chicken was brought to the kitchen and we suspected that it wasn't kosher. The White Angel was very surprised and claimed that it came from the Sphinx, a British store which sold pork!

My very existence must have been a nightmare for Mr. Thomas, because one day, when I had been ill in the hospital for a month, Peninah, who was in charge of the kitchen, returned the supplies as unfit. He moaned, "Obviously, I should have known, she's from Tzila's room."

People do not always reveal their thoughts, and there is no way of knowing what is hidden in their souls, but I am sure that we detainees impressed Mr. Thomas with our integrity and self-respect, never broken by the awful conditions of prison life, and with the way we bore our burdens.

From the moment we arrived in prison till the moment we left, we thought about ways of escaping. For a political prisoner there is nothing final about an arrest, and he devotes all his efforts to returning to the front. Just like the detained men, we kept thinking about how to escape. Here too we had less luck than they, not only because their conditions were better, but because they had more and better opportunities to escape.

In Bethlehem both the prison and the camp in the villa were located in the heart of a hostile Arab city, on an exposed and windy hill. There was a curfew at night, and no one could move on the roads, and the vigilance of the guards in the prison itself was very strict. Trying to escape in such conditions was tantamount to committing suicide.

However, one day we were horrified to hear shots fired in the vicinity of the prison, and we were afraid that the Arabs were attacking. I told the women to lie down on the floor, although a few minutes later we learned that there had been no attack but rather that someone had tried to escape.

The prison director came into the corridor and threw a bloodstained jacket onto the floor. Only then did we notice that Geula Cohen was not there. When we saw the jacket we were afraid that the shots had killed her, but he said, "I am a humane person and will not punish all of you because of her, but tell me to whom this jacket belongs." We told him that we all wore each other's clothes. He and the guards kept up the tension and would not tell us what had happened to Geula. It was only the next day that we learned that by some miracle she had been wounded and not killed outright. (A while later, aided by Arabs from Abu Gosh, she succeeded in escaping from the hospital in Jerusalem.)

✳ ✳ ✳ ✳ ✳ ✳

Chapter Eighteen

Interrogations

The time of the arbitrary arrests could be summarized as a reworking of Judges 17:6: "In those days there was no law in Israel, and every CID man did that which was right in his own eyes."

Emergency regulations had been enacted against the Arabs who murdered Jews during the riots of the 1930s, and these same regulations were now being used against the underground resistance fighters. Under these regulations, anyone could be arrested for an unlimited amount of time. This could be done even if there was no evidence against him, and even without affording him the right to defend himself in a court of law, a basic right given to the worst of criminals, murderers, and rapists. The freedom of action given to the members of the CID, many of whom were the dregs of society and could not find their place in Britain, led to the complete nullification of citizens' rights in Palestine (the Land of Israel). Many alarming incidents occurred.

There is the story, for instance, of a girl who had been going out with a fellow for some years when she became attracted to another man and didn't know how to get rid of the first one. The new boyfriend wrote an anonymous letter to the CID, accusing her old beau of being an underground resistance fighter and of belonging to an illegal organization. The CID arrested him immediately and the happy couple's problems were solved.

There is another story, this one about two partners, one of whom would have done anything to get rid of the other. He too wrote a letter to the CID, and his partner was arrested.

Those who were arrested were never given a chance to prove their innocence. They received a stenciled form from the CID, reading "You must remain in detention," and signed, "Your obedient servant." In addition to this notice, the camp commander would give him an envelope stamped "Secret" with a letter inside informing him that it had been "decided" that he would be interned for six months or a year. Actually the letter was meaningless, because some recipients of such notices were released within a few days, and others remained in prison for years on end and were even exiled. Apparently the CID offices were full of printed forms, and when the time came, the detainee would receive another letter from his "obedient servant" informing him that he would be the guest of the state for six more months.

The CID worked on the fundamental assumption that it was better for ninety-nine innocent people and one terrorist to be to arrested than to let one terrorist go free. When 251 detainees were exiled from the camp in Latrun to Eritrea, the following joke was told: Why were exactly 251 people exiled? Answer: Because one of them was a terrorist, but no one could identify him. And what happened in the end? That one terrorist was released and sent back, while the remaining 250 stayed in Eritrea.

As the number of arrests increased, and more and more people were detained, increased pressure was exerted on the CID by lawyers and family members, forcing it to set up interrogation committees to camouflage its actions. The committees would review each file to determine the possible innocence of the person in question. They would notify the lawyer representing the detainee that on such-and-such a day his client's file would be examined, but he would not be allowed to appear before the committee. And if, to the detainee's bad luck, the appointed day was the same day the underground had chosen to launch an attack, the next day the lawyer would be informed that whereas they had intended to review his client's file the preceding day, and whereas there had been a good chance that his client would have been released, his friends in the underground had ruined everything. When the terrorists desisted from their criminal activities, his client would be released.

The families of the political detainees were willing to do anything to see their loved ones released, and in spite of all the pressure brought to bear against them, tried everything. I convinced my mother that it was bad for her health and beneath her dignity to appeal to the CID on my behalf, and that I had no intention of exerting pressure on them either, and until my ex-husband returned nothing was done.

Interrogations were conducted in Jerusalem, and in the camp the days on which they were to take place were practically holidays. We started preparing early and wore our best clothing. Some of the detainees were "unlucky" and were never sick, so that during all the years of their incarceration they never left the camp for doctors' appointments and examinations. It was not the interrogation or any hope connected with it that caused such joy, but the trip to Jerusalem. Faces shone with excitement and anticipation, hearts pounded, and sometimes the detainees's hands trembled so badly that they needed help getting dressed.

Usually two or three detainees went together, and there was great excitement both when they set out and when they returned. After the CID interrogation they were subjected to a much more thorough interrogation by the other detainees. "What did they ask," we wanted to know, "what did they say to you, what were they most interested in, did they mention any names," and finally and most important, "what are your chances of getting out?"

Each detainee came back with her own story. One of them, for instance, told us only after her return that during her family's last visit they had told her that she would be interrogated, but she hadn't believed them. We thought about it and decided that this was proof that people outside were doing everything they could for the detainees, and that there was a good chance that some of us would be released soon.

There were those who came back utterly disgusted, feeling that they had taken part in a fraud. "I was a puppet," recounted one woman, "a marionette. They asked me all kinds of pointless questions, and I had to give them the answers they wanted to hear. Of course, I didn't give them any information, they didn't even try in that direction because they knew it wouldn't do them any good. But I had to tell them for the hundredth time that I wasn't a terrorist, that I had never been a terrorist, and that after I was released I would behave myself. It was disgusting!"

Another said, "I'll never go back for another interrogation. It was offensive and humiliating. The only reason I went this time was because my family wanted me to and I felt sorry for them. They have done everything they can for me, and if I hadn't gone all their efforts would have been wasted."

Unfortunately the happiness we derived from these trips didn't last long. The CID decided that it was dangerous to take such women out of Bethlehem and let them go to Jerusalem, but they didn't want people to think that the files weren't being reviewed, so they brought the interrogators to the camp. Thus we were deprived of one of the good aspects of prison life: the "field trips" to Jerusalem.

Once the interrogations began to be held in Bethlehem, we were simply told to get ready to report to the office. "Getting ready" meant that we had to dress suitably. Usually we walked around as if we were at home, in robes and bedroom slippers. It also meant that we had to prepare ourselves psychologically, because a certain amount of concentration was needed, at least until the interrogation began.

When one of the detainees went to the office, we would all crowd around and wish her luck and a speedy release.

Usually when someone was released it came as a relief for the rest, but subconsciously it was also depressing. The main thing was that the ice was beginning to crack, and if someone else got out today, maybe I would get out tomorrow. There was a current of detainees being released, and I was sure that one fine day it would sweep me away with it, too.

When the detainee left the office the scene was reminiscent of what happened when someone new came to the camp. She would be surrounded with questions, but this time the questions were different. When someone new came, everyone wanted to know what was going on outside, whereas now everyone wanted to know what was going on inside: what questions were asked, what her general impression was.

One day, out of a clear blue sky, I was told to prepare myself for an interrogation. And I thought of 1 Samuel 10:11, "Is Saul also among the prophets?" Are they going to interrogate me as well? This was the first time since my arrest that anyone had wanted to question me. From my first arrest, in December, 1941, until my current arrest in 1946, which was just one link in a long chain, I was never interrogated or asked any questions beyond purely formal ones. I concluded that it was due to Aryeh's pressuring of the CID. Who knew, perhaps I would be released in spite of all the promises I had received to the contrary. One important thing that might work in my favor was the fact that since my imprisonment, I had been constantly ill. The prison director himself had hinted that my illness might help me: I might receive proper treatment, or . . .

Needless to say, my being called for questioning caused a great sensation in the camp, and everyone tried to guess what it meant.

Several CID officers were waiting for me in the office when I entered. I didn't know any of them, but I recognized one from the accounts of other detainees. His name was Lodge, and he was in command. Usually I spoke English, and all my conversations with Mr. Thomas were in English. Although during our arguments I had never denied belonging to the Revisionist Movement and could express myself perfectly, this time I demanded an interpreter. I had two reasons for this. First, an interrogation is not an intellectual argument, and any faulty answer or misunderstanding could seal my fate. Second, with an interpreter present I would have more time to answer. Every question would be asked twice, and I would be able to think clearly, so as to avoid traps and difficult questions.

The interrogators asked many pointless questions. They wanted to know about a picture of me which they claimed had been found in Abraham Stern's possession. The fool must have thought that I would say, "Oh no, he wouldn't have a picture of me, but David Raziel would." I said that my picture wasn't for sale and therefore no one would have it, and besides, I didn't think Stern collected pictures of women.

The interrogator changed his tack, and from his questions I understood that he thought I was a very important Irgun officer. I said that if that was what he thought, the CID intelligence services were quite poor. When I was free, I had been under house arrest, reporting to the police station three times a day, and required to stay at home from sunset till sunrise. Under such conditions, I wanted to know, how could I be in the Irgun? (My logic was flawless, but they were right. Although under house arrest I had great responsibility and performed many important duties, and the traitor Hilewitz must have informed on me. He was the only traitor in the ranks of the Irgun, and later went to America. Despite his protestations I never believed he was one with us, because he was so careful about his appearance. I knew he would never go to jail.)

Secondly, I claimed that I couldn't be important in the Irgun because I wasn't a member! The interrogator, unmoved by the least fear of insulting or offending me, replied that he simply didn't believe me. All I could do was shrug my shoulders as if to say, "If you don't want to believe me, that's your problem, not mine. It's up to you to decide what you want to believe and what you don't."

He also wanted to know how old my son was. I said that he was nine, and several seconds passed in silence. He seemed to be calculating something. I turned to the interpreter and said, "Doesn't he believe that either?" When he translated what I had just said, the interrogator replied in Hebrew, "No, I believe you, I'm just trying to figure out if he is old enough to join the National Military Organization." I shot back in English, "No, by the time he is old enough to join, there will be no need for a National Military Organization, because by then . . ."

The prison director finished my sentence for me, saying "by then there will be a Jewish state," and puffed furiously at his pipe. "Yes, yes, Mr. Thomas," I said to him, "by then we will have a Jewish state, take note!"

He looked at me, but whether he felt sorry for me or was laughing at my foolish beliefs, I never found out. Unfortunately, he was not the only one. Many others thought the same.

And that was the end of my interrogation.

As I left the room I met all the detainees who were waiting for me. They were excited and impatient, as though it were their fate and not mine being decided. I told them what had been said, especially about my promise that a Jewish state would be established in a few years. As far as I could see, the whole thing had been a show, nothing more. I don't know whether my interrogation had anything to do with my release, but it did come a short time later.

A few years after this I found out that Mr. Thomas had said that if I weren't released he would quit his job, since it was out of the question that one prison have two directors. He complained bitterly that the guards were more obedient to me than to him.

All this was told to me by Anita Miller-Cohen, who heard it after my release when she went to visit her daughter who was ill in the hospital. After I was arrested for one night along with Shoshanah Raziel and Bilhah Hermoni (details in a later chapter), Mr. Thomas said that he was happy when I was released, and had done everything he could to facilitate it, and he was terrified when I was arrested that I might be coming back.

Aryeh Possek, a Betar commander, also told me about Mr. Thomas's ultimatum after my release. To the title "Dangerous to the Empire" was added the title "Director of the Prison at Bethlehem," a job I am willing to hold even in the State of Israel when Bethlehem is ours once again.

❋ ❋ ❋ ❋ ❋ ❋

Chapter Nineteen

Revolt

On July 22, 1942 the prison administration was ordered to separate the Lehi and Irgun fighters. The separation was done on the basis of the suspected affiliations of the detainees at the time of their arrests.

There were two of us from the Irgun, Ruth Halevi and I, and twelve from the Lehi. Since there were only three rooms, it was decided that Ruth and I would have one, and the other twelve would share the remaining two.

That same morning Ruth and I were told to move our things. The decision to change our living arrangements in such a fashion was arbitrary and stupid, because the rooms were too small to house so many women. Before we knew what was happening, Ruth and I were pushed into the room and the door was locked behind us, and the remaining detainees were left standing in the corridor.

At that point the Lehi detainees revolted. They refused to enter the rooms. The guards tried unsuccessfully to force them, while the White Angel shouted commands. She ordered the convicted Arab prisoners to help the guards, and of course some of them always wanted to curry favor even though they hated her, and now they could both show her their loyalty and hit and kick those special Jewish detainees as well. However, several of the Arab prisoners refused to cooperate, both because they had become friendly with the detainees and because they did not want to obey the White Angel.

She tried to seduce them with patriotism, claiming that the
Jewish detainees were the enemies of the Arabs and it was their
duty to help the prison administration. It did her no good,
however, and those who tried to do her bidding received a
thorough trouncing at the hands of the Lehi fighters and quickly retreated, while the others fled to their own rooms, having
lost all desire to participate in a conflict between the prison
authorities and the Jewish prisoners. We decided that it had to
be because they themselves had received so many beatings,
and because we had always treated them so well.

Since the detainees could not be forced into the rooms by
female guards alone, the White Angel took the unprecedented
step of calling for reinforcements: policemen. That had never
been done in a women's prison before.

The small grille set in our door looked out over the staircase,
so we could see who came and went. Suddenly we heard steps
and saw policemen mounting the stairs. We called out to the
other detainees to announce that they were coming, because
beyond informing them of what was about to happen and
encouraging them there was nothing we could do to help.

The policemen made no pretense of hiding their joy at being
able to strike Jewish female prisoners, especially Lehi fighters.
However, it wasn't as pleasant or as easy as they had hoped.
The detainees did not give up easily, and the men had to use
force, and there was a real fight, although eventually they
pushed the women into their rooms. Even Tovah Savorai, who
was ill, put up a fight. Miriam Shuchman fought till she was
bloody. There were times when we thought we would explode
as we watched the policemen mercilessly pulling the women's
hair. When they finally got the detainees into the rooms, there
weren't six in each but only two, because the administration
was afraid of what would happen if a large number of
detainees were together in one room.

The upshot was that instead of four or five detainees in a
room there were only two, and they were allotted six rooms in
all. That was done by crowding even more Arab prisoners
together and putting Rachel Ohevet-Ami in with us, although

the administration had never agreed to do so before. That was not, however, the end of the story. The Lehi fighters began banging on the doors with shoes and everything else they could find, and when the guards wanted to enter their rooms they pushed the beds up against the doors to barricade them. Since the doors opened inwards, there was no way the guards could get in. Finally the guards made a chain, and only then did they manage to break into the rooms. The women threw everything they could get their hands on at them, including their chamber pots, not all of which were empty.

Punishment was not long in coming. Everything was removed from the rooms; every piece of furniture, beds, and even shoes were taken, and only the mattresses were left. The anguish was great, because things which had been acquired only through long and difficult struggles had been taken away in an instant. The detainees remained locked in their rooms, were not permitted to go onto the roof, and were only allowed out in pairs for a few minutes to go to the bathroom. Each room was opened and locked before another one was opened. Ruth and I went down to the kitchen to cook for everyone. We gave the food to the guards, and they opened each door individually and distributed the food.

That was only on the first day, and by the second day we had arranged that we would give out the food, and we used the opportunity to smuggle them cigarettes, pencils and paper, and news, of course. The guards increased their surveillance, but we did whatever we wanted to, right under their noses.

The situation continued for three or four days, and in the meantime I was released and Ruth remained alone, with the result that the prison administration began to permit the Lehi fighters out of their rooms for kitchen duty and general cleaning. Tovah Savorai and Miriam Shuchman were put into solitary confinement in the punishment cells. These are not particularly inviting in any prison, but at Bethlehem they were awful. They were located in the same wing in which the mentally ill women were kept. The very fact that these women were imprisoned was bad enough, but having to live next door to them was unimaginable. The punishment cell was the size of a mattress, and the imprisoned person could not walk around, but only sit or lie down. Yet in spite of everything we managed to smuggle all sorts of forbidden items in to them, pencils and paper and news, and cigarettes to Miriam.

This torture continued for two months until the detainees managed to make contact with the outside world and asked Zeligman and other lawyers to come to the prison. I had already been released and did everything I could to rouse public opinion by appealing to the press and to public figures. Mrs. Danziger appealed to her brother, Dr. Rosen,[49] who later became Minister of Justice, and others. Mrs. Herzog was also very active in this matter. Rabbis were contacted, and all the appeals finally bore fruit.

As Julie said, "We were moved to Villa Salem, but we paid for the move with our suffering. For two years we were denied visits, and they constricted our lives and made us miserable in revenge for having humiliated the prison administration in the eyes of the convicted prisoners. But our prestige rose higher and higher, and they were careful to leave us alone if they wanted to avoid trouble, as the White Angel used to say." And so the underground fighters proved their bravery and heroism even behind bars.

The next and final revolt broke out after the announcement, on November 29, 1947, of the Partition Plan for Palestine. I was not in prison at the time, but Peninah Bejaio told me what happened.

"The atmosphere in Bethlehem was tense and electric even before the United Nations accepted the Plan. The Arabs were

---

[49]Pinchas Rosen (1887—19??), a long-time Zionist activist, headed the Progressive Party from its founding in 1948 until 1961, when it merged with the General Zionists to form the Liberal Party. He headed the Ministry of Justice almost continuously from 1948 to 1961.

running riot in the streets. It is not hard to imagine how a handful of Jewish women trapped in a hostile Arab city felt, but as soon as the acceptance of the Plan was announced our situation became far more tenuous. The British could not be relied upon to keep us from harm. The British policemen openly collaborated with the Arabs, and we saw with our own eyes how they handed out weapons to the Arabs. As far as the Arab guards in the prison were concerned, there was no doubt in anyone's mind but that they would open the gates to the Arab assassins at the first opportunity. The nightmare of the Hebron massacre of 1929 came back to haunt us, but our urgent appeals to the institutions of the Yishuv went unheeded. Rabbi Goldman visited us and saw the danger with his own eyes, but he too was powerless to help, and all he could do was pray.

"We realized that we could not count on help coming from the outside, and remembering that `God helps those who help themselves,' decided to take matters into our own hands. We requested authorization from the Irgun commander in Tel Aviv to start an uprising in the prison, and approval was quickly given. Needless to say, the Lehi fighters joined us.

"They used to lock us in for the night at eight, after the guards had counted us and made sure that no one was missing, so the first step we took was to refuse to enter our rooms; we remained in the corridor all night long. For someone who has never been in prison, that might not seem like much of a rebellion, but in prison its significance was a slap in the face of the `holy of holies': prison regulations. Rules and regulations formed links in the chain binding the prisoners, and if one of the links were broken, the whole chain would fall apart. In the normal course of events, such an action would result in strong measures being taken against the prisoners, but since the British regime was weak and almost over, the authorities did not react at all.

"The next day we went even further, in more senses than one. We broke down the fence separating the two sides of the garden and entered the part that had been closed to us since the

camp had been set up. After that the prison administration was
forced to negotiate with us. Mr. Thomas himself appeared with
the following message: on December 26th the detainees would
be moved out of Bethlehem.

"Our joy was great, as all at once fear was lifted from our
hearts, and we ran from the camp to the prison to tell the
Jewish prisoners. It was obvious to the prison administration
that not only the detainees, but the convicted women, would
have to be moved from Bethlehem. However, the next day we
were surprised to hear a disturbance coming from the prison.
The building was removed from the camp, but the noise was so
loud that it reached us. We immediately contacted the prisoners (we had our own ways of doing this), who told us that Mr.
Thomas had just announced that they would not be moved
together with the detainees but would remain in Bethlehem.
The prisoners, feeling that they had been deceived, announced
that they were rebelling and refused to enter their rooms. Their
situation was worse than ours, because there were only seven
of them, and as prisoners, not detainees, the prison authorities
could take much harsher steps against them.

"British policemen were called to the prison, and they
viciously and sadistically dragged the women to their rooms.
Having learned from their experience in the rebellion of 1942,
when the detainees had barricaded themselves in and attacked
with everything they could find, the police confiscated all their
possessions and left the detainees in empty rooms. Vastly out-
numbering them, they managed to overcome seven women,
but they soon learned that while they might have won the battle, the war was far from over.

"We opened a second front. We broke into the *sanctum sanc-
torum*, the prison office, burned papers, disconnected the telephone, wrested the keys from the amazed guards, and from
there broke into the yard. At that time the police were busy
with the last stages of the battle against the prisoners and had
to regroup to attack us. Here they had a real fight on their
hands. We had prepared everything in advance, and like the

matrons on the walls of Jerusalem, we had pots full of boiling oil and boiling water with which to `wash' the faces of the British policemen.

"We stood in the yard like a wall, while a line of policemen, ready to do battle, advanced toward us.

"It was a case of psychological warfare. The police hoped that when we saw them we would retreat, and then they would be able to return to trying to control the prisoners, but they were surprised and even frightened when they saw that we stood firm. They in turn began to retreat, because they were afraid that they would have to deal not with seven women, but with dozens of women armed and ready for battle. They decided to call in Mr. Thomas. In all his career he had never faced people possessed of such a militant spirit, and he tried negotiations. We said that we would never negotiate with a so-called gentleman who had turned out to be a liar. He had no choice but to call in another `gentleman,' one who had not lied to us, and he called in the Chief Inspector of Prisons himself.

"The inspector came pretending innocence, and trying to remain calm, asked what all the noise was about; after all, we had been given the date for leaving Bethlehem. We said that we would not leave without the seven convicted prisoners, because if the lives of thirty-five detainees were in danger if they stayed in Bethlehem, it was ten times more dangerous for seven detainees alone. He had no answer for this and asked for an extension of three days in which to find a solution. In the meantime he requested that we return the prison keys to Mr. Thomas. We refused and said that we would only give him the keys, and then on condition that if we did not get the answer we wanted, we would reach our own conclusions.

"In spite of our bitterness and the seriousness of the situation, it was a wonderful thing to see: a few dozen detainees, alone and isolated, in the heart of a hostile Arab settlement in the days just before a time of great confusion and upheaval, standing firm and conducting negotiations and presenting conditions to the Chief Inspector of Prisons as though both sides were equal. Or rather, as though our side were stronger.

"We didn't have to wait three days. The following day Jemila appeared to inform us that we would all be moved from Bethlehem, although not on December 26th, because it was the day after Christmas and the policemen would still be drunk. We couldn't be moved on the 27th, because it fell on Saturday, and therefore it would be postponed until the 28th, even though it was a Sunday, the Christian day of rest.

"We told them that this time we would be the ones to tell the prisoners officially, and that the prison authorities would be present at the time, and so it was.

"We immediately began to pack our belongings. We were used to packing for one or two women who were being released, but this time everyone was going. It wasn't like packing possessions, but rather an era of our lives full of suffering and glory, an era of a war of liberation and freedom. We remembered what Winston Churchill had said when he visited Tripoli during the war and saw the Jewish soldiers from Palestine loading munitions on boats: `Fellows, do you know what you're loading? History!'

"We had the feeling that history had reached a turning point. All of our possessions, which would be worthless in the outside world, were important. They were our companions and witnesses to everything that had happened to us here, to the long, gloomy nights of disappointment and despair, to the difficult hours of depression and the great moments of faith that we would overcome in spite of everything, and to the long years we had been waiting for the dawn of Hebrew redemption to break, and for the rays of the sun of liberation to shine and warm our hearts.

"We knew that we were not going home, but to another detention camp——the last station on our road to freedom, on the road to a Jewish state, the thing we had yearned for and fought so long for.

"Therefore we decided that we would not sneak out of Bethlehem like thieves in the night, but go with our heads held high and a song of victory on our lips, the song of the prisoners of Zion, returning to the cradle of the Kingdom of Israel, its historic significance renewed as in days of old!

"With this end in view we took razor blades to cut open the canvas they planned to use to cover the trucks taking us through Bethlehem. We managed to smuggle razor blades to the prisoners as well.

"A heavy guard of soldiers armed with Tommy guns and Sten guns was put in charge of us, but before they knew what was happening the canvas coverings had all been cut off the trucks.

"With overflowing hearts we began to sing as we passed Rachel's Tomb. `Refrain thy voice from weeping, and thine eyes from tears; for thy work shall be rewarded, and they shall come from the land of thine enemy.' As we reached Jerusalem we sang even louder, and called out, `We are the prisoners and detainees from Bethlehem!'

"During the ride it turned out that this could have been our swan song, and we almost lost our lives as a result of our joyful singing. As we passed through the Arab city of Lod, singing loudly, a gala reception was prepared for us by an enormous crowd of Arabs who had been incited against us, and they began yelling, `Jews! Kill the Jews!' To the credit of our British guards, it must be noted that they abandoned their usual pose of neutrality. They crouched into position, ready to fire at the crowd, which suddenly realized that the police were not going to abandon us. The firmness of the guards prevented our being slaughtered at the hands of the Arabs.

"When we arrived in Atlit (near Haifa) we saw that huts had been prepared for us. We refused to get out of the trucks, but when we saw that it was a camp of illegal immigrants we ran to meet them, since most of our war had been fought to save them and bring them to their homeland.

"We moved to a special camp which had been fenced off for us, but we quickly broke down the fences. This made the immigrants happy, and we told them that it wasn't the first time we had torn down a fence. We showed them our calling card: Bethlehem!

"The two camps quickly became one. `The people of Israel live,' we sang, and we joined hands and began to dance with the immigrants, who had escaped from the Nazi inferno and had finally reached a safe harbor and had now met the people who had worked so hard to save them.

"The women's prison in Bethlehem began to fade from our memories like morning mist when the sun's rays shine. It was already turning into a legend, one of those legends wrapped in the glory of liberation and redemption."

This is the story as told to me by Peninah, who was interned in the camp at Atlit. (Two of the women later escaped from the camp dressed as guards, and one staged an appendicitis attack and escaped as she was being transferred to a hospital in Haifa.)

＊ ＊ ＊ ＊ ＊ ＊

Chapter Twenty

Release!

As I recounted in the chapter on holidays, we tried to inject a note of joy into our drab and monotonous lives in Bethlehem. However, there was one special day that we couldn't prepare for the way we could for holidays, birthdays, and visiting days. It not only made us very happy but came as a surprise—-the day someone was released from the camp.

From our rooms we could look over the railing and watch the Bethlehem-Jerusalem road. If we saw a policeman with a white hat on a motorcycle, we knew that he was bringing the prison authorities a release order. When that happened the detainee would be called to the office and given the following laconic message: "Be ready in half an hour. You're going home."

During the time I was in Bethlehem, I never had the experience of seeing my "messiah" ride up with news of my salvation, not on a white mule and not with a white hat, but riding on a motorcycle. I never saw the policeman who brought my release order, because it was done secretly.

On July 22, 1942, two days before I was released, the uprising of the Lehi fighters broke out, so the chances of saying goodbye were limited. My release was effected when the doors to the rooms were being locked, and all I could do was climb up to the grille in the door and touch the hands of those in the room or call goodbye through the closed door.

Being released from Bethlehem was as humiliating as being admitted, although the attendant emotions were not the same.

The situation in the camp was different. Since we were free to roam the camp grounds during the daylight hours, we could turn someone's release into a real holiday.

The process was usually as follows: the detainee would be summoned to the office, something which in itself caused everyone to gather around the office door, since the very fact of being called was important and significant, usually heralding release. If that was not the reason for the detainee's being summoned to the office, as she left she would say, "No, not this time," and only later would we ask why they had called for her.

If, however, they had given her good news, she would come out of the office grinning from ear to ear and announce happily that she was going home. Everyone would rejoice with her, hugging and kissing her as we led her back to her room as though she were a bride being led to the altar. Once inside she would be left alone with her best friends.

Then packing would begin. The detainee always said that she would leave her possessions for those remaining behind, because you could buy anything you wanted "outside." They tried to talk her into taking all her possessions, since there were many things which could not be had outside, and if she had no family or if her family was not well off, those not being released refused to heed her and would even put some of their own belongings into her suitcases.

As we packed we would talk and laugh and tell jokes, until the Arab guards yelled, "Come on, come on, you should have finished by now!" It was strange that everything had to be done in a rush, even leaving. Subconsciously we tried to drag the process out, to prolong the experience and enjoy it longer, because knowing that one was going home was the sweetest sensation in the world.

When the detainee being released held a high position in the Irgun, she had to relay a great deal of information about running things to her successor. For instance, when Esther Raziel was released, Adah Stecklis was appointed to replace her as camp leader, and they had to arrange the codes for official mail (illegal mail had not yet been instituted in the camp). To camouflage their actions and give them time to complete all their arrangements, the process of packing had to be drawn out for as long as possible.

When the packing was finished, the time came to say goodbye. Everyone participated in the leave-taking. The detainees would hug each other and cry with joy; some would ask that regards be given to people outside, and others would ask that important information be relayed, information of the sort that could not be passed on in letters or during visits.

The detainee who left often felt strange. She sometimes felt that she was transgressing by leaving her friends behind. She would try to comfort them, saying that they would all go home soon, and promising to do everything she could to help them and make their lives easier until they were released. These promises were usually kept, and if they weren't, it was not for lack of good intentions but because of the circumstances in which the woman found herself after her release.

As she left a special song was sung for her, one written by David Dannon and played at all Irgun officers' training courses. We really didn't know the words very well, just the melody, and it became the anthem of the detainees released from Bethlehem.

We would watch her until she disappeared from view, that is to say, until she walked through the gate leading to the other building.

The prisoners could hear the song as we sang it, and they would get up on the window sills to watch the detainee as she left, calling out all kinds of last-minute errands and requests.

When someone was released it was as if it were the day before Yom Kippur: all transgressions were forgiven, and all fights and arguments were forgotten. Those who weren't on speaking terms would approach her and amends would be made.

Then she went to the camp office to return everything she had been issued while in prison. If anything was missing, it had to be paid for. The other detainees always paid the sum immediately so that her release would not be delayed.

A vacuum would be felt in the detainee's room after she had gone. Her closest friends would be the sorriest, those with whom she had worked and shared her feelings and spun dreams of release. Those who were left were depressed in spite of their joy, and subconsciously the knife of jealousy would turn in their stomachs and make them wonder why she had been released and not they.

On the other hand, when one of the long-time detainees was released, the others would feel that finally things were beginning to move in the right direction.

After Adah was released and I became camp leader, the question arose of filling the void she had left. She had devised all sorts of handicrafts; who would do that now? Who would teach other detainees how to knit? Who would lead the dances and play the part of Carmen Miranda on the holidays, something Adah had been so good at? In addition, she was a nurse and gave injections when necessary, who would do it now?

When Peninah Effron was released, we lost our English teacher; after Adinah Lior left, we had no seamstress; when Miriam Shuchman left, we tried to console ourselves with the fact that we had lost our heaviest smoker, and now there would be more cigarettes to go around. We quickly discovered that we had made a mistake and there were others to replace her: Sonia, Frieda, Tzipporah, Emma, to name a few. When Hadassah was released we lost our chief cryptographer, and we missed her for a long time. Miriam Birenbaum's release was particularly important; most of the detainees connected her name with rusks, but the few who were in on the secret knew enough to connect her name with the illegal mail which was our lifeline to the outside world.

The release of the younger women was doubly joyous for us. Besides the happiness we felt at seeing them get out of prison, we knew that young people full of strength and eager to work were going back to the front. However, those of us left in the camp really missed them. Hassidah Sonkin and Hassidah Rosenzweig, Tzipporah Molin, Raphaela Olitzky and Zehava Pogrobinsky were young in spirit and more than a little mischievous, and they lightened the atmosphere considerably.

Sometimes the prison would be flooded with waves of new admissionx, for instance when the women came from Jerusalem. They were like visitors who had come to spend the night, and just as they had been admitted wholesale, so were they released. From that wave I remember the Jerusalem lawyer Eliyahu Meridor's wife and sister, Mrs. Fanzer, Abraham Axelrod's sister, and others.

Esther Raziel and Hayah Shwartz were released because they were pregnant, despite the fact that Dr. Ma'alouf had promised them that they and their babies could have private cells. Esther was released first and was very worried until she heard that Hayah had also been released. Esther called her daughter Efrat, another name for Bethlehem in the Bible. We missed them because they reduced by two the number of married women who were entitled to light the Sabbath candles. Naomi Orenstein was the first old hand to be released, and that gave hope to the other long-imprisoned detainees.

Those who remained never forgot the friends who had gone home. They often brought up their name, and a letter or a gift or even regards from one of them caused great joy.

Once in a while we were quite surprised when someone was released, but no one more so than the detainee herself, because the release had been effected without outside intervention. That is what happened to Bilhah Hermoni, whose husband was in the camp in Eritrea, and who had no one actively working on her case. She couldn't believe her ears when they told her, and all she could say was, "Home? I have no home to go to." We tried to comfort her, saying that she had a large, loving family, and was not alone in the world.

Usually there were hints that someone was about to be released, and visitors would say that the chances were good because certain anonymous officials had made promises, or that files had been examined. But often women were promised that they would soon be released and then remained in prison for months and even years. Someone who despaired of being released paid no attention to the promises her visitors brought her; she had heard them and been disappointed too many times. When it was officially announced that she was going home, however, she would tell the other detainees that during their last visit her relatives had told her that she would soon be out, but she hadn't told her friends because she didn't believe it was true.

It was unusual—except in my case—-for anyone to be released and then return to the prison or the camp. Ruth Halevi was arrested the first time at an Irgun training course and then a second time because they thought she was Tzila. She was younger, taller, and prettier than I, and what was ridiculous was that she remained imprisoned even after I was brought to Bethlehem and was released after me.

All the detainees who had been sent home were rearrested after the King David Hotel in Jerusalem, which was the British headquarters, was partially destroyed by a bomb. We were sent to Latrun, however, and only afterwards were some of us brought to Bethlehem, but that is another story.

A few words on my own release, which was complicated and full of strange and wonderful developments.

On July 24, 1942, I was released from Bethlehem, having been there for about eight months. On July 20, Mrs. Graham had asked if any of us was named Kleiman. She didn't pronounce the name correctly, but I immediately answered that there was no such person among us. At the same time, far away at the Mezra detention camp, north of Haifa, they asked the men if there was anyone named Tzila Heller, and instead of merely replying that there was not, and saying that Tzila Heller was a woman imprisoned in Bethlehem, they turned it into a joke and went looking for Tzila Heller in all the rooms in all the huts, and only a few days later reported that there was no one of that name among them, and that I was in Bethlehem. The joke cost me a few more days in prison, and they were fateful ones, because that was when the rebellion broke out. If I had been released earlier, the plan of dividing the detainees into Irgun and Lehi fighters might not have been implemented, because Ruth Halevi would have been alone. As it turned out, however, Ruth and I were still together then, and I was only informed of my release later.

The order came one day after the rebellion broke out. All the Lehi women had been locked in their rooms, so that Ruth and I were doing the cooking for everyone. I was in the kitchen when a guard told me I was wanted in the office. I was certain that it had to do with the rebellion, because the previous day I had spoken to Mr. Graham about how unjust and illogical the room division was. My surprise at being told that I was going home was boundless! Mrs. Graham was also in the room, and took over immediately. She told me that there were special instructions regarding my release and I had to obey them: I was to leave the building without informing any of the other women, and if any of them found out, my release would be postponed and perhaps even canceled. To hide the fact that I was being sent home, a guard would go with me to my room to help me pack and inspect my belongings, and the guard herself would carry my suitcases. And it wouldn't be just any guard, but the head guard herself, Jemila, and she would be responsible for keeping my release a secret from the other women.

It was certainly weird. Ruth had been arrested because they suspected her of being me, and they were releasing me while continuing to hold her, even though by now they knew who was who. In addition, Ruth's relatives were far more active about effecting her release than mine were in my behalf, and they had enlisted many influential people in her cause. It was a mystery, but the opportunity could not be ignored. I remembered that once, because of a simple error, the wrong person had been sent home from the prison in Acco. In addition, no release had ever been more fortuitous, because I could now work from the outside to help the other women and could give an exact account of what was going on behind the prison walls. I decided that saying goodbye to the others wasn't worth waiting even one day, and I accepted Mrs. Graham's conditions. I went back upstairs in a daze. Was it really going to happen? Was I going home, and before Ruth? I began singing that I was going home, and the women in the room across from mine climbed up on the window sill and I hinted to them that it was true, that I was going home but was forbidden to say goodbye. The news spread like wildfire through the prison, but I cried bitter tears at not being able to say goodbye to the women whose fate was linked to mine.

When I got to the office, Mr. Graham asked me why I was crying. I said that it was because I had been arrested openly but was being released underhandedly, and I was unhappy about leaving the other women in such a sorry state, all the while being forbidden to say anything to them. I argued with him about the injustice of the room assignments, and he said that it had not been his decision, but an order from above.

The discussion ended the instant the White Angel came in, trembling in fury. She had heard that the women knew I was leaving. I said that they had guessed it themselves, seeing me leave the building following a guard carrying my suitcases, and I said that she was being arbitrary in not letting me say goodbye and making me leave like a thief. After all, in a few minutes they would know for certain that I had been released, and what was there to be feared if they spoke to me at the last minute? Did she really think that I was a fool?

She stopped me and said that if I liked it so much in prison and wanted to come back, all I had to do was to continue acting and speaking as I had been. As usual, I didn't answer and left the office without so much as a backward glance.

I was very sorry I had listened to her and not gone to bid goodbye to the other detainees. The first thing I did that day was to make the conditions in Bethlehem known, first in Jerusalem and then in Tel Aviv. I don't know if it did any good, but I received promises that the situation would be rectified. Needless to say, my release entailed house arrest, and when I got to the CID headquarters in Jaffa, I asked Wilkins as a special favor to allow me to go to the cinema that evening. He looked around the room and told me to choose one of the men sitting there, saying I could go to the cinema in the company of the policeman of my choice. I answered that I'd had enough to do with police and wanted to spend my time with human beings. He was not pleased but agreed.

The second time I was released (from Bethlehem; I was only released from the prison in Jaffa once) was completely different from the first. The only similarity was the surprise it entailed. The first time I was whisked away, but in the second instance I knew about it two full days before it happened, something that had never happened.

At the time of my second release, due to illness, I had no assigned duties, but whenever I felt better I would help around the kitchen or wherever there was work to be done. It was before Passover and many things had to be prepared. The building had already been cleaned and the utensils made kosher. Whatever might be considered leavened bread had been burned in accordance with the Law. Esther Auerbach and Hayah Ben-Tzvi were in charge of that aspect of the kitchen. We had been told that a rabbi would come to conduct the Passover Seder and would remain until the following day.

The only thing that cast a cloud over the holiday was the fact that the prisoners were not permitted to join us at the camp. Having them with us would have made the holiday atmosphere complete. We shared everything we had with them, so they lacked nothing, and we were somewhat consoled when we heard that they too would have someone from the outside to lead the Seder. It turned out that it would be the same rabbi; he would go to them first and then would come to us.

I felt well enough to help in the kitchen that day, but suddenly was called to the office. I didn't give it a thought, because I was sure it had to do with utensils or food I had demanded, and I went along unconcernedly. Mr. Thomas was waiting for me, grinning from ear to ear, and told me that he had a "present" for me for the holiday: I was going home. I almost yelled at him to not joke with me, but I stopped and asked if I were going immediately. He answered that I would be released after the holiday, that is to say, in two days' time, but he had wanted to tell me beforehand, so as to make the holiday more pleasant.

I didn't hear the rest because I flew out the door and ran back to the kitchen to tell the others. Their excitement was boundless. Peninah broke out in tears, and after her Hassiah and Yaffa, who were my cellmates. Julie came up to me, trembling, Esther, Hannah, and Hayah, and none of them knew what to say. A miracle had occurred for Passover. In Hebrew, when someone wants to say that something cannot be done, he says it is a difficult as the parting of the Red Sea, and indeed, the holiday of the parting of the Red Sea became the holiday of my release.

The excitement was doubly great because of the timing of the announcement, which was usually half an hour before the release itself, and in my case I had received two days notice, which was unprecedented. In addition, no one had ever expected me to be released before the young women whose reputations with the CID were far better than mine.

Nonetheless, we had to recover quickly from our excitement and get on with the preparations for the Seder. I went back to the kitchen. I was so excited that I managed to spill boiling oil on my hand, and I still have a tiny scar as a souvenir. Mr. Thomas came into the kitchen after me and said, "Tzila, you will be pleased to know that after all your demands for a new stove, I can promise you that in a few days the women will receive a good electric stove." And as if that were not enough, he suddenly remembered that the meat grinder, which had been sent out to be fixed, had not yet returned. He told me to come to the office with him and in my presence telephoned the man, a Jew, who was supposed to fix it.

"Sir," he said, "why haven't you returned the meat grinder to the prison? Aren't you ashamed, as a Jew who should want your own people to have everything as it should be, that Passover has come and you still haven't fixed the grinder? One of the most aggressive young detainees is with me in my office at this moment, and she is holding a stick with which she plans to beat me. Aren't you ashamed?"

Then he passed me the receiver so that I could speak to the man, whose name I have forgotten. I told him that while I was not holding a stick, everything else Mr. Thomas had said was perfectly true, and that he had to fix the meat grinder that very day and bring it to the camp. I cannot recall whether he brought it that day or the next, but I do remember seeing it before I left.

On the evening of the Seder, Rabbi Solnick was with us; the rabbinate had sent him. He wasn't the type to fawn and grovel before the prison director and the guards. The Seder itself was quite successful, and its success was heightened by my forthcoming release. The table had been beautifully set, and everyone was in a good mood. I couldn't help remembering the first Seder I had attended in Bethlehem in 1942, and comparing them.

The Seder in 1942 was gloomy and unsuccessful. For some reason we hadn't received all the supplies we needed—no matzot, no wine, and no bitter herbs (although we had enough bitterness)—and we had to make do with a package of candy brought by Dr. Yunichman to one of the detainees; it served to replace all the missing items. In addition to our sorrow at the holiday's being ruined, there was the mocking look in the guards' eyes, which seemed to say that everyone had forgotten us. Nevertheless we were in good spirits, we told jokes, and

Gertel Herzl (she was related to Theodor Herzl) and Miriam Shuchman made us laugh with their awful Viennese Hebrew.

This time, however, nothing was missing, and after the service and the meal we sang and danced. I could not really participate in the festivities, because I knew that I was leaving so many friends behind, despite the fact that lately I had been nothing but a burden to them, unable to work because of my illness, which forced other women to work in my place.

We spent the next day praying and again ate a festive meal, and before Rabbi Solnick left he said that the paradox was that we wanted to leave, whereas he wanted to stay. It was easy to understand. A collection of such liberated and independent women would have been hard to find in the freedom outside the prison walls.

That night we couldn't fall asleep. We stayed awake for a long time, talking about the future. We built castles in the air and knocked them down, and talked about what we thought we would do once we were free and then changed our minds, and discussed everything under the sun. I can still remember how we talked about the homeland, about freedom and independence, and how far away they still were. We talked about meeting in ten years for a picnic on the grounds of the prison in Bethlehem. Perhaps someday we may still do it.

In the morning we began to pack my private belongings, books I had been sent from the outside or given to me with special dedications, all kinds of things—three suitcases full of gifts. I took almost nothing else with me. I didn't have much, but what I did have I left behind. While we were packing Yocheved Gargi was called to the office. A few minutes later she returned bursting with the news that she, too, was going home.

The surprise was so great that all the women crowded around her, leaving me alone with my suitcases. Fortunately we had almost finished packing, and I too could go to congratulate her. She immediately became the center of attention, and everyone wanted to help her, especially the other women from

Jerusalem. We had to hurry because we had been told that Sonia was to be taken to a doctor in Jerusalem, so we would all go straight there in the CID car.

Thus we were all ready when the car came, and in order to make a good impression, Mr. Thomas had the guards help me with my suitcases. They had already helped me once before, but that time they had been willing and I had been unwilling, and now they were bitter about having to act as my servants. I, however, was perfectly happy about it, especially as it was most unpleasant for one guard who was particularly anti-Jewish.

The policemen were very gracious and helped us put the suitcases into the car. But they reached the heights of thoughtfulness and consideration when we passed the Tomb of Rachel and asked them to stop so we could pray, giving thanks to God for our release and praying for the release of the other detainees. They granted our request but wouldn't let Sonia out because she was still a detainee. Yocheved and I got out of the car, lit candles near the Tomb, and prayed. When we returned to the car, one of the policemen asked if we had merely prayed, or cursed as well.

We arrived in Jerusalem and from there went straight to Tel Aviv. A few relatives were waiting for me. They knew that I was due to be released but didn't know on which day. My mother was not in Tel Aviv, she had gone to my sister for the holiday, so I went directly to my brother's house. My ex-husband and son were also not in Tel Aviv. I sent a message that I had arrived and a short while later they came. We were all very excited and emotional. By that time my son was nine years old, and my ex-husband had just returned from the POW camp. This was a special time for us, because Aryeh and I had decided to remarry, and we knew that now we were going back to being a family.

✳ ✳ ✳ ✳ ✳ ✳

Chapter Twenty-One

Going "Home"

As soon as the Irgun declared war on the British, I knew that I had to be ready to go "home" at all times, that is to say, to prison.

My first two releases were the result of pressure put on the authorities to fulfill promises made by Catling and Giles, the heads of the CID. My first release (from the prison in Jaffa) came after negotiations at the end of 1941 because of Widenfeld's kidnapping, and my second release only came after long months of negotiations. Having spent almost two years under house arrest, I knew that the CID would be only too happy to send me back to Bethlehem at the first opportunity.

And that opportunity soon presented itself. After an uneasy ceasefire which lasted from 1940 to 1944, the war we had been preparing for so long broke out. During that period the Irgun had been closing ranks in the wake of a split with the Lehi and training its fighters for battle. Any money collected was earmarked for officers' training courses. Some of it went for the purchase of weapons, but usually we got our weapons from the British storerooms for free.

One day I learned that Esther Raziel and her husband, Yehuda Naor, had been arrested. I knew that her elderly parents had been left to take care of their two small children, one almost three and the other barely eighteen months old. It was dangerous to go anywhere near Esther's house because the CID took note of anyone entering or leaving, but I had nothing to lose, or at most a few days of freedom. The risk was worthwhile, especially if it meant contacting old people who had suddenly found themselves alone. In addition, I was an expert when it came to the ins and outs of the Jaffa prison, and that would make things much easier for Esther and her parents.

I went to her house, did what I could for the children, and made up a couple of packages containing everything Esther would need, including food. A few days later Grunia Kimchi, who had brought me food when I was in the Jaffa prison, told me that they were going to send Esther to Bethlehem. I called a taxi and took Esther's parents to Jaffa, and exploiting all my connections in the prison, I tried to arrange a meeting between them, because there were no visiting facilities there. Fortunately I was successful. On the way back, Esther's mother told me that it all seemed like a bad dream, an old wound being reopened: first their son, David, had fallen trying to protect the homeland, and now Esther and Yehuda had been taken away, and who knew for how long?

Esther's parents were strong in the face of their suffering and pain. During that time several underground operations were launched, and when I was late coming to their house, something I did every day, her father's first question was invariably whether the operation had been successful and everyone had returned safely. He was also worried about me, because it was obvious to him that my position as a free citizen was temporary at best, and that every day I remained out of prison was a miracle.

Another thing that gave witness to their bravery and heroism was the following incident: One day, while I was visiting them, someone knocked on the door. I went to the door and through the peephole saw Menachem Begin. I told Mrs. Raziel that someone had come to see her and went into another room. Despite the danger involved, he had come to see how the family was making out after the children's arrest. When he came into the living room, he asked if there was anyone else in the house, and hearing that I was in the next room, said that I should join them.

It was a difficult and complicated problem. The Irgun had decided not to deal with individuals, since that might lead to discrimination against the Lehi fighters, who were not members of the movement. Now that Esther (who was pregnant) had been arrested along with her husband, two small children who had to be cared for were left. The question was whether or not to make this case an exception. The answer of Esther's parents was an unequivocal no. Their children would be treated like everyone else.

Every day brought news, mostly about arrests. It was like a tree from whose branches fruit was being picked.

The British believed that every arrest weakened the underground, and as a matter of fact, we feared that they were right. But that's not what happened. Every time someone was taken, his or her place was quickly filled by a new recruit, just as when living tissue is injured and repairs itself so that the organism may continue to function. Thus the arrests did no real harm to the Irgun.

One day, as I was walking along Herzl Street in the heart of Tel Aviv, I met a friend who told me about some "funny" arrests. It was ridiculous the way the CID's intelligence service failed, and they arrested people who had never been active in the underground. After speaking to him I went to the police station where I had to report every day. Usually I stopped at my mother's on the way and said hello to her, and sometimes I left things there, but for some reason this time I went straight to the police station. I was to pay for this oversight by having to set out on a long journey without being able to say goodbye to her.

I was used to walking into the station house, signing my name, and leaving. It was only when I had something that I wanted to leave in the police station, such as some Irgun fliers, that I would pass through the gate in the railing as though I were looking for someone, go into the next room, leave whatever I had in one of the drawers, and continue on my way. This time I had nothing to leave and no reason or desire to pass through the railing, but the CID had other plans. They decided that I myself was illegal material, body and soul. When I tried to sign my name as usual and leave, the sergeant on duty told me to cross over to the other side.

No explanation was necessary. Automatically I tried to back out and leave so that I could run and say goodbye to my mother, but I never got the chance. Several British policemen appeared. Having no choice, I went in. Once I was left alone with some Jewish policemen, I begged them to go to my mother with a list of the things I needed. Taking advantage of the fact that I had not yet been searched, I destroyed certain documents in my purse which I thought best not to let fall into CID hands.

It was noon, and most of the policemen were not on duty. Some of them were on the top floor of the building, where there was a kind of lounge. One of them went upstairs to look for someone who could go to my mother. It was hard for me to overcome my feelings of thanks and relief at that moment when I saw how willing the police were to help a "terrorist." I only regret that I cannot remember the policeman's name. This incident, by the way, was to repeat itself.

An officer with three stars on his epaulets told me yet again what a danger I was to the British Empire. When I had come to sign in, one officer said to another, "What do you want from this young lady? She has been coming here day in day out for years," to which the second officer replied in English, "Of course, she's dangerous to the British Empire." I blushed at hearing such a compliment from an officer. Laughing, I saluted and thanked them.

Again I was taken to the police station on Yehuda Halevi Street. The name "Yehuda Halevi"[50] had lost its original meaning for me and had become a synonym for "train station" on the way to Bethlehem. Unconsciously I made an association with the words of the poet for whom the street was named: "Zion, surely thou wilt ask after your prisoners . . ." I sat there for about two hours, and then it was "home" again, to the Jaffa prison.

I was happy that I was the only one there and no one else had been arrested, because it meant that in general the mass arrests had stopped. I entered the prison like a tenant returning home after an absence. I went back to my old cell, but I had been demoted; I was no longer "very dangerous," and was not permitted a room to myself. My cellmates were women who were real or suspected underground fighters. There I met Sonia Rakuzin and Dinah Markoshwitz. This was my first meting with Sonia; she was suspected of belonging to the Lehi.

In the meantime one of my food parcels arrived and it made everyone very happy, since no one on the outside was responsible for these women and they had no food. I had both my own family and my ideological family, the Irgun. When I received the package I realized that yet another family was worried about me: the Raziels, parents and children.

The room looked like a campsite on a field trip of some kind. As we did on field trips, we both ate and slept on the floor, but this was one trip not destined to end after a day or two. In case we forgot, the presence of the guard in the corridor reminded us, because if we forgot for a minute where we were and wanted to wash a dish or get some water, we had to ask the guard to unlock the door, and if it was evening, we had to wait until the next morning. We had no clock, and officially no writing materials, although I had managed to smuggle some in——there is no substitute for experience.

---

[50]Yehuda Halevi a Jewish poet and philosopher who lived in Spain in the eleventh century.

From outside we could hear the waves breaking, and it seemed as though they were breaking against the walls of the prison, trying to penetrate. It sounded to us like the muffled sobbing of invisible mothers: mine, Esther's, and all the other mothers whose only protest was their tears, and the prayer in their hearts that the sacrifice would be acceptable, and not in vain.

Once again the call of the muezzin cut the air, coming from the minaret of the mosque across the way, its monotone cadences enough to drive us mad. It was like the proverbial Chinese water torture. I often thought that the Arabs had to be patient and phlegmatic to be able to bear the call, and I suppose they are, but only when they pray. The muezzin finally finished, and the sudden silence was deathly. Only the sea kept sending waves to break on the shore, and they never stopped their assault on the land.

It was not the first time I'd had such thoughts, all those things had occurred to me during my first "visit," and I waited anxiously to fall into the arms of Morpheus. Suddenly I heard a bell, one of those sounds that never brought good news. At home when a bell rang it meant guests, but here it meant new prisoners. Who was the unfortunate woman who had been brought here at such an hour?

It seemed to take the guard an endless amount of time to return. Everything was dark, and only a faint light filtered in through a barred window set high in the wall. We could hear the door creak and then the faint sound of footsteps echoing on the stairs. The old guard was dragging herself along. But for heaven's sake, they hadn't brought an old woman, why were the guest's footsteps so faint?

The light in the corridor went on, and the door to our cell opened. Exhausted and barely able to walk, a very young, dark-skinned girl with two long, black braids came into our cell. I made room for her on the *burshes*; no one was going to get her a clean one of her own at that hour. It also seemed to me that she was badly in need of encouragement and warmth. I

invited her to lie down next to me. It didn't occur to me to ask
her name or why she had been arrested. I thought it would be
best if she rested until the morning and regained her strength,
but she had ideas of her own. She asked me what my name
was, and when I told her, she said, "Oh, that's good, that's very
good. I know who you are. I've heard about you."

I asked her if she lived in Tel Aviv, because I knew the Irgun
girls from the Tel Aviv area. She said that she did, and I immediately understood that she was a Lehi fighter. In the morning
I recognized her, she was Hayah's sister. I knew that they were
looking for Hayah, and the resemblance between them was
very strong.

We were able to continue talking quietly because the other
two were asleep. She told me that she had to speak to me without delay. That night she told me the story of her arrest, a horror story if ever there was one, punctuated continually by the
sound of the waves breaking, one after another . . .

"My name," she began, "is Tzipporah Weiss, at least that's
the name I was arrested under. They surrounded the house I
was living in with my boyfriend. He managed to escape. They
chased him, but I hope and believe that he got away from them.
They took me outside and arrested me there. It was a Lehi
house, and it had a storeroom for weapons. Members of the
Haganah betrayed us to the police. I was not interrogated, they
merely asked a few questions, but they behaved very rudely.
They will interrogate me tomorrow morning. Actually, I will
probably receive the death penalty, but that isn't what bothers
me. It breaks my heart to think of the quantities of arms they
captured and that a Lehi safe-house has been destroyed. Who
knows better than you how hard it is today to find a place to
`work' that is hidden from the eyes of the CID and the
Haganah informers and the Palmach.[51] It is so hard to work
under such conditions, and everything was lost all at once."

She was trembling with unhappiness over the success of the

---

[51]The Palmach was the fighting arm of the Haganah.

authorities and the informers, and she was so upset that she couldn't concentrate and think about the answers she would have to give at her interrogation the next day.

I tried to calm her and bring her back to reality; I also wanted to tell her how to behave and what to say to the CID. They had already captured the weapons, and no amount of midnight conversations in the Jaffa prison would get them back. I told her that she would not receive the death penalty, probably "only" life imprisonment, because women were not sentenced to death.

She was tired after her experiences and fell asleep. I, however, could not sleep and stayed awake thinking. "Oh, Lord of the universe," I thought, "how miserable is the world You created, and how miserable the creatures in it. This young girl, like others in the underground, risks her life with burning faith for an ideal, while others, who have no faith, are not content to stand by idly and do no damage, but sabotage the works of those who do act. Here is a girl who fell into enemy hands and she does not weep for her youth, which will end behind prison walls, but for a load of weapons and an underground safehouse! Protect us from the fratricidal hatred which drives men mad to the point at which they betray Hebrew weapons which were paid for with blood; weapons and fighters betrayed to an alien, oppressive regime."

I only managed to fall asleep as dawn was breaking.

zsipporah had many names, and she had to inform the Lehi under which one she had been arrested. I found a solution to her problem. I told her to write what was necessary on a small piece of paper; I would add a few words to Adah Stecklis, and she would make sure that the note was put into the right hands. The only problem was getting the note out of the prison. I knew that my mother would come to visit, and all she needed was the slightest hint to understand everything. She would not be searched by the prison guards, and they would not ask any questions, since I had excellent relations with them as a result of my previous arrests.

I took some strands of wool and wrapped them around the note until a small ball was formed. On my mother's next visit, I gave her the ball and said that I was knitting something and needed more yarn of the same shade, and that she could get it from "Aunt Annie." Mouthing the name "Adah" but not saying it aloud, I said that I needed it urgently, because I couldn't continue until I got it.

My mother understood everything, including how serious the situation was. This was my first experience with sending illegal mail. When my mother left the prison she went directly to the National Health Fund, where Adah worked, and gave her the ball of wool, and that same day the note reached its destination (it took some time before we found out, however).

They called Tzipporah in for an interrogation and it proceeded along the lines I had expected it would. When she returned to the prison, she was less upset than she had been the previous night; the shock had passed. She knew for a certainty that her boyfriend, Joshua Cohen, had not been arrested and that his identity was not known to the CID. Thanks to the Haganah he was arrested, but that was only to happen later, and they hadn't asked her any questions about him at all.

We were in the Jaffa prison for several days, and this time as well we weren't spared the mentally ill. There was one poor woman who had lost her son in the war and had never recovered from the trauma. She was very clean but nervous and overexcited, and made a lot of noise. We took her into our room; she ate with us, and at night we watched over her lest she have an attack. The other two women had made contact with people on the outside who sent them packages of food and personal items, so they lacked nothing material. Despite the fact that visits were forbidden, I met unofficially with my mother and son.

Then we were moved to Bethlehem. This time the journey was more pleasant than it had been on previous occasions because I had company. A policewoman named Rebecca Sidney was our guard, and I knew she could be trusted. I decided to check again the belongings which had been returned to me when I left the prison in Jaffa, and I gave her all kinds of documents which might be useful and told her to pass them on to my mother, and so she did.

This time we didn't stop at the prison in Jerusalem, because there were no other prisoners with us, and we went directly to Bethlehem.

Through the slits in the sides of the *zinzaneh* I could see people in the streets, and I thought about how strange and cruel life could be. Inside this closed, stifling vehicle sat four young women whose only crime was wanting freedom for their people. We would have to spend our time behind bars, while there, on the streets, were people who couldn't stomach the thought of freedom and betrayed the fighters, and as their prize they received: freedom! But I was not jealous, for I compared ourselves, the underground fighters, to a tree planted near a sure source of water, knowing that it would bear fruit when the time came, and that every leaf would thrive and flourish. The informers were like a Christmas tree, decked out for the holiday and with people dancing and singing around it, but only for one evening, and when it withered and died, our tree would still be standing.

People were running to catch buses before they left the station, to get tickets to the cinema, running every which way with the motto "Eat, drink, and be merry" on their lips. But among all those frantic people it was possible to discern a young man with glasses walking along slowly, and a few steps before him a young woman carrying a suitcase or a package, walking as though nothing in the world concerned them. They were deliberately acting, disguised not only on Purim but all year long to fool any spy or traitor who might be looking. The line at the cinema might be their meeting place. They might enter the theater, but I doubted if they could tell anyone the plot of the film. For them the show began when the film ended and they left the theater. They could be seen through the slits in the *zinzaneh*, and my heart filled with envy because they could continue their activities while my freedom had been taken from me. I could only say a silent prayer that those brave young men and women would succeed, so that the people of Israel might rise and flourish.

The *zinzaneh* reached the Jaffa Gate of Jerusalem, and we sent our prayers and looked with longing at the Wailing Wall. Only a few months before I had used my visit to Jerusalem to go to the Wall and add my tears and prayers to those already sent to the God of Israel, that He might hear our voice and have mercy on us, bringing redemption to the people of Israel so that we could build His house in Jerusalem, and again I repeated the prayer.

I knew the road from the other times I had been sent to Bethlehem: Allenby Camp, the governor's mansion (on whose rule we had declared war to the death), and then the Tomb of Rachel. "Rachel wept for her children," but tears alone were not enough. It was our war, mixed with tears, that would bring redemption to Israel.

A sharp turn left, a drive uphill, and we were "home" again, this time the prison in Bethlehem. We got out of the van and saw that a heavy guard had escorted us all the way. As usual the bell by the great black door rang for a long time. Revolutionary things had happened in the world, but here nothing had changed. The expression on the guard's face changed dramatically when she saw who had arrived. I laughed and went in first, like a guide eager to show the new women the way, but they separated us on the spot. Tzipporah stayed in the prison building because she was going to be tried, whereas I went to the villa, that is to say, to the detention camp.

The search was easier this time. Tzipporah had no packages or baggage with her, except for her emotional and intellectual baggage, but that could be neither examined nor taken from her. The search performed on me was superficial; I got along well with the guards. The other two underwent baptism by fire and were subjected to the humiliating search I had first been subjected to, but I had prepared them for it on the way, so at least it didn't catch them by surprise. I said goodbye to Tzipporah, who asked me to say hello to the other women. We saw some of the convicted women in the prison building and spoke to them briefly, and then went to the camp.

A surprise was waiting for me there. I knew that the women had moved to a camp near the prison, but I wasn't familiar with it.

Again a bell was rung, and again the guard was amazed to see me. My heart began to beat with excitement when I thought about meeting the women I had been in prison with. It was ironic that instead of meeting Esther as I usually did, outside at work, I was going to meet her here. For some reason the women did not climb up on the window sills when they heard the bell ring and the great key grating in the lock. They were sitting in Esther's room listening to her read a letter from her parents, to which I had added a few words, although I hadn't signed my name because I knew it was unnecessary.

When we entered the room, all the women fell upon us, about twenty of them, and began to hug us. I introduced them to the new women, while Esther held the letter, excited and smiling from ear to ear. "I was just reading your letter," she said, "and I told them what a diplomat you were, writing a letter without signing your name, and at the very same moment you yourself appear. What a diplomat! That's no way to behave!"

I hadn't even taken one step forward and Miriam Shuchman came running up to me, her hair wet, saying "Tzila, it's good you came, do you have a towel?" Julie said, "They caught you again and sent you back to the cage with us." Bella Schechter and Frieda shook my hand like old friends.

Miriam exploited the fact that I had come "just in time" and took the towel from my suitcase. I went straight to Esther's room and marveled at the nice airy rooms, which were like paradise compared to the prison. I told Julie that Tzipporah (whose real name was Necha Israeli) had been arrested. I gave special regards to Leah Oshrov, who hadn't been known as a

Lehi fighter till then; Tzipporah had been Leah's commander. Chubby Nellie made the effort to come up from the basement to say hello to me, smiling her special smile. She looked so good-hearted and charming, so different from the rebellious terrorist she was supposed to be. Tovah was sick in bed and I went in to say hello. Some of the old hands had been released and new faces had replaced them; most of the new women came from Haifa.

Now I learned the meaning of the proverb about casting one's bread upon the waters. While on the outside I had sent supplies to the women in Bethlehem, especially for the holidays. Since I had been arrested just after Passover, there was a wealth of goods at the camp. I recognized the wine glasses I had sent and the other things which seemed to pave my way back. I hadn't bought them with my own money, but with money from the Tel Hai Fund and from the Irgun, but it was I who had, with Adah, made the purchases and mailed them.

I was assigned one of the rooms in the basement because there was no space anywhere else. We didn't want to put any more beds on the second floor as long as there was room downstairs. Going to the basement was a terrible mistake, because it was not fit for human habitation. I was included in the work schedule right away, and everything went so smoothly that it was hard to believe I had ever been away. The guards couldn't understand how I could be there again, and they expressed their surprise by cursing the government and the cruelties of life, and the injustice done to a poor wretch like me.

The next day the bell rang, heralding the arrival of another guest: Shoshanah Raziel.[52] This depressed us no end, Esther especially. One of her eyes was bandaged, and we knew that her health was bad. Esther knew how worried her parents would be. They worried about her all the time and had faith

---

[52]She was the widow of David Raziel, commander of the Irgun, who had been killed in the line of duty while helping to overthrow the pro-Nazi government in Iraq.

that the authorities wouldn't arrest her because of her ill health. However, nothing could stop the CID, not even the memory of David Raziel, who had fought side by side with them against their common enemy, the Nazis.

The mood passed. Shoshanah became well integrated into camp life and was assigned to Esther's room. Since she was a patient of Dr. Ticho's, an effort was made by people on the outside to make sure that she could continue being treated by him. She used to go to Jerusalem from time to time for appointments.

I didn't let the opportunity go by, and since I had a small growth in a corner of one eye I decided to annoy them by threatening that I might go blind. It was a brilliant idea, given to me by one of the detainees, and I exploited it to the hilt. The prison authorities permitted me to join Shoshanah on her trips to Jerusalem, and thus several times I got to see how life flowed along in the big city, since as far as life in Bethlehem was concerned, we might as well have been on Mars.

Once, when we returned from a doctor's appointment escorted by high-ranking officers and a heavy guard, we passed by the Jewish Agency building. As we did, one of the officers turned to us and said that we would do better to put our bombs there, because they were the ones who had betrayed us. Naturally we told him that we didn't plant bombs anywhere, but it pained us deeply to hear such a thing coming from him, and we knew that what he was saying was true.

On another occasion we were having a conversation with the officers, and one of them couldn't resist saying, "If I do something wrong, you can tell your Irgun to kill me." We told him that we neither gave nor received orders and did not kill people, but it showed us how much they and other officers like them feared us.

Chapter Twenty-Two

The Criminal Always Returns
to the Scene of the Crime

On July 21, 1946, about a month after I was released, I went to see a doctor in Jerusalem. It was a Friday, and I decided to stay there for the weekend. I had been invited to the home of Shoshanah Raziel, and there I met Bilhah Hermoni. The three of us decided to go to the Western Wall, of course. When we got to the Jaffa Gate we saw the bus-stop for Bethlehem, and we saw that the first melons had appeared on the market. We thought it would be a good idea to buy some melons and take them to the prisoners and detainees in Bethlehem. We got on the bus and decided not to get off at the gate, which is where the bus stopped, but to continue and go all around the camp, that is to say, the Villa Salem, which lay to the north of the prison, so that we could wave to the women, and only after that go to the main gate to deliver the melons.

We were certain we wouldn't arouse the suspicions of the guards on the roof, because who would be able to identify us as Jewish women or as former inmates of the prison? Unfortunately we didn't know the way, and when we got off the bus we began to walk around without knowing where we were going. The guards saw a group of women wandering about near the prison and the camp with packages in their hands, and we had forgotten that only a few days previously British officers had been kidnapped in Jerusalem.

We were still trying to find our way either to the main gate or to the road when Shoshanah told me that Jemila was calling us. I replied that I wasn't a prisoner and Jemila wasn't my guard and I didn't have to come running when she called. At the same moment I noticed a path which would lead us to the road. I called out that I had found a way, and had barely finished the sentence when I saw Mr. Thomas walking toward us with a gun in his hand. It was only two days after the kidnapping and that is why he was armed, because otherwise he never would have had a gun.

Mr. Thomas was as white as a sheet. He ordered us to go with him, because we were trespassing and it was illegal for us to be where we were. I demanded that he put the gun away and precede us; only then would we agree to accompany him. I followed him along the same path I had intended to take a few moments before. We entered the prison and he went to his office. Shoshanah asked to be allowed to call home to let her family know where she was. He refused, and when I asked to speak to him, he refused again. He didn't know Bilhah at all, because she had always been a quiet person and he had never even noticed when she had been released.

Shoshanah and Bilhah weren't familiar with the prison at all because they had only been in the villa, but I was an old hand. We were put into a small dark room which was usually reserved for convicted criminals. In the rooms which had previously housed detainees, there were now four Lehi fighters who had been captured during an operation at some small workshops in Haifa and had been brought to the prison a few days earlier. It was interesting that only shortly before this arrest, one of Frieda's relatives (she was one of the four) had come to me to ask me to help him contact her, because she had been wounded and was in the hospital. I told him that if she was in Jerusalem I could do something, but there was nothing I could do in Haifa. He explained that he himself could not act openly because he was afraid of being arrested, but he wanted to send her certain things and to know how she was.

Strange are the ways of the world, for I was fated to be arrested and to meet Frieda in prison, who in the meantime had been brought there. I didn't know she was there, but I did know about Malcah Grenyevich and Esther Beckman because they were Irgun fighters and I had once been their commander. Hassiah Shapira and Tzipporah Weiss Serulowitz Cohen (Necha Israeli), with whom I had been in the Jaffa prison, were also there.

When we arrived at the prison the women were already in their rooms. We waited till morning, climbed up to the small grille set in the door, and called to them. Tzipporah and the others were startled and ran to the door, and through the cracks we told them what had happened. When I asked about Frieda, they told me that she was there. A sweet-looking blonde girl smiled at me and said, "I'm Frieda, what can I do for you?" I gave her regards from her relative and asked what she wanted me to tell him, because in all innocence I thought we would be going home the next day. All the woman came close to the door to see us, and we all laughed at the situation which had led to our being arrested.

The only thing that worried us was Shoshanah's family, for as far as Bilhah and I were concerned, our families knew we were in Jerusalem, but Shoshanah had left home without telling anyone where she was going and hadn't returned. We decided to rebel.

First of all, we wouldn't go up onto the roof. Besides the fact that we were protesting we had another reason. The detainees in the villa used to stand at their window when the hour for exercise on the roof came around and count the number of prisoners and identify them. Seeing three more on the roof would only make them unhappy, and we wanted to avoid that at all costs.

Second, we would refuse to accept food. We would demand to be released, since walking around Bethlehem was not a crime and therefore there had been no reason to arrest us. Incidentally, the guards at the villa and the prison had trained their rifles on us, and the detainees in the villa had noticed but without knowing why.

It was 8:30 in the morning. The doors were unlocked and the prisoners ran to the bathroom, because after that they would be locked in again until they were taken up to the roof between ten and eleven. In the meantime there was no sign of Mr. Thomas, and no guard came to tell us that we were to be released.

Fortunately I was familiar with the building, and I knew that knocking on the door made an awful racket due to the space between the door itself and the bolt which locked it from the outside. We began banging on the door, and when the noise was loud enough a guard appeared. She wanted to know what we wanted, and we told her that we had to talk to Mr. Thomas and only to Mr. Thomas.

The other guards were very surprised to find us in prison again when they came to work that morning.

We banged on the door until a furious Mr. Thomas opened it and literally threw himself into the room. What was going on, he wanted to know, what was this, a kindergarten, a bunch of hooligans, what was all the noise?

No, we said, the hooliganism was in arresting us in the first place, when all we were doing was going for a walk around Bethlehem. We wanted to go home.

He raised his voice and so did I, and in an instant what had been a semi-polite conversation became a shouting match. All of a sudden he stopped and asked me why I was shouting. I asked him why *he* was shouting.

He told us to sit down and started to leave the room. I said, "Listen, Mr. Thomas, yesterday you didn't want to speak to me, and now I am telling you, you are responsible for our incarceration, not the CID, as you told us yesterday. You arrested us and you will release us."

He began to argue with me again, and asked what we were doing in Bethlehem, especially what I was doing in Bethlehem, since I had been forbidden to leave Tel Aviv as a result of my house arrest. I said that I had received permission to go to a doctor in Jerusalem.

"Jerusalem," said Mr. Thomas, "is not Bethlehem."

I said that they were in the same region, and he said that they were not, not at all.

"Perhaps you have forgotten," I reminded him, "but every time I complained that there wasn't enough water, you would tell me that there wasn't enough water in Jerusalem either, and that it was the same area. If it was the same area then, it's the same area now."

He mumbled something and then began to shout at me again: "You always argued with me about regulations and were quite an expert, and now all of a sudden you don't know that the area around the prison is restricted." I said that I did know the regulations, and I knew that our arrest was illegal and that he had to release us at once. He said that the matter had been turned over to the CID and was no longer in his hands. I said that was fine and we wanted to see someone from the CID immediately.

Now I was treading on dangerous ground, because going to CID headquarters would mean riding on Saturday, otherwise we would have to stay where we were, and who knew for how long? We discussed it among ourselves and the three of us decided that it would be best to go today, even if it meant desecrating the Sabbath. We refused to back down and continued to demand to be taken to the CID, telling him that until then we would neither eat nor go up onto the roof, and if our incarceration continued we would continue banging on the door. We refused to give in, and the argument became heated and bitter. The other women tried to make out as much of our argument as they could from the other side of the door and later told us that they were very happy with the tongue-lashing we had given him.

Mr. Thomas left, and a short while later we were called into his office. Our property was returned to us, that is to say, our handbags and everything in them. He laughed pleasantly and asked us if everything was all right. We asked if he meant our purses, in which case the answer was yes, but if he meant our arrest, then the answer was no. CID officers were waiting for us and they took us to their headquarters in Jerusalem. It was not a pleasant sensation to be riding on Saturday, but we had no choice.

When we got to Jerusalem, Shoshanah went in first. I didn't have a chance to ask her anything because Bilhah was called as soon as Shoshanah came out, and she wanted me to go in with her to translate.

We went into the office together. Two officers whom I didn't know were waiting for us. Actually I didn't know anyone from the CID, because my only contacts with them were when I was interrogated in the prison before my release and when they escorted me to the hospital.

The interrogation began. I decided to pretend we were stupid and to turn everything into a joke. I told the officer the truth about the melons, explaining at length about how we couldn't find the road leading to the prison gate. After all, it was the first time we had gone there by ourselves. Every other time we had been brought right up to the gate in a closed car, and this time we had to tell the bus driver where to let us off and we simply made a mistake. We must have stayed on the bus for one stop too many, and then we got lost looking for the gate and wound up being arrested. I said that I had wanted to see what the prison looked like from the outside.

Once again we argued about the area, Jerusalem or Bethlehem, and once again I was told that I was forbidden to enter Bethlehem since I had only received authorization for Jerusalem, and I repeated everything I had said to Mr. Thomas. I asked, by the way, with whom I had the honor of speaking. The officer's face, which had worn a smile all through the interrogation, suddenly became serious, and he asked why I wanted to know. I said that it would make the conversation easier, but if he didn't want me to know who he was, I would simply call him "Sir."

The telephone rang, and without thinking he picked up the receiver and said, "Curtis here." I began to laugh, and I knew that he understood Hebrew. I also knew that Bilhah knew who he was, because he was involved in her efforts to free her husband, still exiled in Kenya. I said to her, in Hebrew, "Why was he afraid to tell me his name? The minute we got out of here you would have told me who he was." I deliberately spoke in Hebrew, knowing he would understand. Into the phone he said, "You certainly fouled things up. There is a woman sitting here who was very interested in knowing my name, and because of you, now she knows." He finished his phone conversation, turned to me, and said, "In fact, I should send you back to prison, but I think it would be better if you had your husband supervising you." My husband knew him well, because he had negotiated with him for my release. He told me that I needed my husband's supervision, but he had asked my husband what he needed someone like me for, I was sick and would never get well.

Bilhah told me that during the interrogation one of the officers was sitting behind us and kept laughing as I told the story of how we had gotten lost. So in the end it turned out that playing dumb was the right thing to do, and we went home none the worse for our experience.

✳ ✳ ✳ ✳ ✳ ✳

Chapter Twenty-Three

From Here to Egypt and Back Again

The population of the prison in Bethlehem was varied and intellectual. There were schoolteachers, kindergarten teachers, high school graduates, office workers, and more. It was a cross-section of Jewish youth at its finest, and only one element was missing: a native-born soldier fighting in the ranks of the Allies against Fascism, and eventually representatives of that group were sent too.

One day several soldiers were brought to the prison: Hassiah Luria and Yaffah Greenberg, who belonged to the Women's Army Auxiliary Corps, and a short time later, Adah Leibowitz and Ruth Grossberg from the Royal Air Force, who had gone to Egypt like the patriarch Jacob. They, however, had not gone looking for food in time of famine, but for weapons to smuggle to the underground army, which sorely needed them.

As the underground resistance movement grew and expanded even beyond the borders of Palestine, so did the activities of those who preferred to collaborate with the British and wanted to sabotage the war of liberation.

What brought Hassiah to Bethlehem? Hers is a long story, full of the bravery and glory of the men and women who smuggled "iron" into the country. It is a story of the sacrifices and risks taken by the soldiers from Palestine, who even in the heat of war knew that when the war with Fascism ended and they no longer had to fight for the physical survival of their people, there would be other battles to fight, and another war would begin, this one for resurrection and independence. Under their foreign uniforms beat true Hebrew hearts, and under the canvas covering the trucks of His Majesty's army, the weapons of deliverance were being smuggled in.

Egypt, the heart of the British fortress, served as the site of the Allied GHQ in the Middle East. It was there, in a hostile Arab country, that a center for smuggling weapons was established, headed by a young Jewish woman who took it upon herself to set up her activities in the lion's den. Her name was Lifsha Segal-Yankowitz, and according to her old CID file, she was "pretty, with braids."

In those days she was a young wife who had followed her husband to his home in Cairo. Before she got on the train which was to take her to Egypt, she gladly accepted the offer of being the secretary of the Irgun in Egypt.

A Jewish newspaperman who worked on the editorial board of *La Bourse Egyptienne* was a frequent visitor at her house. One day he told her about a secret meeting about to be held by a group of Communist students at El Azhar University, many of whom were Jewish. The Jewish reporter had been sent to cover the meeting, which would deal with the ways in which they could join the fight of the Arabs in Palestine who were actively opposed to the Yishuv. However, he was too busy to go and wanted Lifsha to replace him if possible and to infiltrate the meeting and then give him details at some later date.

The fact that she had come from Palestine opened the club's doors to her; it was on Kasr el-Nil Street in Cairo. She sat there for a long time, controlling herself as she listened to the recriminations and accusations spewed out by the students. A short blond young man stood up and was introduced as Jewish. Lifsha recognized him as a member of a family she knew well. He told the other students that the Jews in Palestine were well equipped with dangerous weapons and large amounts of money with which they were planning to deprive the Arabs of their land. "There has never been one case in history," he said, "in which land was bought with money and not blood. We have to sign a petition expressing our solidarity with the Palestinian Arabs and help them raise money for their holy war against the Jews."

His speech ended to thunderous applause, and Lifsha asked to take the floor. She agreed with the speaker, she said, for in her opinion money was not an appropriate means by which to express the ambitions of an ancient people which desired to return to its legal homeland. However, Lifsha's objective was to keep the Jewish students from signing the petition, and she said, "The same history has taught us that Jews will never be safe as long as they live among non-Jews." How, she wanted to know, could they add their names to a political document aimed against the last place of refuge for the Jewish people without first receiving assurance that their lives would be safe?

The next day she went to the Jewish quarter and at the branch office of Carmel Mizrachi told the workers what had happened at the meeting the previous evening. (The student was ambushed and beaten by people from the National Workers Party on his way home that same day.) From there she went to Rabbi Nahum Effendi, the Chief Rabbi of Cairo. He became very angry when he heard what she had to say, and invited all the Jewish students who had participated in the meeting to his home. In Lifsha's presence he said, "I am the only person authorized to sign a political statement in the name of the Jews of Egypt. Don't you dare sign any petition whatsoever!"

The students' petition was publicized during the bloody riots in 1936, but not one Jewish name appeared on it.

In September 1939 the Second World War broke out, and the British Red Cross asked for volunteers from the European population. Lifsha offered her services and received card number 000365, which identified her as a volunteer worker with the Middle East Forces. The first volunteers began streaming in from Palestine, and their numbers steadily increased. The British nurses and doctors in hospitals found that they had a common language. Lifsha was fluent in Hebrew, English, French, and Arabic, and she asked the hospital directors to prepare and update a list of everyone from Palestine who was admitted. The army cooperated with her and she quickly became a well-known figure; they called her the mother of the Jewish soldiers. She organized shipments of Hebrew newspapers, opened Hebrew-language libraries in the hospitals, and announced to one and all that her apartment on Novar Pasha Street was an open house where any Jewish soldier would be welcomed with open arms.

Dr. Aryeh Altman,[53] one of the leaders of the National Movement, arrived in Cairo early in 1942 and called all the Irgun fighters and members of the Revisionist Movement in the capital to Lifsha's house. He told them that it had been decided to outwardly separate the Irgun from the movement, and told Lifsha that from that day forth she would work for the Irgun and would no longer serve as secretary of the Cairo chapter of the movement. She became the link connecting the network of women workers in Egypt and the Irgun headquarters in Palestine.

The first thing she did to raise the morale of the Jews in Egypt was done on her own initiative and not at the suggestion of headquarters. During her routine visits to the hospitals she saw how the Jewish nurses from Palestine were discriminated against and humiliated by the British nurses, and she became extremely angry. The British Army Medical Corps, yielding to the pressure exerted by the English nurses, did not give the Jewish nurses regulation uniforms. Instead of white uniforms, nurse's caps, and shoes, they had to wear khaki uniforms and brown shoes with hob-nailed soles. Lifsha went to the matron, that is to say, the head nurse, and received the cynical answer that it was due to the fact that the war effort was so expensive

---

[53]Aryeh Altman (1902—1982) was active in the Revisionist movement in the United States and Palestine, and served as president of the Palestinian organization from 1936 to 1949.

for the British that they couldn't afford to dress all the nurses in white.

Next Lifsha went to Mrs. Widon, a member of Jewish Cairo's high society, and told her how the army was humiliating the Jewish nurses serving in British hospitals. Mrs. Widon, ever jealous of the respect due her people, promised to furnish the nurses with white uniforms out of her own pocket. Within a few days the matron received a shipment of 250 white uniforms, nurses' caps, and pairs of shoes.

There was a note accompanying the shipment, signed by Mrs. Widon for the Egyptian Women's Association for Jewish Soldiers, and it informed the commander of the Nurses' Corps that they "were happy to help Great Britain finance the war." That same day 250 Jewish nurses took off their khaki uniforms and donned white ones.

At that time there were five hundred Irgun fighters spread throughout the Middle East. They were organized, in accordance with the structure of the Irgun, in squadrons and companies, each with its own commander. They arrived on every train out of Palestine for Cairo and were sent to stay in hotels, and a smuggling network was secretly set up. Hundreds of members of the Revisionist Movement serving in the British army cooperated with them, and the focus of all these activities was a small woman with failing eyesight who, at the end of every day working in the hospital, stood behind the counter at the Jewish Soldiers' Club.

Jewish soldiers who were off duty in Cairo used to go to the Club for something to eat or drink. When they went to pay Lifsha, who was sitting at the cash register, in addition to their checks they would secretly give her packages of pay books that had been "extracted" from the desks of paymasters in various army units. Lifsha would fill out the pay books with particulars copied from a list of names of soldiers and officers which had been "borrowed" from the offices of Army Intelligence. Soldiers going home to Palestine on leave would take the filled-in pay books, and these would return to Egypt deep in the pockets of Irgun fighters disguised as British soldiers.

Lifsha went from one Jewish store to the next and discovered that many of the merchants were more than sympathetic. They wanted to help even if it meant endangering themselves, and readily agreed to open their storerooms to the network of Irgun smugglers.

She gave the addresses of these storerooms to the men of the various units, and vast quantities of weapons—machine guns, submachine guns, rifles, pistols, hand grenades, ammunition—began to flow from the army stores into Irgun depots on Cairo's main commercial streets. Lifsha organized the paperwork and wrote out reports about how many weapons were to be found in each storeroom, made contacts, and coordinated the Irgun fighters disguised as British soldiers who were given home leave, making sure they took with them British arms intended to be used against the British themselves.

All the time the weapons were pouring into the storerooms of the Jewish merchants, Lifsha was also dealing with quantities of medical supplies, the need for which was increasingly felt by the resistance fighters in Palestine. She could come and go as she pleased in the hospitals, and there were crates of medicine open in front of her. She would take what she wanted and pass everything along to the messengers who brought the weapons to the depots. Before long she found a legal way of sending medical supplies to the Irgun commander in Palestine. From the offices of the Red Cross she took a thick pad of the consignment slips which accompanied shipments of medical equipment when they were sent to the units, and she wrote "A present from the British Red Cross to the Red Magen David in Palestine" on them; these too she would give to those going home on leave.

Lifsha was never interfered with until May 5, 1944, when a frightened Jewish merchant appeared at the Soldiers' Club and told her that when a shipment of arms had arrived that morning, he had gotten the impression that his store was under surveillance, and he begged her to have the arms removed while there was still time. He said that if the shipment was not removed within twenty-four hours, he himself would take it and throw it into the Nile.

Lifsha hurried off to look for some Irgun colleagues. She ran from one hotel to the next, knowing exactly where their rooms were, and as if fate were deliberately conspiring to make her angry, she couldn't find a single one. She went back to the club, still trying to decide how to solve the problem, when a young man came in, and having said hello, told her that the next day at dawn he would be going to Palestine. His name was Joseph, he was young and full of energy and had been born in the country, and was known to Lifsha as one of the Haganah contacts in Cairo. She made up her mind quickly, having faith in his having been sent by fate to help her out of the situation. She asked him to take the package of weapons and deliver it. He agreed, and Lifsha called a young uniformed woman over and introduced her to him as Hassiah Luria from Tel Aviv, instructing her to give the package to the man from the Haganah. A few days later he returned to Cairo and told Lifsha that she had nothing to worry about and the package had been delivered as planned.

October 26, 1944, was a fateful day for Lifsha. She got a telegram from Rishon le-Zion informing her that her father was ill and she had to come home. She did so, and that same day noticed two suspicious young men lurking around her house. As she left the next morning she was surprised to discover that they were following her.

It took her a whole day to lose them. Then she kept a scheduled secret meeting with Jacob Meridor.[54] When she told him

---

[54]Jacob Meridor (1913—1994) became temporary commander of the Irgun in 1941 after the death of David Raziel. When Menachem Begin became commander in 1943, he served as his deputy and was in charge of military operations.

about being followed he said that it was no wonder, since she had a thick file at the CID.

After her father regained his health, Lifsha went to the CID to ask for an exit visa. She left her passport with the clerk and waited in vain for six weeks. The CID officer to whom she complained about the delay invited her to sit down. He opened a file containing dozens of original documents, some of them handwritten and some of them typed. He was very polite, but stressed that the file was full of material about her activities in Cairo and contained a detailed description of everything she had done since her return to Palestine. He wanted to know if she knew a female soldier named Hassiah Luria. The connection between the Haganah man in Cairo and the CID's sudden interest in her became only too obvious.

The British officer promised to let Lifsha return to Cairo, and the next day a motorcycle officer arrived at her father's home to deliver her passport, stamped with the required exit visa.

At the gates of the city of Gaza the train suddenly stopped and plainclothes policemen got aboard, striding down the aisle of the passenger car until they came to Lifsha. They searched her baggage for a long time, and not finding anything, allowed the train to continue on its way.

On March 23, 1945, Eliyahu Hakim and Eliyahu Beit Zoori, two Lehi fighters, were hanged for having assassinated Lord Moyne.[55] A Cairo resident named Sadovsky, ignoring the security rules, laid flowers on their graves. A company of riflemen, who were guarding the grave lest someone try to remove the bodies to Palestine, saw him, arrested him, and left him to the tender mercies of the CID. When they searched his apartment they found among his belongings an old list of names of Revisionist Movement activists, and among them the name of Lifsha Yankowitz, the movement's secretary in Egypt. In the

---

[55]Lord Moyne (1880—1944), anti-Zionist and anti-Semitic, was Britain's Resident Minister in the Middle East from 1942 to 1944. The two men who killed him were Lehi operatives.

middle of the night on April 11, 1945, the doorbell rang at the Yankowitz house. The part played by Lifsha Segal from Rishon le-Zion in the Yishuv's struggle for liberation from a foreign power came to an abrupt end in cell number 3 in Cairo's Bab el Hadir prison.

This was the story of a modern-day flight from Egypt, as told to us in the women's prison in Bethlehem by detainees who had arrived from Egypt.

Chapter Twenty-Four

On the Altars of the Enemy

The prisoners in Bethlehem fought bravely on the front before they were arrested, and continued to fight even after they had fallen hostage. Like their male counterparts, they knew how to turn a courtroom into a battlefield on which to attack the enemy, never letting them forget that they had betrayed the trust given them by the League of Nations. Instead of defending themselves they attacked, and made the representatives of British "justice" listen to their accusations.

Some of the speeches of the Lehi fighters were published in the book *Unknown Soldiers*, by Jacob Banai. The speeches of some of Lehi's women fighters follow below.

BRACHAH BIRENBAUM

Your Honors, the war of the Hebrew youth against your rule in Palestine is a defensive war in the truest sense of the word. By force of arms you are trying to turn the homeland of the Jewish people into one of the countries of the Jewish exile, of the Diaspora. To put it another way, you want to sentence our people to generations of exile and slavery, the end of which will be our extinction, whereas we are trying to release our homeland from your oppressive hand and return it to the Jewish people forever. In fighting this war of liberation we are in fact defending our people. However, it cannot be denied that besides this definition of the word "defense," which for us is holy in itself, there is another, narrower one. For the twenty-five years of your rule here, pogroms have been organized by Arabs who were British agents. That is not a matter of opinion but of fact which has been certified not only by neutral sources but by British observers as well. The world is not the same naive place you knew it to be fifty years ago. What is in your opinion a stroke of genius and a total secret known only to a few high-ranking people is actually, in this era of radio broadcasts, known to the man in the street everywhere. Therefore, the time has come to ask the question: why did you initiate the attacks on the Jewish population, since after all is said and done, it is never pleasant for any government to have such events laid at its door? The restraint you have exercised toward the Arabs proves that your regime is not what you claim, a regime of freedom, justice, and democracy, and proof of that is your feverish activity against us, against the Jewish youth fighting you. You exiled three hundred Jews to a concentration camp in the Diaspora; how many Arabs did you exile after they rioted and slaughtered more than a thousand Jews? What punishment is exacted from Jews who carry weapons, what punishment from Arabs?

And in spite of everything you have done, you still do not rule over us. The duty you have, the duty of destroyers of the peace, going against all wisdom and logic, can only be explained in the task your government took upon itself when it took the rule of Palestine into its own hands: your government decided to put an end to the Yishuv here, and with that goal in mind decided to prove to the world that the process, which is without equal in its historical justification, is in fact unjust and has only met with the continued resistance of the local Arab population and entails endless bloodshed and, as the British commander and traitor Bulls said, "the humanitarian duty to defend the weak Arab from the aggressive Jew." Something had to be done, Jewish blood had to be spilled by murderers, mass pogroms had to be carried out, so that Malcolm

MacDonald[56] could go before the Mandates Commission of the League of Nations and say, with his well-known hypocrisy (and I quote): "Despite the fact that the Arab movement of rebellion has been disgraced by many murders committed by assassins of the worst sort, it is stamped with the undeniable imprint of widely based national patriotism."

Needless to say, it was not because of your great love for the Arabs and for their own good that you organized those "protests" by Arabs in all those countries of which you are the true rulers. The Arab population grows from year to year, while east of the Jordan River there is a famine. Yes, you certainly worry about the Arabs, and what you honestly think about them can be learned from Mr. Spicer's open-hearted proclamation, he who was Chief Inspector of the British Police in Palestine. When asked why he and his friends objected to the Jews, he answered that there were many reasons. He said it was easier to deal with the Arabs; when you told them to go home, they went home without making any trouble.

You need people who will serve you without argument.

One thing should be made clear to everyone: we have absolutely nothing against our Arab neighbors. We want to live peacefully with them. The Hebrew state will be their home as it will be ours. And I, as a representative of an extremist group, say this to you, because our patriotism, Your Honors, is not based on hatred of the non-Jew, but on brotherly love. First and foremost we are in favor of our own people and homeland, but we know the value of other peoples and cultures, and we are willing to be friends. The condition, of course, is that we receive friendship in return. We feel that way about every people, Arabs included.

---

[56]Malcolm MacDonald (1901—19??) was the British Colonial Secretary who issued the White Paper of 1939, which severely restricted Jewish immigration to Palestine as well as land transfers to Jews, and rejected the idea of a Jewish state. Appearing before the Permanent Mandates Commission, he denied that the White Paper was a violation of Britain's Mandate over Palestine.

I would like to conclude what I have to say. As I said at the beginning, the goal of Jewish youth is not self-defense against Arab attacks, nor is that what gives us the right and the duty to bear arms and to use them. We are the last generation of slaves and the first of redemption, and we came here not merely to live, but to bring about a renascence. We didn't come to protect ourselves but to bring our brothers here to live. Self-defense is not enough. If we find ourselves in a situation in which we are cut off from those of our people living beyond the borders of this country, it is our sworn duty to fight with all our strength to put an end to that crime, and if that isn't enough, defense against the rioters will be necessary and we won't forget that either as we stand accused of bearing arms. Jewish youth will carry weapons because it is our duty to defend our own lives and the lives of our brothers against rioters, as it is our duty to fight the oppressive regime which uses bloody riots as a political tool to achieve its own dark ends.

DEBORAH SHAPIRA

Your Honors, we know from history that women, to whom the spirit of war is utterly foreign, have actively participated in wars of liberation against oppression and enslavement, overthrowing the chains that bound their people and endangering themselves. We are anxious about the future of the next generation, and that anxiety commands us to go out and do battle. The very fact that in the dock sit both men and women accused of the same crime clearly proves that the war now being conducted in Palestine against your oppressive and treacherous regime carries within itself clear signs of the wars of liberation known to us from history. And if the example of us women, who are not afraid of your punishments and your prisons, causes thousands of youths to arise to a war of national liberation, I will always know that when we were being tested, the flame of love for my people burned and its light guided me.

DEBORAH KALFUSS
(captured in Bat Yam, tried in a military court in Jerusalem in 1946)

Gentlemen, after you sentenced two young Jews, Eshbal and Simchon, to death, they stood at attention and sang with an enthusiasm you will never understand. They sang our national anthem, "Hatikvah." The British radio in London reported it, as did others, when in a few short sentences they showed the world how without surrendering, proud Jewish fighters accepted their fate. I have no idea to what extent this influenced you, but I am sure that in these dark days of fearful cruelty you cannot deny that their conduct renewed every free man's faith in human nature, idealism, and morality.

It was not enough for the radio to merely broadcast the facts; slavishly following your political dictates they found it necessary to provide editorial comment, and included the announcement that "The two men who were sentenced to death sang a song in the courtroom called `the Jewish national anthem.'" Not simply the "Jewish anthem," but what you call "the so-called anthem."

I will explain why I want to speak about the radio announcer's deliberate choice of words, and what the connection between them and our trial is. Meanwhile, there is another fact I wish to bring to your attention, and while it is not officially connected to the trial, it is morally connected to it, or at least to the factors which brought it about. The fact was publicized in one of your government's official announcements: in the middle of the ocean a British destroyer—in accordance, apparently, with international piracy law—stopped a ship carrying Jewish immigrants, people being repatriated to their homeland in spite of everything you could do. When your naval officers boarded the ship they noticed the flag it was flying, the blue-and-white flag of the Hebrew nation. However, your officers reported—and the announcement was made public—that the ship was flying an "unknown flag."

These two facts are symbolic of the war between us, and they also explain, perhaps even more than anything we could say, the legal background for our mass trials. You, the British, refuse to recognize our anthem and our flag, and since there is no nation without an anthem and a flag, your position is clear: you don't recognize us as a nation. In other words, ideologically you identify with Adolf Hitler. He also said that Israel was not a nation, but merely a collection of subhumans, and his idea was to kill us all. You accept his theory, and during the war you helped him put his plan into action, and as for the eleven million Jews still left in Europe, who in your opinion have neither anthem nor flag, that is to say, who have no nation, you are fully prepared to make them line up for the extermination camps, the way you helped the Nazis with six million of their brothers.

That is your plan, and to implement it, or perhaps as a result of it, you took our country away from us, and now you want us to continue as Wandering Jews, stateless and with no flag or anthem, or rather with an "unknown flag" and a "so-called national anthem." In your evil, or perhaps in your stupidity, you assumed that we would bow our heads and prefer to live like slaves rather than go to war (even though war costs lives) to gather our people into our own country, where we could fly a flag recognized by all peoples everywhere as the flag of a free and independent nation. Your hopes were not to be realized, and the main reason was that, in the words of our anthem, our hope has not been lost. No, gentlemen, we have not lost hope.

If, after two thousand years of exile, the Jewish people still lives, our hope has not been lost. If after a generation of persecution and slaughter, humiliation and degeneration, we are still alive and have Jewish soldiers who are fighting an armed battle for the liberation of their homeland, our hope has not been lost.

If, after the nineteen hundred years which have passed since the suppression of the Bar Kochba revolt, we have lived to rebel anew, led by the sons of Judah excelling in bravery, our hope has not been lost.

If, after the terrible slaughter of six million Jews, the faith in the eternal future of Israel in its own country has not only not been weakened, but has been strengthened, our hope has not been lost.

If young men stand in the shadow of the gallows and sing our national anthem, our hope has not been lost.

Our hope has not been lost. . . . Do your hard-hearted, stupid rulers know what the song means to us? The Jewish *heart* has sung it for two thousand years; Jewish youth sing it as they go out to battle and when they return. Do you know who else sang those simple yet great words? I will tell you: our parents, brothers, and sisters sang "Hatikvah" as the Nazi butchers, murderers all, forced them into cattle cars. When the best of our people, our scholars, our old men, and our young children marched in line to the gas chambers, they sang "Hatikvah."

"To return to the land of our fathers" were the last words on the pale lips of millions of victims, they lifted their eyes "to the East" before they closed forever. And this song, this anthem which more than any other in the world has been sanctified by blood, you call the "so-called anthem"?

Know, then, gentlemen, that we, the children of Israel, will fight you until we have realized the hope of the millions who were slaughtered because you, with your partner Hitler, did not recognize our anthem and our flag, because you took our homeland from us. In this war of liberation our nation has been reborn, and we will force you to recognize us and our right to a homeland and to all the symbols of independence accepted in the civilized world. Whether you recognize our country willingly or unwillingly, that is your decision, but recognize us you shall. And when the day comes and we have correct relations with all the countries of the world, the captain will look at the ship passing his and see the flag and recognize it. When that day comes, and someone, near or far, hears the sad strains of

"Hatikvah," he will stand at attention and pay his respects to the anthem of an independent nation, as we, the soldiers of Israel, are willing to honor the anthems of other countries. That day will come, and we give our souls for it.

AMALIAH SANDER

(In September 1945, Amaliah Sander, age seventeen, and Judah Cohen, sixteen, were tried in a military court in Haifa for posting Irgun fliers on walls in the city.)

Your Honors, I admit that I wanted to hang the fliers, but I don't admit to being guilty of any crime. On the contrary, I am certain that I was only doing my duty. If the British were in my position, every one of them would do what I did, and with your blessing. Eretz Israel is my homeland, it is the homeland of the Jewish people. You conquered it and closed its gates. As a result, six million Jews were slaughtered, and thousands more are dying; they want to come here and you won't let them. That is an evil whose only precedent is the cruelty and atrocities of the Germans. Therefore, every Jew must fight against you. And every Jew will fight, even if you send us to your prisons and concentration camps. The motto of every young Jewish person is, "We will do it anyway!"

※ ※ ※ ※ ※ ※

Chapter Twenty-Five

The Home Front

One of the most touching and painful chapters of the war of liberation is that of the families of the detainees and prisoners, their parents, the wives and children who bore their burden with pride and bravery, living in the midst of people who were alien and indifferent, hostile, and rejoicing at someone else's misfortune.

Whenever a husband or a son or a daughter was arrested, the people who suffered the most were their families. The natural burdens of taking care of the children and supporting the family were increased by the stress and frustration involved in trying to effect the loved one's release. The ordinary routine of life was disrupted and turned into a long, hard battle whose end could not be predicted. The families stood firm, and sometimes managed to break through the walls of apathy and hatred.

Where did they find the moral and physical strength in those hopeless days? That was one of the secrets of the war of liberation. The expression "detainee's wife" turned into a nightmare for the officials of the institutions of the Yishuv in Palestine, and they dreaded the thought of a meeting with one of them. One way or another, the wives found out about every committee meeting or conference and made their way there, and the expression "The detainees's wives are coming!" turned into a kind of war cry, striking fear into the hearts of the assembled company.

Everything there is to say about the home front could not possibly fit into one chapter. A book could be written about the subject, and I hope it will be someday. I will only retell a few select episodes, as recounted to me by one of the wives.

One day a rumor spread that 251 detainees would be expelled from the country. As soon as they heard the news, the wives and mothers, without stopping to organize a demonstration, marched on the Tel Aviv city hall. A meeting of the local council was in progress, headed by the late mayor, Israel Rokach.[57] They interrupted the meeting, spoke to Rokach, and were promised that the council would act in the matter, but they weren't satisfied and decided to go to Jerusalem.

When they got there the invading force divided in half. One group went to the King David Hotel, the seat of Mr. Schultz the chief secretary of the government in Palestine, and the other to the offices of the National Council, which would eventually become the government of the State of Israel. Those who went to the British had a far easier time than those who went to the Jews. In the absence of the Secretary, the women were received by Mr. Scott and his two interpreters. He politely invited them to sit down and allowed them to voice their complaints. The embittered women protested strongly against the expulsion, and pointed out that the Bermuda Conference was currently in session to solve the refugee problem.[58] At the Conference it was being claimed that there were no funds available for transport-

---

[57] Israel Rokach (1896—1959), a leader of the General Zionist Party, was mayor of Tel Aviv from 1936 until 1947, when he was arrested and sent to Latrun. He subsequently resumed the mayoralty, and also served as Minister of the Interior and as Deputy Speaker of the Knesset.

[58] American and British diplomats met in Bermuda on April 19—30, 1943, to deal with the growing wartime refugee problem. Perhaps by

ing refugees, while at the same time, at the height of the war, the British government had managed to press thirteen planes into service for the purpose of exiling 251 men from their homeland. They demanded that the detainees be released from the prison in Bethlehem where they were being kept in subhuman conditions, and returned to the country, and that funds be allotted to support the families left without breadwinners. Mr. Scott listened patiently and said that he would write a memorandum.

The situation of the wives and mothers who went to the National Council was far different. They were not permitted to enter the building because at that time an "important" meeting was being held by members of the National Council and the Jewish Agency: Eliyahu Golomb was explaining how he thought the war against terror should be fought.[59] A clerk held the women back and promised that the National Council would receive them in a short time. It was obvious that this was a ploy to silence the women until the leaders finished the meeting and left. However, the trick was discovered and the women began shouting and forced their way into the building and ran up to the second floor. When they reached the conference room they found it empty, although smoke was still rising from the quickly extinguished cigarettes left in the ashtrays. The leaders had simply run away . . .

From that time onward a sentry was stationed at the National Council headquarters to protect the leaders from the wives and mothers of the exiles and detainees. Moreover, a special intelligence unit was set up at the Tel Aviv bus terminal to inform Jerusalem whenever a large group of women were on the way. It reached the point at which the women decided to go by Arab buses to avoid being detected.

---

design, according to some historians, the conference was totally ineffectual.

[59]Eliyahu Golomb (1893—1945) helped found the Haganah and was its leader until his death.

One day the families were informed that a joint National Council—Jewish Agency meeting was going to be held. At that time letters had been received from the detainees describing the terrible conditions in which they were being held in the new camp. The sentry went out to meet the women and told them that they would not be received. There was a man from the "information service"[60] walking around among the women, laughing whenever he saw them crying. Two clerks who worked for the Jewish Agency could not bear to see their suffering; they came downstairs and quietly encouraged the women, urging them to speak out. Rabbi Blum, the prison chaplain, left the building to prevent them from breaking in. At the same time one of the male clerks locked the other door. The women overpowered him and succeeded in entering the building. Behind the door was a "very important person" and some of his aides. The women asked him why he had deceived them, why they had been told that there would be no one in the office before six o'clock. One of the guards, who was on the women's side, whispered that he himself had heard the important person call the police and ask that Arab policemen be sent along with a Jewish commanding officer. He had been afraid that Jewish policemen might have pity on the women. The police came and began to force them from the building. That did not faze them in the least, although one woman fainted, and as a result of the disturbance the National Council sent a statement to the effect that it would receive the women at six o'clock.

The VIP began by speaking bitterly against the terrorists, and when one of the women objected to the use of the term he said sarcastically that they weren't terrorists, because only one sixteen-year-old boy had been caught with a machine gun. Then he turned his accusations against the women themselves, asking by what right they had come to lodge complaints. After all, they were guilty of having brought their sons up to become terrorists. One of the women stopped him in the middle of his

---

[60]After statehood it become Israel's intelligence service.

speech and said that the leaders of the Yishuv were in favor of too much self-restraint, and that Golomb, who collaborated with the CID, was a Quisling. The VIP shouted at her to shut up.

An old woman, simple and innocent, turned to Shazar[61] and told him that he and the Committee were their "government ministers" and as such were duty bound to help the women's sons. What kind of ministers could they be, he wanted to know, if they didn't have a country? The woman expressed her faith that the war their sons were fighting would lead to the establishment of a state which would have ministers, and it turned out that this simple woman knew more about what the future would bring than did the leaders.

The women were brave and undaunted from going to the Governor's Mansion in Jerusalem. When they heard about the exiles' hunger strike, three hundred women and their children went to Jerusalem in a caravan of buses to demonstrate at the Mansion. Of course the CID or its collaborators had been informed about what was going to happen, and when the buses approached the site, a man jumped out of one of them, ran to an Arab Legion post, and from there telephoned the Governor's Mansion to tell them that the demonstrators were on their way.

When they arrived they found the way blocked by a living wall of Arab policemen accompanied by the commanders of the CID, Catling, Hamilton, and Curtis, all of whom had their hands in their pockets.

One of the officers approached the women to discuss their demands. The women said that in the first place, as "gentlemen," they should take their hands out of their pockets when speaking to ladies, and in the second place they wanted to meet with Lord Gort. The officer answered that Lord Gort was very busy and could not see them. The women announced they would hold a hunger strike at the gate of the Mansion.

---

[61]Zalman Shazar (1889-1974) was Israel's third President.

It was a very hot day, and a dry east wind was blowing from the desert. There was no shade, and they soon became terribly thirsty. The went to the offices of one of the Histadrut's women's organizations and asked for water for the children, which was given, but not graciously or willingly. Someone important came out of the office and tried to persuade the demonstrators to leave. She said that she was afraid of the Arabs and that the region was full of snakes. To be even more convincing, she asked them if they knew that one of their great leaders, Eliyahu Golomb, had died that day.

When the sun went down the strikers were forced to leave. Not one single charitable or public institution in Jerusalem bothered to send three hundred women and children so much as a cup of water. The voice of the striking women was like the voice crying in the wilderness . . .

Was there any place the women didn't go and anything they wouldn't do to help the prisoners of Zion? Like Banquo's ghost they appeared at every public celebration and put an end to the festivities.

Nazi Germany was finally conquered, and people went wild with joy, forgetting that the victory had cost the blood of six million human beings whose existence had gone up in smoke through the crematory chimneys, and that the Jewish people had received no political recompense. Crowds danced in the streets and there was universal rejoicing—and the "ghosts" appeared. At Tel Aviv's city hall there was a meeting of the Council. Sentries guarded the door and tried unsuccessfully to prevent the women from entering the building, but they broke into the room in which the meeting was being held. They told the surprised members of the Council that it was too early to celebrate a victory, because the war had not yet ended, and they forced the assembled company to discuss the problem of the men exiled to Kenya and to decide what could be done to bring them back.

Dramatic news arrived from Kenya; the men had gone on a hunger strike to strengthen their demand to be returned before the confusion planned by the British government could begin. They knew that as soon as it began the routes back through the Arab countries would be closed. Their families immediately announced a sympathy strike, and gathered in the central synagogue in Tel Aviv. In the plaza in front of the synagogue they used a megaphone to announce the demands that the exiles be returned and that the population be made aware of the situation. From there the demonstration moved to the office of the regional governor on Ahad Ha'am Street, where they met with the regional officer, Kissilev.

Suddenly the demonstrators were informed that Golda Meir[62] had returned from America that very day. They organized a delegation of women to go to her hotel. In the hotel waiting room they met Pinchas Sapir and Israel Rokach, who were waiting to see her. Someone approached Sapir and with no further ado told him that when he met with Mrs. Meir he was to tell her that a delegation of families of the Kenya exiles was waiting to see her about their return. Rokach overheard, and said he was willing to draw her attention to the problem.

The delegation sat in the waiting room for three quarters of an hour until Sapir and Rokach came out. They asked Sapir if he had told Mrs. Meir that they were waiting to see her, and he said that he had, but that she had answered that the hotel was no place to receive delegations and she would only be able to see them the next day, at her office.

Her attitude infuriated them and proved how intense and fratricidal her hatred was, in that it could make her act in such a fashion toward women whose suffering was so great.

When Knesset member Esther Raziel mentioned the incident from the podium during a Knesset session, Golda Meir interrupted and denied everything. Israel Rokach, who was chairman of the Knesset, blanched and said that he remem-

---

[62]Golda Meir (1898—1979) was Israel's Prime Minister from 1969 to 1974. In the early 1940s she was the head of the Histadrut's Political Department.

bered the entire incident, and was ready to testify before any and every committee that Golda Meir had in fact done exactly what Esther said she had. Pinchas Sapir confirmed that the story was true and said that he too was willing to testify. It took years, but the collaborators finally admitted what they had done.

The unscheduled meeting with Dr. Ralph Bunche,[63] the representative of Trygve Lie, the Secretary General of the United Nations, reads like a mystery story.

One day a delegation of representatives of the families of the exiles visited the Newspapermen's Union. They went to ask the late Mr. Haftman, the union's president, to have the papers devote their lead stories to the demand that the exiles be returned. Haftman received them with his usual courtesy and did his best to put them at their ease, and in fact, the lead articles were devoted to the demand.

As the delegation left his office and was waiting in the corridor, Esther Raziel overheard a conversation between two newspaperwomen, one asking the other if she was going to Dr. Bunche's press conference. Esther immediately realized that it could be the chance of a lifetime to bring the exiles' plight before the deputy of the Secretary General of the United Nations. She asked where the conference would be held. One of the newswomen said that she didn't remember, while the other looked at her suspiciously and asked which paper she worked for. Esther replied that her paper appeared "on every wall." She went back to the delegation and told them there was a chance that they could speak to Dr. Bunche.

Hardly believing their ears, they decided to go to the Dan Hotel, which was where press conferences with important people were usually held. As the delegation neared the hotel Esther ran forward, rushed up the steps, and without waiting

---

[63]Ralph Bunche (1904—??) was secretary of the United Nations Special Committee on Palestine in 1947 and director of the U.N.'s Trusteeship Division from 1946 to 1955.

for the doorman to ask what she wanted, demanded to know if the conference had already begun.

When the delegation reached the room where the conference was being held, the newspapermen were amazed to see "Banquo's ghosts" and began to wonder what the women were up to and how they had found out about the conference in the first place.

Mr. Weissfisch, a member of the delegation who was fluent in several languages, wrote a note in capital letters which said "We have to meet with you about an urgent matter," and passed it to Dr. Bunche, and on the spot he prepared a memorandum about the Kenya exiles. When the conference was over, Dr. Bunche asked who wanted to speak to him. As he walked toward the exit, the delegation began to explain the problem and gave him the memorandum. When Dr. Bunche said that he was not responsible for the orders, Esther answered, "But you are responsible for order."

✳ ✳ ✳ ✳ ✳ ✳

Chapter Twenty-Six

Irony

The more I look back at those days, the more it all seems like a tragicomedy orchestrated by history. The most gifted playwright could not have imagined a story like the detention camp at Latrun—the Mapai government version, that is.

Year after year the underground fighters sat, ostracized and outlawed, in the detention camp at Latrun. In those days, the arrests could not be reported. A fighter was arrested, sent to Latrun, and disappeared like a stone thrown into water. Except for his close friends and family, no one cared what happened to him. People avoided the family like the plague. If the names of the detainees were mentioned, it was only to revile them as terrorists, dissidents, a tiny sect of madmen who were threatening the existence of the Yishuv. The poor families had to move heaven and earth to get anything at all for the detainees of Latrun, whether it involved visits by a rabbi for religious purposes or their own visits. For a long time the detainees in Latrun were denied what the worst criminals—murderers and rapists—were permitted: the right to be visited by their families once a month and on holidays.

This difficult time in Latrun was known as the era of "Whose visitors are you?" It was not unusual in those days to see the figure of a man or woman, sometimes more than one, dragging along in the heat on the way to the camp, loaded down with packages. At the same time hundreds of detainees would gather behind the barbed wire, trying to guess who the figures were. Each hoped they were his relatives, and as they approached they could hear the detainees shouting, "Whose visitors are you?"

The visitors in turn would shout the name of their relative. Their voices would rise in the air of Latrun like the voice crying in the wilderness. It was enough, in those days in Latrun, for someone to walk past the huts and say "Whose visitors," and in a flash everyone would run to the fence, leaving the hut empty. To make them easier to recognize, the men would tell their wives to wear dresses of specific colors, but sometimes two women wore the same color, and then an argument would break out between two or three men, each insisting that the figure 300 yards away was his wife. The same thing would happen when they saw children waving.

No one knew or wrote about their suffering, or, more to the point, no one wanted to know, and the families bore it alone.

However, as if someone had waved a magic wand, everything changed. Suddenly, the leaders of the Yishuv found a new spot to settle: Latrun. The nod was given and resources began to pour in from the national coffers. A "new world" had been discovered no farther away than the Jerusalem-Jaffa road, and its name was Latrun.

Something very simple had happened. After many years of resisting the idea, the various fighting organizations—Irgun, Lehi, and Haganah—were forced to cooperate, and in the wake of the mass arrests, as a result of which Haganah members also went to prison, something that had never happened before, everything changed.

All the newspapers trumpeted the fact that "the hearts of the people have been pierced by the barbed wire of Latrun." They made a great noise about the cruelty of the arrests, and even— ironic as this may sound—began to count the *hours* that the detainees had been incarcerated without an interrogation. In 24-point type the headlines screamed "48 Hours and No Interrogation," "96 Hours!" . . . "120 Hours!" . . .

They began to print lyric, sentimental editorials about the experiences and feelings of children who had not seen their fathers *for a week!* A reporter for *Ha'aretz* interviewed a child who had gone with his mother to visit his father behind barbed wire and was deeply moved. The same reporter, however, remained utterly indifferent when mothers were torn from their children and put behind bars not for a week but for years and years on end, and when the children of those who had been exiled to Eritrea and Kenya were deprived of both parents for endless years; he and his fellow reporters remained apathetic when they heard that there were men in Eritrea who hadn't even seen their newborn children.

The demonstration by the women whose husbands had been imprisoned gave witness to how intense their suffering was, and it was widely covered by the press. The papers didn't write, as did the official Haganah newspaper after the demonstration by the wives of the Kenya exiles, that "any money given to the families would be construed as supporting terror."

The camp at Latrun quickly turned into a kind of branch office of a local agricultural cooperative. The Jewish settlement opened its coffers for its "loyal sons," who had but lately joined the ranks of the underground and begun doing what the Irgun and Lehi had preached and done for years. Fate was having its revenge in the new relationship between the foreign rulers and their collaborators. It was as though the echoes of Ben-Gurion's voice could still he heard in the void, calling for collaboration with the British and the betrayal to the CID of the Jewish fighting forces. As for the danger threatening the nation as a result of the activities of the underground, the official line did a complete about-face. Where was the man who had called for collaboration? He too was behind bars, not exactly in Latrun or Rafiah, but in Paris. An "encouraging" telegram was sent to the leaders of the detainees signed by Ben-Gurion, "incarcerated in Paris."

The whole situation was very amusing for those who had already been imprisoned for seven years (the term of slavery in the Bible) and for the handful of families who, ostracized and alone, had to endure their suffering, asking themselves from time to time if they might be wrong or if the entire Jewish settlement had lost its mind.

And then, all of a sudden, they proved to have been right after all. Everyone, if only for a short time, was doing what they had been doing all along. But it was too hard for them to continue, even being "imprisoned in Paris" was too hard.

What follows is a description of the second camp at Latrun, established on June 29, 1946, and what happened to the wives of the detainees and to the kibbutzniks who were arrested, the men and the women we were to meet there.

When I was released from Bethlehem I was terribly ill, and the first thing I did was to go to Kfar Etzion, near Jerusalem, to rest and to receive medical treatment for complaints whose nature still hadn't been diagnosed. When I returned, in June 1946, I made an appointment to see Professor Mendel, an orthopedic specialist, and as it turned out it was for the day after the bombing of the King David Hotel. When I arrived in Jerusalem I saw the "parade" of thousands of people going to look at the Irgun's handiwork. I have to admit that there was a lot to see, and it was a pity that the criminal Shaw, the chief secretary of the Palestinian government, had been unwilling to prevent the loss of human life; he had ignored the warnings sent to him, and the fact that there had been Jewish victims was particularly painful.

When I left the doctor's office I hurried back to Tel Aviv. I had a feeling that it was unwise for me to stay in Jerusalem, lest someone say that I had taken part in the bombing. I returned to Tel Aviv exhausted and went to sleep.

At three o'clock in the morning the doorbell rang, again and again. I got out of bed, and my husband woke up as well. I said through the closed door that I had to get dressed and opened it. I thought that one of my women friends had come to see if I was at home or off on Irgun business.

I was still saying "Hold on a minute," and there stood a

group of policemen. One of them said, "Get dressed. You're coming with us." He told my husband to give me what he thought I would need, like a toothbrush and a towel and some food. My husband stood there, alarmed and embarrassed. He had just returned from a POW camp, I myself had just been released, we were starting our lives over again, and everything was being destroyed. I got dressed, took what I could, said goodbye to my husband, and left.

As I walked down the stairs I saw that there were armed soldiers on every landing, and that encouraged me no end and even amused me. The hallway leading into the building was fairly long, and it was lined on both sides with soldiers. I smiled to myself, although it was no time to be laughing. They put me into a strange vehicle, something between a tank and a pickup truck, and there I met not only Isaac Gurion, but to my surprise, his fifteen-year-old daughter, Na'ama. Neither of them knew where we were going.

The vehicle continued its rounds until morning, stopping every so often to take on more prisoners, most of whom I didn't know. I only remember that one of them told me that it had been hard for him to say goodbye to his little girl and she had cried a lot. Gurion dryly remarked that he had been smarter; he had brought his daughter with him.

At dawn we stopped at the main garage of what is today the Dan bus company. The soldiers and police didn't permit us to speak, not even with each other. But since the general mood toward people who had been arrested was not as severe as it had been, and since no one knew who we were, some young people took the risk and gave us cigarettes. Later on, when they found out who we were, some of them may have been glad that they had an opportunity to help, even a little, people who had fought and suffered to liberate the nation.

In the morning we arrived in Jaffa, where men and women were separated. I took it upon myself to be responsible for Na'ama Gurion, and when they wanted to take her away from

me I refused, saying that she was still merely a child and needed her mother, or at least an older woman to take care of her.

When we went up the stairs and entered the women's cells,
I felt for the first time what imprisonment really meant,
although it was the fifth time it had happened to me. There was
a crowd of women, all wearing robes and with their hair
uncombed, lying on the floor, and because of lack of space to
lie down or even sit, they were practically one on top of the
other. There were women of all ages, all of them tired, but as
usual in good spirits, with nothing but contempt for the situation, determined to overcome no matter what happened.

From time to time one of the women would climb up to the
small window set high in the wall, almost near the ceiling, to
talk and joke with the men who were standing downstairs.
There were women whose husbands and brothers were there,
and fathers whose daughters were with us. Nothing happened
for several hours.

We began trying to guess where they were going to take us.
There was no room for us in Bethlehem, and Latrun was a
men's camp. Were they perhaps going to send us into exile?
No, not women. Some of the women had loved ones who were
already in Kenya, and they were overjoyed at the thought of
going to join them. We kept guessing until the order to move
came and brought us down to earth.

They took us out, men and women, through the rear gate
instead of the main gate, and we were able to speak to each
other. Hundreds of Arabs in the neighboring buildings
watched us go. It was Friday and the Arabs were at home. We
left the building singing and laughing and making jokes at the
expense of the English. There was a crowd of curious onlook-
ers, and in it I saw my husband and my mother. I waved, but
they didn't see me.

We got into a vehicle and rode off, and once again we didn't
know where we were going. Once we turned left off the
Jerusalem road, it was no longer necessary to guess; the desti-

nation was Latrun, not the men's camp, but Latrun II. We arrived at the camp tired, hungry, and road-weary. However, we walked into the camp singing a popular song, "We have brought you peace," and we were answered in song by the detainees from Jerusalem, Haifa, and other cities.

Entering the camp, we began shaking hands with women with whom only yesterday we had been imprisoned in Bethlehem. We saw others who stood off by themselves, and when we asked who they were we were told that they were women from the kibbutzim who had been arrested. I couldn't help remembering how we had always behaved to new arrested women, even if they wore blue shirts!

It was hot outside and even hotter inside the corrugated tin huts. One of the detainees had left a sick baby at home and couldn't stop worrying about him. It was also the first time she had been arrested; until then she had only known house arrest. Esther Raziel and I decided to take the younger women into a hut with us so that we could help them. The women split up into groups based on the cities they came from. The next thing we did was to meet with the camp commander to demand kosher eating utensils and to bring up the issue of medical care. The mother who had left her baby demanded to be returned; Esther was worried about her three children, and in addition to my child I was worried about my husband, who had just returned from a POW camp.

The commander acceded to our demands for kosher utensils by giving us new ones, and let us use the services of the Italian POWs who were in the camp and a sergeant who would do what we told them needed to be done. After everything I had been through I had an attack of my illness and had to lie down, but from my bed I told the Italians and the sergeant how to mark the pots and the silverware for meat and milk products. That's how we spent the first day we were there, that is to say, Friday. We didn't have time to prepare anything to eat for the Sabbath, and we had to eat dry food. To my great surprise, my husband managed to find out where I was. He was the first person to visit the camp, and even brought some packages.

Our meeting with the kibbutz women, whose ideological upbringing had theoretically been in the spirit of comradeship, was another story altogether. When someone was newly admitted to Bethlehem, we never asked her anything about herself. We knew that she had been arrested, and that it was our job to make things easier for her and to encourage her. I have already told that part of the story.

But what happened here was just the opposite. We needed their help, and what did they do? Among the arrested women was one from Jerusalem, the mother of a small baby. She was fairly experienced and had decided to bring the baby with her. The women from the kibbutz weren't even willing to give her a cup of water. On the other hand, the treatment she received at the hands of the camp commander was quite correct (he was new in the country). He did his best to find suitable food for the infant, and as a result of his efforts the mother was released the same day.

An entire book would be insufficient to describe the kibbutz women's complete and total lack of the spirit of comradeship and human feeling, these women who had been educated in the school of international brotherly love. As soon as they were arrested, the Hadassah organization took it upon itself to see to their needs, something it had never done for those in Bethlehem during all those awful years. It even sent *sheets* for these delicate and spoiled women. The only thing they really needed was something they were never sent and never seemed to have: a little humanity and some real team spirit.

Since most of the kibbutz detainees were released and didn't take the sheets with them, the remaining ones had extra sheets. We had been brought to the camp after a sleepless night and didn't even have a change of clothing, let alone something to sleep in. In our group there were pregnant women and very young girls, but not one of the kibbutz women thought it might be a nice gesture to give a sheet to a pregnant or sick woman or a child.

Incidentally, when we heard in Bethlehem about Black Saturday, when the leaders of the Jewish settlements were arrested, we were certain that Golda Meir would be brought to the prison.[64] Many years later she claimed that she hadn't been arrested because there was no detention camp for women at that time, although the walls of Bethlehem and the detainees of the camp attested to the opposite. The detainees had even held a meeting at which they decided how to treat the expected honored guest and which duties she would not have to perform. The general feeling was that her age should be taken into consideration and that things should be made as easy as possible for her.

A week later the women on the roof saw an elderly woman being escorted to the prison by a policeman, and they were sure it was Golda. A few minutes later, however, they realized that they had been mistaken. It wasn't Golda, it was the late singer Hilda Dolitzkaya. So it seems there was a women's prison after all.

Friday passed at Latrun, and so did Saturday. The kibbutzniks didn't share their food with us, but put all the crates of fruits and vegetables and everything else they got directly into their hut.

On Sunday my husband came again, bringing packages for Esther, Na'ama, and me. We shared them with the young women and with those women who, because they only ate kosher food, wouldn't eat things cooked in the camp kitchen, Our own kitchen had not yet been set up. One day I went into the shower and happened to meet one of the kibbutzniks. She said that in my place she wouldn't eat the food the Yishuv sent them, because they were the Yishuv and the Yishuv was them, whereas we were outlaws and beyond the pale. There was no

---

[64]On June 29, 1946, known as Black Saturday, the British arrested the members of the Jewish Agency Executive and imprisoned them in Latrun. In their absence Golda Meir became the acting head of the Jewish Agency's Political Department.

way I could respond to her tone of voice, but I said that money had been taken from me against my will, a special tax everyone had to pay to the Yishuv every time he or she bought something, and that now I was getting it back by eating their food.

Once some of the kibbutz women burst into our hut and asked us to return the books we had taken from the library. When Esther asked if the books were their own personal property, one of the kibbutz women answered that they had been sent by the Yishuv (by which she meant the official institutions, not the kibbutz), and since they were about to be released, they wanted the books back. It was hard for us to restrain ourselves, but we did. They also intended to take the radio with them when they left. Then some unfortunate things happened to them. Dr. Katznelson came to visit the camp, and we asked her to send us what the Yishuv had sent the kibbutzniks, since we also officially belonged to it. She became angry, saying, "What, didn't they give you sheets? They have more than enough for themselves. And they also should have given you dairy products for the sick women." After that things went along fairly smoothly for us, against their will but also out of their hands.

One day Rabbi Goldman came to the camp. I heard people outside calling my name and telling me that he was there. I was so angry about the way the kibbutzniks were behaving that I decided not to go out and see him. A few minutes later the camp commander came to my hut, driving a strange kind of vehicle I had never seen before (it was a jeep), and invited me to come meet with the rabbi. Out of respect for him I went to the dining room.

When Rabbi Goldman saw me he smiled and said, "If Tzila is here, I know that everything is all right." I replied that everything was not all right, and told him the whole story of the antisocial way the kibbutzniks were behaving, and how, on their release, they were planning to take the Yishuv's radio with them. He didn't let me finish, but burst into their hut, furious. A few minute later shouts could be heard as he told them in no uncertain terms that they were behaving badly. When he came back he told me that I could rest assured that the radio and the books would remain in the camp.

It is worthwhile pointing out that these things happened during the days of the revolt, when terrorism, until then defamed, had been given the official stamp of approval of the Yishuv institutions. One can imagine how they would have acted under "normal" circumstances.

One day I was called to Latrun I as a representative of the camp. Our people in the camp had appointed Esther Raziel and me as their representatives without asking our permission. For some reason Esther decided not to go, but I went, as did two kibbutzniks, including the one who had spoken so eloquently in the shower. When we got there we met Joseph Becker, the representative of the camp, and Isaac Gurion. I told them about everything that was going on in our camp, and the other women listened and became very angry, but they also heard the men's answer, which was that David Remez[65] and Moshe Sharett[66] were in Latrun and were interested in having peace prevail, so they calmed down somewhat.

During the curfew which lasted four days (it had been put into effect three days after the bombing at the King David Hotel) some women and girls were brought to the camp. One of the women was quite old. They also brought women who were active in the Irgun, and we regretted that very much— another limb lopped off the tree.

One of the new women was pregnant. I knew that when the women from the kibbutzim had been arrested, one of them had miscarried. The doctor was a decent person, and so was the camp commander, who had just arrived in the country and hadn't had time to absorb the prevailing mood of hatred and

---

[65]David Remez (1886—1951), a long-time Histadrut official, was chairman of the National Council from 1944 to 1949.

[66]Moshe Sharett (1894—1965), Israel's second Prime Minister, was head of the Jewish Agency's Political Department from 1933 to 1948.

anti-Semitism. I asked him if there was any chance that the newly arrived detainee would miscarry as well. I neither knew nor cared who she was, all that was important was to save a woman from imprisonment, whoever she might be.

The doctor told me to watch her, and if I saw any change for the worse in her condition, to inform him immediately. He was a young man, and when he spoke about pregnancy he blushed like a child. Her condition did change for the worse during the night, and in the morning I told him in no uncertain terms that she had to be released, otherwise a tragedy might occur.

She was released the same day, and since the curfew was still in force she was returned home in a British army ambulance. When they came to take her the doctor requested that I accompany her, for in his eyes I was her nurse. Esther Raziel told me that in her opinion I should tell the doctor that Adah was a registered nurse and let her go; that would give her official standing in the camp. It was a great sacrifice for me to give up an opportunity to leave the camp, especially since the woman's home was near my own, and it would have given me the chance to see my husband and son.

Adah promised that she would go to my home and take care of anything I wanted her to, and that she would also give my regards to my family. She not only went to my house but to Esther's, and came back with packages. I am still glad I took Esther's advice, because it gave Adah a considerable amount of status in the camp, and whereas I was released a short time later, Adah was forced to stay for several weeks.

Relations between the kibbutz women and us improved after our visit to Latrun I. They must have been given orders by their leaders to behave better, and life with them became somewhat easier.

Since we were in Latrun, not Bethlehem, conditions for us were similar to those for the men. We were free to walk around all day long. We could even sit outside at night until quite late, which was fortunate because it was very hot in the huts. The cleaning was left to the Italian prisoners. When we came to the

camp we taught them that they were not to enter the huts without first knocking and receiving permission. In the evening,
when they had to use flashlights (there was no electricity, and
the radio worked on batteries) they would back into the room
and ask in English if they might come in.

The doctor was active in getting me released because he saw
that I was in pain. I was having severe attacks of amoebic
dysentery and my liver was painful as well. I hadn't received
any treatment because I was still undergoing tests.

One day a group of CID men came to the camp, and I looked
for Curtis among them. I remembered that when Shoshanah
Raziel, Bilhah Hermoni, and I had been released, he had said
that my husband should keep me under control. I asked the
CID men if Curtis was with them. The officer in charge wanted
to know why. I responded by asking him to remind Curtis that
I had been under my husband's supervision, just as he had recommended, so why was I now under the supervision of so
many other men? They laughed aloud, but made a note of
what I had said.

For his part, my husband did not sit by quietly. He had not
been a member of the Irgun before he was drafted into the
army and his name was not on any list. As a result he managed
to knock on all the doors and gain entry to all the offices, and
his efforts must have led to my release.

One Saturday morning I was called to the camp office and
told that they were waiting for my release orders to come from
Jerusalem. To my great joy my husband was there, and he too
knew that I was about to be released, for they had promised to
tell him. I was now faced for the second time with the problem
of whether or not to leave the camp on a Saturday. I decided
that the sooner I left the better, because they might change their
minds at any minute, and as usual, something might happen to
lead to my being rearrested, and who knew for how long. The
other women advised me to go and I took their advice.

My husband and I left the camp, took an Arab taxi to Jaffa,
and from there went home, where my son was waiting for me.

I rested for a while and then went back to work, both for the prisoners and detainees still in Bethlehem and for the Irgun.

Naturally house arrest was a condition of my release every time I was arrested and released. That was the case for everyone who was released in order to curtail their activities and make it easier for the police to watch them. I had to go to the police station to sign in three times a day: morning, noon, and evening. From sunset to sunrise I was forbidden to leave the house, but I didn't pay too much attention to the order and was often away from home in the evening. I couldn't help feeling that "the sun never set on me."

Some of the police officers were on our side, and they would warn us when "house calls" were going to be paid, and on those days I would stay at home. With several we had a gentlemen's agreement; they would tell us that a visit to the house was due but would simply mark down that they had been there without actually coming over. One unfortunate evening a policeman noted that he had been to my house and found me in, but another visit that same night by a British policeman found me absent, and I had a great deal of trouble the next day to whitewash the incident.

On Saturdays and holidays I refused to go to the police station to sign in; they had no choice but to capitulate. On Yom Kippur I stayed at home, and as a result the CID ordered me to go to Jaffa to be interrogated. Asked, through an interpreter, why I had not gone to the police station, I answered that I hadn't wanted to desecrate the sanctity of the holiday. That made my interrogator angry, and he told the interpreter to tell me that I was under the orders of the military commander in Palestine, not the Irgun, the National Military Organization. The last three words were said in Hebrew, and he ground his teeth while doing so.

My year of house arrest ended in April, 1947. A few days earlier they had called me in to sign an extension, and I was told to sign a document written in English. I refused and asked that it be translated into Hebrew. Even in Bethlehem, I had always demanded a Hebrew translation when I had to sign papers.

A few days later, when the year ended, a policeman who lived in the same neighborhood (Yad Eliyahu, in south Tel Aviv) came to my house. Visibly shaken, he told me that I had to report to Mr. Wilkins at CID headquarters in Jaffa. It was his understanding that I was about to be arrested again, and he begged me not to resist but to sign. I refused. He left and I went back to what I had been doing. It was almost Passover, and I was busy preparing food for the holiday. I called to my neighbor, who was in the kitchen (in those days two families shared a common kitchen) and told her that if I didn't come back, my family was to dine with her. She began to cry, but tried to encourage me and told me that she hoped I would be back soon.

I said goodbye to my son (my husband was not home) and left. When I arrived at the CID in Jaffa, the police looked at me with a mixture of pity and admiration. Wilkins was a fat but athletic Englishman with a florid face. Overcome with pleasure, he said, "So, dear lady, you don't want to sign?" I answered that I had nothing against signing, but in Hebrew, not English. I proposed a gentlemen's agreement; I would sign in Hebrew and in English (till then I had only signed in Hebrew) if they would agree to do the same thing, filling out the form in both languages. He refused unconditionally. "In that case," I said, "I won't sign! I have never signed only in English and am not about to start!"

"What if we prove that you did once sign a document in English?" he asked. I said that if he could prove it, I would sign. I was certain that I had never done any such thing.

Wilkins left and came back twenty or thirty minutes later, smiling victoriously and waving a piece of paper in front of me.

Was it possible? It was. When I was arrested the first time and released after six o'clock in the evening, I had been ordered not to make trouble and to do anything as long as it meant being released. They had handed me a document and I signed.

So I laughed and said, "This time you win. I'll pay for my mistake, but I promise you that I won't make the same mistake again," and I demanded that a note be attached stating the reason for my agreement.

I signed and went home, to the joy of my family. The policeman who warned me came by to shake my hand and say how glad he was that I was back home. He told us that the other officers at the station house had understood my position and were happy that everything had turned out as it did.

The second incident occurred when a curfew was declared after Dov Gruner[67], Mordechai Alkachi, Yehiel Dov Dresner, and Eliezer Kashani were hanged. Some British officers came to my house to see if I was at home or participating in an Irgun operation. They searched the entire neighborhood, asking everyone where I lived, until they found my apartment. I was not known to my neighbors as Tzila Heller, but as Tzila Teplitzky. Several people knew who I was but were in no hurry to help the British police. They wanted to warn me first, and it was a good thing they did, because it gave me a chance to destroy certain damaging papers.

Suddenly a number of well-armed officers appeared at my door, asking if "Madame Heller" lived there. I said that I was Madame Heller, and they began arguing among themselves in English about whether or not I was telling the truth. I ended the argument by saying in English, "Yes, I am Madame Heller." They broke out laughing and said that they were now certain that I was who I claimed to be, begged my pardon, and left.

The neighborhood children had gathered around the house to watch. Adults, too, friends and people who were simply curious, came on all sorts of pretexts. I was saved from their curiosity by the curfew in force in our neighborhood, because they all had to return to their homes. However, people who lived in the adjoining buildings continued to look in my direc-

---

[67]Dov Gruner (1912—1947), an Irgun fighter, was captured during an attack on a police station and was executed by the British.

tion, and the hatred in their eyes was plain to see, as if they felt
that my comrades and I were responsible for the curfew. But
when the curfew was suspended, people I had never seen
before came to shake my hand. I became the local heroine; the
neighborhood was small then and had only a few dozen inhab-
itants.

A funny thing happened once when someone who wanted
to give me regards from people outside of Tel Aviv tried to find
me, and no one would tell him where I lived because he looked
English (even though he spoke Hebrew) and that aroused their
suspicions. It took him a long time to find me. He wanted to
know if it was possible that no one knew me, and asked what
my real name was. I told him not to be angry, but that he did-
n't look Jewish, he looked English, and therefore people didn't
want to tell him where I lived. He showed us the Star of David
on a chain around his neck, explaining that he wore it because
more than once he had been beaten up by people who thought
he was English.

Despite the fact that I was under house arrest and had been
forbidden to leave Tel Aviv, I used to go to Netanya, Jerusalem,
Petach Tikvah, and other cities. Once I went to Jerusalem and
had to remain overnight. At that time Gershon Gerdovsky,
called Chaim Brenner, lived there. He was there as a "refugee,"
having been forced to flee Tel Aviv. A machine gun had been
"rescued" from a British camp, and while he and some others
were trying to find suitable ammunition for it, one bullet was
fired, causing everyone to flee from his apartment.

Gershon was a real bookworm and used to spend every
penny he had on books. He had worked for the electric company, but had been fired when he did not volunteer for the
British army, and now supported himself by doing odd jobs.
He was completely devoted to the Irgun, and was a commander in my squadron. He managed to escape alone. His apartment, with all his books, was confiscated by the British. What
could two "criminals" like us find to do in Jerusalem? We

decided to go to the cafe in the King David Hotel (this was before it was bombed) because no one would think to look for us there, in the lion's den.

We didn't have enough money for more than a glass of wine. We looked around at the other people, who were mostly high-ranking functionaries with Jewish women at their sides. We saw how champagne was served and drunk, and met two men who later helped us with Irgun matters. When we left we began to laugh, because it really was the safest place we could have gone.

Gershon was captured a long while later in one of the Irgun's military actions and exiled to Eritrea without being identified. His excellent handwriting caused Joseph Winitzky, the editor of the exiles' newspaper, to press him into service to "print" the paper. His identity was only discovered some months later when his fingerprints were examined, and he was returned to the country to stand trial. He died a hero's death when the prison at Acco was broken into.

※ ※ ※ ※ ※ ※

A Mother Confesses

Brother, do you know where the Messiah will be born?
In a prison, brother . . .

—Yair (Abraham Stern)

Here, at the end of the book, I feel I have to clarify something that caused me sleepless nights more than once, and for which I was often taken to task: how could I, the mother of a small child, leave him alone while I did things that could—and did—lead to my arrest and my being separated from him?

On my son's first visit to me in Bethlehem, when he was barely four and a half years old, the prison director asked me how I dared desert him to play politics, neglecting him and leaving him to suffer, miserable without his mother. I denied belonging to any underground organization and said that her accusation was itself proof that I was didn't belong to any illegal group. Many people asked the same question in many different situations, and I was never able to give a proper answer. Therefore I will use this opportunity to reply, and give the same answer I gave myself when I decided to devote such strength as I had to the war of liberation.

The duty of a mother is to assure her child's welfare and future; there was never any doubt about that. The only question is about how to define "welfare." There are two possible definitions: one of them is fairly limited, and can be summed up by saying to the child, "Come, eat the nice banana." That is the answer of the mothers who run after their children with food and drink, and think they are doing everything they can for them. These were the mothers who, to our great tragic sorrow, could not keep their well-cared-for children from going to the gas chambers. As it turned out, all their loyal, devoted care was of no avail when the time came; not did it do any good during the pogroms. Is there any tragedy worse than having children die before their parents? Everything they did was for the immediate, transitory good of their children, but it did not solve the basic problem, the one which Jewish mothers have had to deal with for the past two thousand years of murder and blood, namely, how to assure that their children would live free, normal lives, would breathe the air as did other men, without having mud thrown at them while hearing the cry *Zhid* in whatever language it might be, and without having to fear the assassin's waiting knife.

The problem of the children's future cannot be separated from the future of the Jewish nation. It is not enough to worry about feeding and educating children. There are mothers who want their children to be musicians, scientists, businessmen, but the prerequisite for these professions is that the child live! If a child becomes ill, his mother will move heaven and earth to help him get well. She will take him to the best doctors and buy the best medicines, put him into the best hospital—anything to have him get well. But when it comes to the worst disease of all, the cancer of exile and anti-Semitism, the Jewish mother ignores the threat and brings up her child to be enfolded in the arms of death.

Zionism discovered the cause of the disease and a cure for it: a Jewish national homeland. But the drug didn't work. The assassin's axe was not wielded over the Jew in the Diaspora because he was a merchant and not a farmer, but because he was a Jew, and defenseless. In a very short time it became clear that in its distorted socialist form, the Zionist solution solved nothing. Jews were being killed in Palestine as they were in the Diaspora. Kishinev was no worse than Hebron and Safed. Decapitated heads, mutilated bodies, crushed skulls, and defiled women were the common denominators of socialist Palestine and the Diaspora.

When I saw my dear sweet child on the other side of the barbed-wire fence, my heart broke with longing for him and the tears stood ready to gush forth. I looked into his innocent eyes and said to myself, "All this is only for you, my dear son." I knew that I could be at home with him, running after him with "a nice banana," sitting next to him at kindergarten parties and watching him grow instead of leaving him alone without father or mother, one imprisoned by the enemy, the other by an "ally." How sweet it would have been to go straight home with him, to hold him in my arms and forget about the rest of the world. With God as my witness, I would have given anything to be able to do that.

Everything I did was for my son and his future. Throughout our history there were parents who sacrificed their children, but I was neither Abraham, ready to sacrifice Isaac, nor Hannah, with her seven sons. I would sacrifice myself and my youth for my son and his future, so that he might grow up free in a country of his own, where he would walk proudly with his head held high like a prince, a scion of an ancient race whose youth had been restored. I hadn't willingly chosen the path I walked on, but took it because there was no other choice, no other path.

I sat in prison so that someday my son's wife might sit quietly at home and raise her children as honorable men, not as victims stretching out their necks for the assassin's knife. I was bone-weary of murderers and the slaughter they had wreaked upon us. Behind prison walls I was actively forging freedom for my people; there, in that stifling atmosphere, young Jewish girls sang the lullaby for all the children yet unborn who would live freely and proudly. From the darkness of the prison in Bethlehem shone a beacon which would light the world.

My son was too young to understand such things, and no wonder. People older and wiser than he didn't understand them either, but someday, when he grew up, he and his whole generation, everyone would understand that Bethlehem was again the cradle of the Kingdom of Israel.

It was a great dream, and we dreamed it on the darkest nights, and my joy was immeasurable when the dream became reality. The sighs of pain at hauling tanks of water became sighs of pleasure when I saw my son in a tank belonging to the victorious Israeli army, which will one day return to Bethlehem.